T0034997

Usborne

# Timelines of World History

Jane Chisholm

Designed by Keith Newell, Mike Olley,
Melissa Alaverdy, Robin Farrow & Julia Rheam

History consultant: Dr. Anne Millard

Managing designer: Stephen Wright

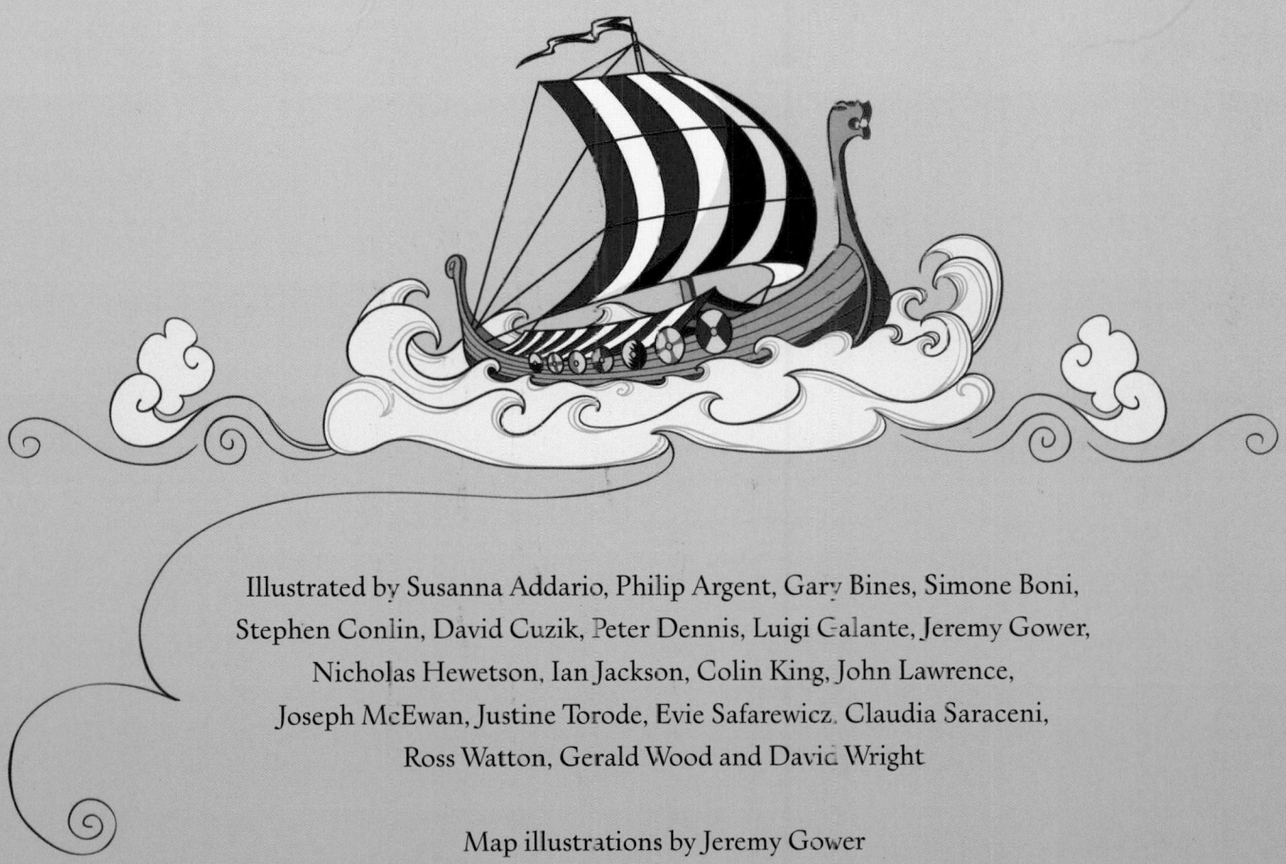

Illustrated by Susanna Addario, Philip Argent, Gary Bines, Simone Boni,
Stephen Conlin, David Cuzik, Peter Dennis, Luigi Galante, Jeremy Gower,
Nicholas Hewetson, Ian Jackson, Colin King, John Lawrence,
Joseph McEwan, Justine Torode, Evie Safarewicz, Claudia Saraceni,
Ross Watton, Gerald Wood and David Wright

Map illustrations by Jeremy Gower

# Contents


3 How to use this book

**4 The Ancient World**
6 10,000BC
8 2000BC
10 1000BC
12 500BC
14 250BC
16 AD1

**18 The Middle Ages**
20 500
22 700
24 900
26 1000
28 1100
30 1200
32 1250
34 1300
36 1350
38 1400
40 1450

**42 The 16th Century**
44 1500
46 1525
48 1550
50 1575

**52 The 17th Century**
54 1600
56 1620
58 1640
60 1660
62 1680

**64 The 18th Century**
66 1700
68 1720
70 1740
72 1760
74 1780

**76 The 19th Century**
78 1800
80 1820
82 1840
84 1860
86 1880

**88 The 20th century**
90 1900
92 1915
94 1930
96 1940
98 1950
100 1960
102 1970
104 1980
106 1990
108 1996

110 Glossary
112 Prime Ministers and Presidents
114 Kings and Queens
117 Internet links
118 Index

*The Pyramids at Giza in Egypt, built in c.2500BC*

# How to use this book

This book is divided up into seven sections, with dates arranged in columns according to geographical area. This means you can look up what was happening in different parts of the world at the same time.

To help you put the dates in context, the columns also contain short features on important themes in world history, such as the Renaissance, or the Industrial Revolution.

Dates that appear in brackets after a person's name, such as Isaac Newton (**1642-1727**), refer to his or her life. In the case of kings, queens and emperors, such as Maria Theresa (**1740-1780**), the dates of the reign are shown instead.

Experts often disagree about dates in very early history, so you may find that some of the dates shown are slightly different in other books.

**Abbreviations**

**c.** stands for ***circa***, the Latin for 'about'. Early dates often begin with **c.** because experts have only been able to find an approximate date for when something happened.

**AD** stands for ***Anno Domini***, meaning 'Year of the Lord' in Latin. It applies to all the years after the birth of Jesus Christ, but it is normally only used with very early dates, to avoid confusion with **BC** dates.

**BC** means 'Before Christ', and so **BC** dates are counted backwards from **AD1**. However, many historians now believe that the year of Christ's birth was probably about **5BC**, rather than the year **1**.

# THE ANCIENT WORLD

10,000BC - AD499

# EUROPE

10,000BC

## THE FIRST ARTISTS

The world's first known artists were the Palaeolithic (Old Stone Age) people of Europe. Animal paintings, including bison, reindeer, horses and hunting scenes, dating back to **c.35,000-18,000BC**, have been found on the walls of caves in the Dordogne region of France, and the Pyrenees region of Spain.

*Cave painting of a bison found at Lascaux, Dordogne, France*

**c.6000BC** Groups of farmers, possibly from Turkey, reach Crete, mainland Greece and the Aegean islands.

**c. 6000-5000** A village is built at Lepenski Vir, on the banks of the Danube in central Europe.

**c.6000-4000** Farming spreads throughout northern and western Europe.

**c.4500-1500** Building of megaliths, large stone monuments such as temples, tombs and henges (circular areas, often made of stones), in Malta, Brittany, the Iberian peninsula (Spain and Portugal) and the British Isles.

**c.4000** Copper is worked in the Balkans.

**c.3800** The Sweet Track is built, one of the first walkways in England. It stretches for 1.8km (just over a mile).

**c.3500** The first of several temples is built at Tarxien, Malta.

**c.3200** Stone circles are built in north-western Europe.

**c.3100** Skara Brae, a village in the Orkney Islands, is built from local stone.

**c.3000-1500** Stone circle built at Stonehenge, Britain.

*Stonehenge, the most spectacular of many megaliths in Britain*

**c.3000** Olives, vines and grains cultivated in the Aegean islands.

**c.2500** Bronze, obsidian (volcanic glass) and flint are traded.

**c.2500-2000** Corded Ware and Beaker cultures spread in northern Europe.

2001BC

# THE MIDDLE EAST

*Wild goat*

## THE FIRST FARMERS

The earliest people lived as nomads, moving from place to place, hunting and eating wild plants. Farming probably first developed in about **10,000BC** in an area of the Middle East called the Fertile Crescent (see map). As people adopted farming, they began to build permanent places to live, and so the first towns grew up, such as Jericho and Çatal Hüyük (see below).

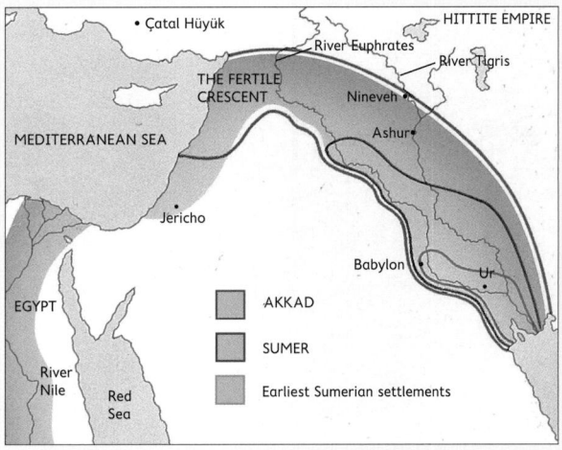


**c.8000BC** Jericho, in Jordan, has about 2,000 people.

**c.7000** Pottery, spinning, weaving and hammering metal are in use.

**c.6250-5650** Çatal Hüyük, in Turkey, has over 5,000 people.

**c.4000** People learn to extract copper and gold.

## MESOPOTAMIA

One of the world's earliest civilizations grew up in Mesopotamia, an area of fertile land between the rivers Tigris and Euphrates in what is now Iraq. Cities developed from about **4000BC**, with impressive public buildings and organized political and legal systems. In southern Mesopotamia, known as Sumer, the wheel was invented, and a form of writing, known as cuneiform. Between **3100BC** and **2800BC**, small states were set up around the cities of Ur, Eridu and Uruk.

*Necklaces of gold and semi-precious stones*

*Gold dagger and sheath*

*Treasures from the royal Sumerian tombs at Ur c.2500BC*

**c.3500** The wheel is invented in Sumer.

**c.3300** The Sumerians develop writing.

**c.2350-2150** The kingdom of Akkad is established in Mesopotamia.

**c.2100BC** Ur rules Sumer and Akkad. A ziggurat (a vast stepped tower with a temple on top) is built at Ur.

## AFRICA

**c.6000BC** People in the Sahara Desert tame cattle.

**c.5000** The Sahara Desert, once green, is still fertile in parts and there is evidence of cattle herders. As the Sahara continues to dry out, many people migrate to the Nile Valley.

**c.5000** Farming begins in Egypt. Pottery, linen making and, later, metal working are developed.

**c.4000** The Sahara grasslands have turned to desert.

### ANCIENT EGYPT

The remarkable civilization of Ancient Egypt grew up along the banks of the great river, the Nile. By **c.3300**, the country was organized into two kingdoms: Upper and Lower Egypt, and the Egyptians developed a form of picture writing, which we call hieroglyphics. In **c.3100**, Upper and Lower Egypt were united by a king called Menes. The Ancient Egyptians produced fine works of art and architecture. They also demonstrated extraordinary feats of engineering, building the pyramids (see below) as tombs for their kings.

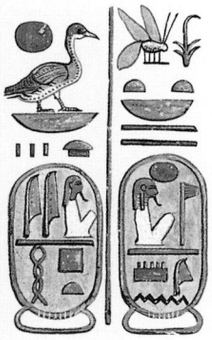

*Egyptian hieroglyphs*

**c.2686-2181** Old Kingdom in Egypt: dynasties III to VI. The pyramids are built.

**c.2180-2040** First Intermediate Period in Egypt: dynasties VII-X.

**c.2040-1720** Middle Kingdom in Egypt: dynasties XI-XIII.

*Pyramids and Sphinx at Giza, Egypt*

## ASIA

**c.9000-5000BC** Jomon Period in Japan: people hunt and fish.

**c.5000** Gradual adoption of farming in China. The Yangshao culture grows up around the Huang Ho River. Farmers grow millet, fruit, nuts and vegetables and keep pigs and dogs.

**c.4000** Farming develops along the Yangtze River in China. Beginning of the cultivation of rice.

**c.4000** Farming communities settle in the Indus Valley in India.

**c.3000** Hunter gatherers living on Japanese islands. Use of pottery.

**c.2700** Silk-making begins in China.

**c.2500** Longshan period in China. Farmers are better organized and keep chickens, cattle, sheep, goats, and buffalo.

*Baked clay figure from Indus Valley*

### THE INDUS VALLEY CIVILIZATION

From **c.2500-1800**, the Indus Valley Civilization flourished in India, based on farming, with contacts as far west as Mesopotamia. The Indus Valley people had large cities, with public buildings and good sanitation, and a form of writing. The best known sites are Mohenjo-Daro and Harappa.

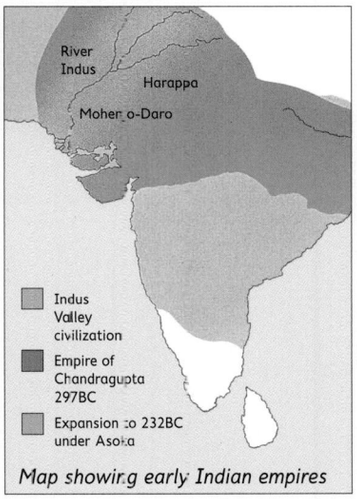


*Map showing early Indian empires*

**c.2500-1500** Bronze Age culture in Bactria, in Central Asia.

**c.2205** Traditional earliest date of Xia (or Hsia) dynasty in China.

## THE AMERICAS

**c.15 000BC** First people arrive in North America, crossing over from Asia via a bridge of land and ice.

*Crossings were probably made over land bridges that appeared when the sea froze and water levels dropped.*

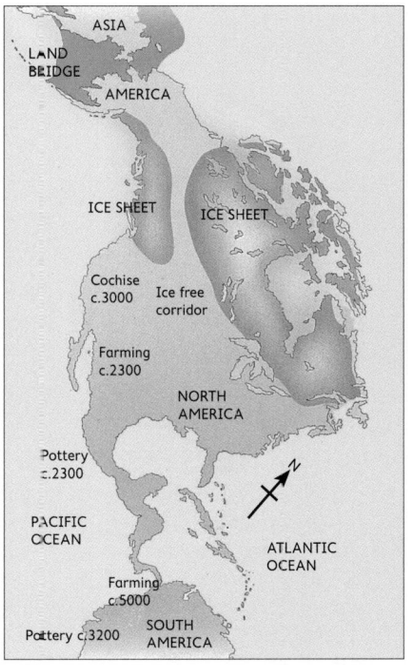


**c.10,000-8000** Early North Americans hunt large animals.

**c.8000-1000** North America: people spread out across plains, woodlands, deserts and icy wastes and gradually change from hunting to a more settled way of life.

**c.5000** Corn farming in Central America.

**c.3500** The llama is first used as a pack animal in Peru.

*Llama*

**c.3200** Pottery is in use in Ecuador.

**c.3000** Hunter gatherers known as Cochise are living in the southwest of North America.

**c.2300** The introduction of farming leads to settlement in permanent villages in Mexico.

**c.2300** Use of pottery spreads to Mexico and Guatemala.

## EUROPE

2000BC

**c.2000BC** Horses and wheeled vehicles are used in eastern Europe.

### THE MINOANS

The earliest known European civilization developed in Crete between **c.3000-2000BC**. It is known as Minoan, after a legendary king called Minos. The Minoans had well-planned towns, skilled craftsmen and good trading links with the Mediterranean. Their golden age is known as the First and Second Palace Periods (**c.2000-1700BC** and **c.1700-1450BC**): they built large and spectacular palaces, including Knossos, Mallia and Phaistos. The Minoans introduced a form of writing, known as Linear A, from **c.1650BC**.

*This bull's head is actually a vessel, called a rhyton. It was used for pouring liquid offerings to the gods.*

**c.2000-1500** Wessex culture in southern Britain.

### THE MYCENAEANS

From **c.1600-1200BC**, Greece was dominated by people known as Mycenaeans, after Mycenae, the site where their remains were first discovered. They lived in small kingdoms, each based around a city, took over the prosperous Minoan trade routes, and developed Linear B, an early form of Greek writing, in **c.1400BC**.

**c.1450** Volcanic eruption on Thera (an island near Crete).

**c.1450** Fall of Knossos. Mycenaeans invade Crete.

**c.1300** Bronze Age culture in central Europe, known as the Urnfield culture.

**c.1250** Trojan Wars, between Mycenaeans and Trojans (from the city of Troy, in Turkey), end in the destruction of Troy.

*Mycenaeans tricked the Trojans with the gift of a wooden horse, with soldiers hidden inside.*

**c.1200** Mycenaean cities are gradually abandoned.

**c.1100-800** Dark Ages in Greece: Mycenaean civilization collapses, old cities are destroyed, people disperse and the art of writing is forgotten.

1001BC

## THE MIDDLE EAST

**c.2000BC** Hittite people arrive in Anatolia (Turkey).

### BABYLON AND ASSYRIA

In **c.2000BC**, a desert tribe called the Amorites set up kingdoms around the old city-states of Mesopotamia. Two of these - Babylon and Assyria - grew into great empires. Under King Hammurabi (**c.1792-1750BC**), Babylon conquered Akkad and Sumer, and other territory. Hammurabi was also a great administrator, and was concerned for the welfare of his people.

*Assyrian gold*

The Assyrian kingdom was based around the cities of Ashur and Nineveh. The Assyrians were an aggressive, militaristic people. Under King Shamshi-Adad and his son, Ishme Dagan, the Assyrians built up their first empire (**c.1814-1754BC**).

*Painting of an Assyrian*

**c.1650-1450** Hittite Old Kingdom: Hittites set up small states in Turkey. They sack Babylon in **c.1595**.

**c.1550-1200** Most of Canaan is ruled by Egyptians.

**c.1500** Aryans settle in the land now called Iran.

**c.1450** Assyrian empire is taken over by the Mitanni people.

**c.1450-1200** Hittite New Kingdom: their territory stretches from the Mediterranean to the Persian Gulf.

**c.1400** First mention in Egyptian records of groups of raiders, known as the Sea Peoples, in the Mediterranean.

*A reconstruction of a sea battle between Egyptians and Sea Peoples, based on a carving at Luxor in Egypt*

**c.1375-1047** Middle Assyrian empire.

**c.1300** Medes and Persians settle in Iran.

**c.1250** Hebrews arrive in Canaan.

**c.1200** Sea Peoples conquer Cyprus and Mediterranean cities, destroying most of the Hittite empire by **c.1195**.

**c.1200-1000** Rise of Phoenicians in Lebanon. They found cities at Byblos, Sidon, Beirut and Tyre. Their alphabet forms the basis for Greek, Latin and modern Roman scripts.

**c.1150** Peleset (or Philistines), a group of Sea Peoples, settle in Canaan, later called Palestine, after them.

**c.1020** Saul becomes king in Israel.

**c.1010-926** United Jewish kingdom of Israel.

## AFRICA

**c.1720BC** Egypt is invaded by people called the Hyksos.

*Egyptian model of fishing boats, found in a tomb*

**c.1674-1567** 2nd Intermediate Period in Egypt: dynasties XIV-XVII.

**c.1600-1000** Egypt rules Kush (Sudan).

### THE NEW KINGDOM IN EGYPT

The Egyptian New Kingdom (dynasties XVIII-XX) lasted from **c.1567-1085BC**. This was the period when Egypt's power was at its height. Their warrior kings, known as pharaohs, conquered a vast empire, and were buried in brightly decorated tombs, deep in the cliff sides of the Valley of the Kings, near Thebes.

*Egyptian mummy*

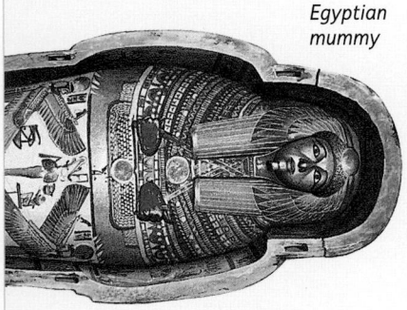

**c.1500** Cattle and goats are domesticated in West Africa.

**1490-1468** Reign of Hatshepsut, female pharaoh of Egypt.

*Carved head of Hatshepsut*

**c.1450** Egyptian empire reaches its greatest extent.

**1364-1347** Egypt: reign of Akhenaten. He tries to impose the worship of one god, but fails.

**c.1285** Battle of Quadesh between Egypt and Hittites: neither side wins.

**1280** Ramesses II of Egypt makes peace with the Hittites.

**1190** Ramesses III of Egypt defeats the Sea Peoples.

**c.1085** Nubia and Kush regain their independence from Egypt.

**1085-656** 3rd Intermediate Period in Egypt: dynasties XXI-XXV. Egypt begins to decline.

## ASIA

**c.1800BC** The Indus Valley civilization starts to decline, partly due to the arrival of Indo-Europeans, or Aryans, from the northwest from **c.1500**, and partly to the flooding of the Indus, which destroys cities already in decline. Aryan control spreads as far east as the Ganges river.

*This statue may be of an Indus Valley ruler or priest.*

**c.1766-1027** First known Chinese dynasty, the Shang, rules China. A feudal state, with walled cities and temples ruled by priest-kings.

*The Bronze Age in China began with the Shang dynasty. Elaborate containers like this were used in religious ceremonies.*

**c.1500-600** Vedic Period in India. Religious poems called the *Vedas* are composed, and passed on by word of mouth. They become the basis for the Hindu religion. The Aryans set up several kingdoms, each ruled by a *rajah*, and divide people into social classes: priests, warriors, farmers, traders and Dravidians (non-Aryans). This is the origin of the Hindu caste system.

**c.1400** First examples of writing in China.

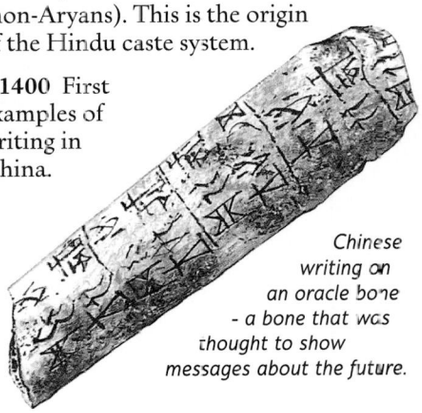

*Chinese writing on an oracle bone - a bone that was thought to show messages about the future.*

**c.1027-221** Zhou dynasty overthrows the Shang in China. Period of trade and economic growth, but also of instability and wars.

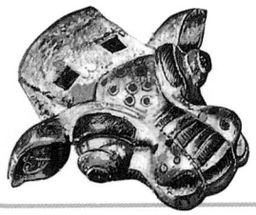

*Ornament for a horse's chariot, found in a grave near Loyang, the Zhou capital*

## THE AMERICAS

2000BC

**c.2000BC** People settle in the Arctic.

**c.2000** First evidence of farmers growing corn and metal-working in Peru.

**c.2000-1500** Pottery spreads among farmers in Peru.

**c.2000-1000** The beginning of Mayan culture in Mesoamerica (Central America). This is known as the Early Pre-Classical Period. Farmers begin to settle in villages.

**c.1800-900** The Initial Period in Peru. People settle in permanent villages, and there is evidence of social and religious organization. The use of pottery spreads.

**c.1500** North America: agriculture reaches the southeast and, rather later, the midwest.

**c.1500BC-AD200** Rise of the Olmec culture on the coast of the Gulf of Mexico. The Olmecs use hieroglyphics (picture writing) and calendars. They build ceremonial architecture at La Venta and other sites, and carve huge heads from a stone called basalt and small jade figures.

*This huge head was carved from a single block of stone.*

**c.1200** A series of temples is built at San Lorenzo, Mexico, by the Olmec people.

**c.1200-300** Chavín people create the first civilization in South America. Skilled stoneworkers, they build huge temples filled with sculptures and are the first people in South America to make things from gold.

*This gold ornament may have been made for a Chavín priest.*

1001BC

## EUROPE

1000BC

**c.900BC** The Etruscans are established in northern Italy. They are skilled at working in metal.

**c.800** Greek poet Homer composes the *Iliad* and the *Odyssey*: epic poems describing the Trojan Wars.

**c.800** First evidence of a Celtic culture in Hallstatt (Austria).

*Etruscans made many statues of warriors like this one.*

### THE FOUNDING OF ROME

From about **1000BC**, groups of Indo-Europeans, skilled in working in iron, settled in Italy. One group, the Latins, built villages on the edge of the Tiber river, which grew to become the city of Rome. Traditionally founded in **753BC**, Rome became the focus of a great civilization which lasted nearly 1000 years. The early Romans were ruled by kings until **510-509BC**, when a republic was set up.

**776** Traditional date for the first Olympic Games in Greece.

**c.750** Greek city-states begin to found colonies in Turkey.

**c.700-500** Bronze Age culture named after Hallstatt in Austria, with evidence of salt-mining and iron-working.

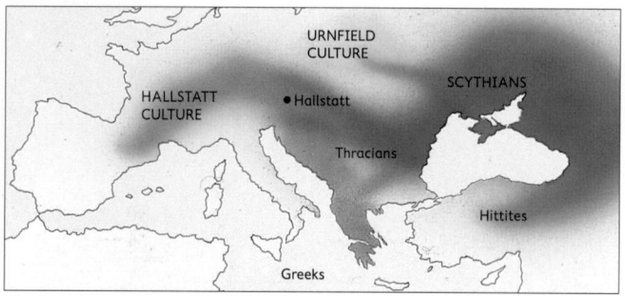


**c.700** Indo-European people called the Scythians spread from central Asia to eastern Europe. They raid nearby lands from **c.700-600BC**.

**683** Athens replaces its hereditary kings with nine archons (chief magistrates), chosen yearly by the nobles.

**c.600-500** The Archaic Period in Greek art.

**594** Solon is made sole archon of Athens. He introduces government reforms.

**514** Scythians fight off an attack by Persians.

**510** Roman republic is established. It is ruled by the Senate, a group of 100 men, called senators, from leading families.

**c.508** Greek politician Cleisthenes introduces reforms which lead to democracy in Athens.

*Scythian horseman*

501BC

## THE MIDDLE EAST

**c.1000BC** The Arabs tame camels.

**c.965-928** Solomon rules Israel. Temple built at Jerusalem.

**c.926** Israel splits into Israel and Judah.

### THE NEW ASSYRIAN EMPIRE

The New Assyrian empire lasted from **c.911-609BC**. At its peak, it covered Mesopotamia and mountains to the east, Syria, Lebanon, Palestine and Lower Egypt. The Assyrians built great cities with palaces and temples.

*Ashurnasirpal II (883-859BC)*

**874** First evidence of Nabataean people in Arabia.

**835-825** Kingdom of Urartu (or Ararat) around Lake Van, Turkey, major base for iron and copper trade. Conquered by Assyrians **(721-715)**, then Scythians and Medes (610).

**c.800** Kingdom of Phrygia is established.

**c.730** Babylon becomes part of the Assyrian empire.

**722-705** Reign of Sargon II of Assyria. Height of Assyria's military power. He conquers Israel and sacks Babylon.

**704-681** Reign of Sennacherib of Assyria. He conquers Phoenicia **(701)** and builds a new capital at Nineveh.

**c.700-546** Kingdom of Lydia. First to develop coins.

**c.700-600** Kingdoms of Persia and Media are set up.

**689** Babylon is destroyed by the Assyrians.

**668-627** Reign of Ashurbanipal of Assyria.

**625-605** Reign of Nabopolassar, who becomes King of Babylon, setting up the New Babylonian empire.

**612-609** Assyrian empire collapses.

**605-561** Reign of Nebuchadnezzar II. Rebuilds Babylon, making it a great city. Destroys Jerusalem in **587**.

**560-546** Croesus of Lydia takes control of most Greek colonies in Asia Minor (Turkey).

**559-530** Cyrus II rules Persia. Conquers Assyria in **550**, Lydia and cities in Turkey in **546** and Babylon in **539**.

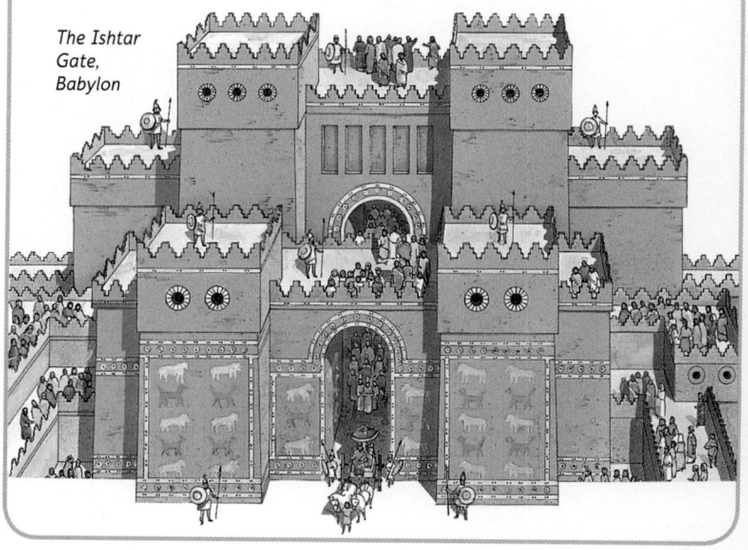

*The Ishtar Gate, Babylon*

## AFRICA

**814BC** Founding of Carthage in North Africa by the Phoenician princess, Elissa of Tyre.

**750-664** Egypt is ruled by kings from Kush (dynasty XXV), who are later driven back south, where they set up the kingdom of Meroë.

*King Taharka of Kush (**690-664BC**)*

*A pyramid at Meroë*

**c.700** Cattle and sheep are domesticated in West Africa.

**671** Assyrians conquer Egypt.

**664-332** Late Period in Egypt: dynasties XXVI-XXX. Egypt is reunited by princes from Saïs.

**663** The use of iron tools and weapons spreads in North Africa.

**c.650** Carthage builds up her fleet to protect colonies in the Mediterranean.

**c.590** Meroë becomes the capital city of Kush.

*Sahara rock painting of herdsmen with their cattle*

**525-404** Persia conquers and rules most of Egypt.

**510** First of several treaties between Carthage and Rome, ensuring Carthage's trade monopoly in the western Mediterranean.

## ASIA

**c.800BC** Hindu religion spreads into southern India.

*Hindu symbol known as the 'wheel of life', representing the cycle of life, death and rebirth*

**660** Legendary date for the founding of Japan under Emperor Jimmu. In fact, Japan was probably not united under a monarchy until **c.120.**

**c.650** Iron-working begins in China.

**c.600** Probable date for the introduction of the religion and philosophy of Taoism, by the Chinese philosopher Lao-tze.

*Taoist symbol representing the harmony between the two opposing forces of the universe, known as yin (female) and yang (male)*

**c.560-480** Life of Gautama Siddhartha, known as the Buddha, Indian founder of Buddhist religion.

*Head of the Buddha from Gandhara, India*

**c.551-479** Life of Kung Fu-tze, also known as Confucius, Chinese philosopher. He lived in a time of warfare and believed peace could only be restored if people followed a strict code of conduct.

*Confucius*

**512** Indian provinces of Sind and Gandhara become part of Persian empire.

## THE AMERICAS

**1000BC**

**c.1000-300BC** The Adena people are based around the Ohio River Valley in North America. They live in small groups, farming corn and beans. They also construct burial mounds and earthworks for ceremonial buildings.

*Snake-shaped Adena burial mound*

**c.900** Mexico: San Lorenzo is destroyed. Olmecs build the first ball court at La Venta, for use in religious festivals, rather than sport.

**c.900-200** The Chavín culture flourishes in Peru, producing fine work in gold and silver.

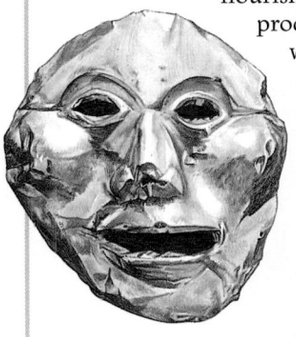

*Chavín gold mask*

*Olmec jade sculpture*

**c.700** Founding of Monte Albán, sacred city of the Olmecs, in Oaxaca, Mexico.

**c.600** Oaxaca becomes the base for Olmec culture.

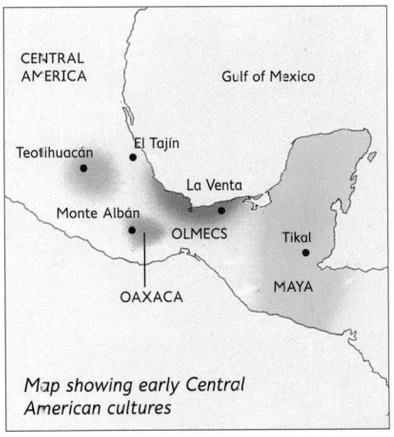


*Map showing early Central American cultures*

**501BC**

# EUROPE

500BC

## CLASSICAL GREECE

The period from **c.500-338BC** in Greece is known as the Classical Period. It was the great age of the Greek city-states. Ideas of art, architecture, literature, drama, politics, philosophy, science and history developed at this time provided the foundations for European civilization. Much of the activity was based in Athens, where commerce, as well as culture, thrived. Rivalry between the cities, and between Athens and Sparta in particular, led ultimately to the Peloponnesian Wars, which tore the Greek world apart and ended the Classical Period.

*A reconstruction of the Parthenon temple in Athens, built between c.447-438BC*

**500-494BC** Greek colonists in Turkey rebel against Persians.

**490** and **480-479** Wars between Persia and Greece.

**490** Greeks defeat Persians at Battle of Marathon.

**479** Greeks defeat Persians at Battle of Plataea.

**461-429** Pericles is active in Athenian politics.

**c.450** Celtic culture, named after a site at La Tène in France.

**431-404** The Peloponnesian Wars in Greece.

**c.390** Rome is sacked by the Gauls, a Celtic tribe.

**359-336** Reign of Philip II of Macedon, in northern Greece.

**338** Philip II defeats Greek cities at Chaeronea.

## ALEXANDER THE GREAT

Alexander (**336-323BC**) came to power after the murder of his father, Philip of Macedon. A brilliant military commander, he extended his empire as far as India, earning the title Alexander the Great. After his death in **323BC**, at the age of 33, his generals, the Diadochi, fought for control of his empire. By **281BC**, it had split into three kingdoms, ruled by the descendants of three Diadochi: Ptolemy, Antigonas and Seleucus. Although his empire did not last, it spread Greek language and culture over a wide area. The period **323-30BC** is often described as the Hellenistic Age, after *Hellene*, meaning Greek.

*Mosaic of Alexander defeating the Persians at the Battle of Issus, 333BC*

**280-168** Antigonid dynasty rules Macedonia.

**279** Celts attack and rob the Greek temple at Delphi.

251BC

**264-241** 1st Punic War between Carthage and Rome.

# THE MIDDLE EAST

*This painting of one of the Persian elite warriors, known as the Immortals, is taken from the palace at Susa, Persia.*

## THE PERSIAN EMPIRE

The Persians first arrived in the area now called Iran in **c.700BC**. King Cyrus II (**559-530BC**) united Persia with the rival kingdom of Media in **550BC** and expanded his territory, taking over Lydia, Greek cities in Asia Minor and Babylon. The empire was at its height under Darius I (**522-486**), who made Persia the largest empire the world had ever seen. He also established a fair and efficient administrative and legal system, and built roads linking Persia with its far-flung provinces.

*Persian armlet made of solid gold*

**c.500BC-AD100** Kingdom of Sabaea on the south coast of Arabia is at its most powerful.

**486-465** Xerxes I rules Persia.

**4th century BC** Nabataeans build a city in rock at Petra, Jordan. They dominate rich trade in goods as far as India.

**332** Alexander conquers Phoenicia.

**331-330** Alexander conquers Persia. Persepolis is burned.

**304-64** Seleucid empire controls Asia Minor, Mesopotamia, Persia and India, but is gradually reduced in size.

**c.280-47** Kingdom of Pontus, founded by Mithridates I.

**279** Celts set up kingdom of Galatia in Turkey.

*Ruins of the city of Petra, in the Nabataean kingdom*

**279-74** Kingdom of Bithynia established.

**263-133** Kingdom of Pergamum, founded by Eumenes I.

**247BC-AD277** Kingdom of Parthia established.

## AFRICA

**c.500BC-AD400** Nubian kings move their capital south to Meroë. A new phase of cultural development follows, with the building of towns, temples, palaces and pyramids, all showing Egyptian influence.

**c.500BC-AD200** Nok civilization in Nigeria.

*Nok sculptors made life-size pottery heads.*

**c.500BC-AD500** Bantu people move through Africa.

**343-332** Egypt is conquered and occupied by Persia.

**332** Egypt is conquered by Alexander the Great.

**323-30** The Ptolemaic dynasty (descended from Ptolemy, one of Alexander's generals) rules Egypt from Alexandria. It becomes an important base for learning and invention, and the largest city in the Greek world.

*Alexandria lighthouse, one of the wonders of the ancient world*

## ASIA

**500BC-AD300** Yayoi culture in Japan is influenced by people who come from China and Korea with bronze-making skills. Rice farming and metalwork begin.

**481-221** The Warring States Period in China: all seven kingdoms of China are at war with each other.

**327-325** Alexander the Great campaigns in India.

**321-185** The first Indian empire is founded in northern India by Chandragupta Maurya, who begins the Maurya dynasty in India. He seizes the kingdom of Magadha and then takes control of much of Pakistan and Afghanistan.

*Indian war elephants*

**272-231** India: reign of King Asoka of the Maurya dynasty. He unites northern and central India and builds a network of roads. Despite his early reputation as a warrior, he later becomes a Buddhist and abandons military conquests.

*Capital of a column erected by Indian King Asoka*

## THE AMERICAS

500BC

**c.500BC-AD200** The Paracas culture in southern Peru. The people are skilled at weaving and embroidery.

*Paracas embroidery*

**c.400BC** Mexico: Olmec city of La Venta is abandoned.

**c.300** Gradual decline of the Olmec culture in Mexico. Rise of Zapotec culture in Oaxaca region.

**c.300BC-250AD** Rise of the Maya in Central America: the Late Pre-Classical Period. Important political and religious bases develop around stone cities such as Monte Albán, Teotihuacán and El Tajín.

**c.300BC-550AD** North America: the Hopewell people displace the Adenas. They are great mound-builders and traders.

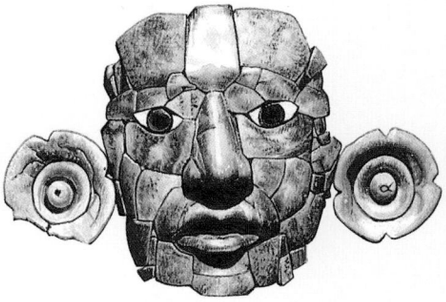

*Mayan mask*

*Part of a Mayan calendar. Dots, dashes and curved lines indicate dates.*

251BC

## EUROPE

250BC

**218-201BC** 2nd Punic War between the Carthaginians, from North Africa, and the Romans: Hannibal of Carthage crossed the Alps into Italy, with an army that included 40 war elephants.

*Hannibal's army crossing the Alps with his war elephants*

**215-205, 200-197** and **171-163** Wars between Rome and Macedonia end in the partition of Macedonia.

**149-146** 3rd Punic war between Rome and Carthage ends in Roman victory. Carthage is destroyed.

**146** Greece becomes part of the Roman empire.

**110-106** Scythian lands are conquered by King Mithridates of Pontus, on the Black Sea.

**102-101** General Marius defeats Germanic tribes invading the Roman empire.

**82-79** Sulla becomes Roman dictator, followed by Pompey **(52-46)**.

**58-51** Julius Caesar, a Roman general, conquers Gaul (France).

**45-44** Caesar is Roman dictator. He is assassinated and civil war follows.

**31** Battle of Actium: Caesar's heir, Octavian, defeats Roman politician Mark Antony and Cleopatra, Queen of Egypt, and becomes ruler of Rome.

*A Roman legionary (foot soldier)*

## THE MIDDLE EAST

**247BC-AD277** Parthian kingdom is founded in Central Asia. Mithridates I **(171-138BC)** extends control in Persia and Mesopotamia.

**168** Judas Maccabeus leads Jews against the Seleucids.

**133** The last king of Pergamum in Asia Minor bequeathes his kingdom to Rome.

**c.100BC-AD150** Nabataea (Jordan) is rich and powerful.

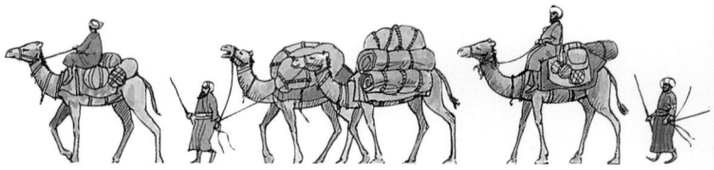

**88-64** Kingdom of Pontus is gradually reduced in size after war with Rome.

**74** Kingdom of Bithynia passes under Roman rule.

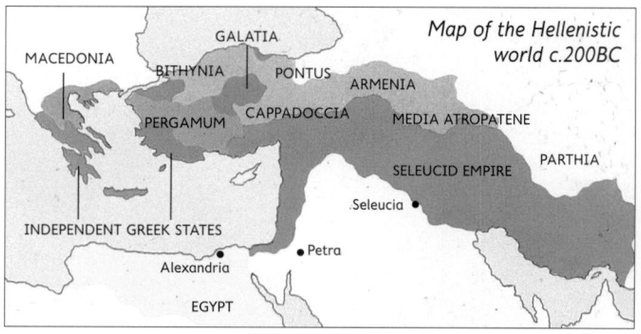


*Map of the Hellenistic world c.200BC*

**64** Palestine becomes the Roman province of Judea.

**47** Battle of Zela: Julius Caesar conquers the kingdom of Pontus.

**37-4** Rule of Herod the Great, King of Judea.

**c.5** Birth of Jesus Christ in Bethlehem, Judea.

*Jesus's mother Mary on her way to Bethlehem*

## THE ROMAN EMPIRE

1BC

*Emperor Augustus*

In **27BC**, Octavian became the first Roman emperor, taking the title Augustus, and ruling until **AD14**. The empire lasted about 500 years. It expanded across the whole of the Mediterranean, reaching its greatest extent under emperors Trajan **(AD98-117)** and Hadrian **(AD117-138)**. But from **c.AD200** its borders were frequently under attack by barbarian tribes and the empire was beset by other problems: economic recession, civil wars and a succession of weak or corrupt emperors. In **AD476**, the empire finally came to an end.

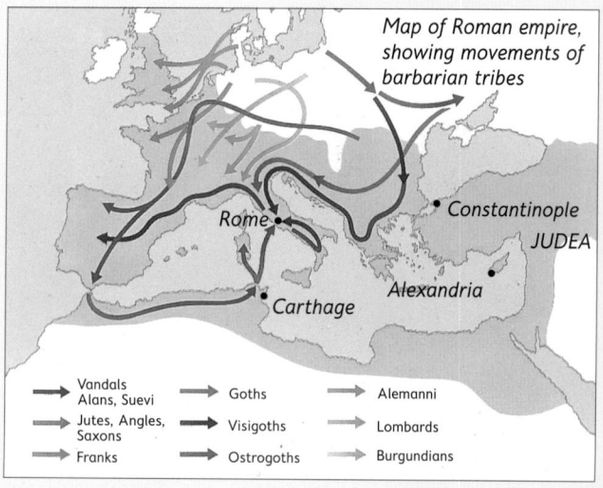


*Map of Roman empire, showing movements of barbarian tribes*

## AFRICA

**203BC** The Romans defeat the Carthaginians at Tunis, North Africa.

**202** The Romans destroy the Carthaginian army at Zama, Tunisia.

**146** Carthage is destroyed and becomes a Roman province.

*Roman legionaries, the well-trained soldiers who conquered a huge empire*

**111-105** Jugurtha of Numidia, in North Africa, is defeated by the Roman general Marius, and his kingdom is absorbed by Rome.

**30** Egypt becomes a Roman province after Queen Cleopatra is defeated by the Roman leader Octavian.

*Queen Cleopatra VII, shown in this Egyptian style portrait, was the last of the Greek Ptolemy dynasty to rule Egypt.*

## ASIA

### THE QIN DYNASTY

In **221BC**, the Qin (or Ch'in) kingdom conquered the six other kingdoms of China and the Qin ruler named himself Shi Huangdi, or 'first emperor of China'. In **214BC**, he built the Great Wall of China, a 3460km (2150 mile) wall to protect China from invaders called Hsiung-Nu (Huns). When the emperor died in **210BC**, he was placed in a vast tomb, watched over by an army of terracotta (pottery) model soldiers.

*The Great Wall of China*

**c.200BC** Three kingdoms in South India.

**c.200** India is invaded by Bactrians and Parthians. Small Greek states are set up in the Punjab from **c.170**.

### THE HAN DYNASTY

There was unrest in China after the death of Shi Huangdi. Then, in **202BC**, the Han dynasty took control, when a soldier named Liu Bang made himself emperor. His dynasty ruled until **AD220**, and China grew in size and prosperity.

*Chinese nobleman*

**c.185** India: end of Mauryan empire.

**c.150BC-AD50** Bronze age culture in North Vietnam, named after the village of Dong-son.

**140-87** China expands under Emperor Wu-ti to include Korea and North Vietnam. He develops an efficient civil service, reduces the power of the nobles, and builds a network of roads and canals.

**c.100s** North India is invaded by Greeks and nomadic tribes.

## THE AMERICAS

250BC

**c.200BC-AD200** Paracas Necropolis culture flourishes in Peru. Brilliant embroidered textiles have been found in a cemetery from this period.

**c.200BC-AD600** Peru: regional development and technological experiments among the Moche people of the north coast and the Nazca people of the south coast.

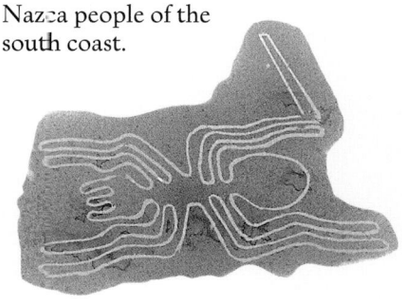

*This 45m (148ft) long giant spider was carved in the desert by the Nazca people.*

**c.200BC-AD700** The rise of the culture of Teotihuacán in Mexico.

**c.100BC** North America: Hohokam people in the southeast build ditches and dykes to irrigate their crops. They also build platform mounds and ball courts.

*Nazca pottery*

*South American vegetables*

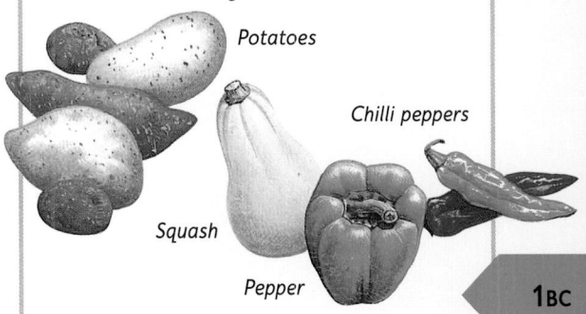


1BC

## EUROPE

1

**AD43** Romans conquer Britain.

**61** Queen Boudicca of the Iceni, a British tribe, leads a revolt against the Romans in East Anglia.

*The Arch of Titus, commemorating the capture of Jerusalem by Rome in AD70*

**72-80** The Colosseum is built in Rome.

**79** The volcano Vesuvius erupts in Italy.

**98-117** Reign of Emperor Trajan: the Roman empire reaches its greatest extent.

**122-127** Hadrian's Wall is built to mark the northern frontier of the Roman empire in Britain.

**c.200** Germanic tribes attack the frontiers of the Roman empire.

**286** Emperor Diocletian splits the Roman empire into East and West.

*Portrait of a Christian family in Roman times*

**312** Constantine becomes emperor of the Western Roman empire.

**313** Edict of Milan: Christians granted freedom to worship in Roman empire.

**324-337** Constantine reunites the Roman empire.

**c.370** Huns invade Europe from Central Asia.

**378** Battle of Adrianople: Roman emperor Valens is killed by barbarian tribes called Goths.

**391** Emperor Theodosius makes Christianity the state religion in the Roman empire.

**395** Roman empire is permanently split into East and West.

**401-413** Visigoths invade Italy and sack Rome. The Roman capital is moved to Ravenna, Italy.

**c.410-520** Angles, Saxons and Jutes settle in England.

**415** Visigoths found kingdom of Toulouse.

**443-534** Burgundian kingdom in Rhône-Saône area, France.

**451** Battle of Châlons, France: Romans and Franks halt the invasions of Huns in Europe.

**455** Barbarian tribes of Vandals sack Rome.

**456-711** Visigoth kingdom established in Spain.

**457** Anglo-Saxons establish seven kingdoms in Britain.

**476** Rome is sacked: the end of the Western Roman empire.

**481-511** Reign of Clovis, King of the Franks. Founds the Merovingian dynasty. He becomes a Christian in **496**.

**493** Italian kingdom of Theodoric of the Ostrogoths.

499

## THE MIDDLE EAST

**AD26-36** Pontius Pilate is governor of Judea.

**c.29** Jesus Christ is crucified.

**45-48, 49-52, 54-58** Paul of Tarsus makes missionary journeys around the eastern Mediterranean, spreading Christianity. He travels to Rome in **58-60**.

*Paul of Tarsus*

**66-73** Jewish revolt against the Romans in Judea. The Romans sack Jerusalem in **70** and destroy the Jewish stronghold of Masada in **73**.

**106** The Nabataean kingdom becomes a Roman province.

**115-117** Jewish uprisings in Egypt, Cyrenaica and Cyprus.

**131-135** Unsuccessful Jewish revolt, led by Bar Cochba. Jerusalem is destroyed.

*Roman ruins at Palmyra in Syria*

**227** The Sassanid dynasty is established in Persia by Ardashir I.

**260** Shapur I of Persia defeats the Romans and captures Emperor Valerian.

**268-272** Queen Zenobia of Palmyra conquers Syria, Mesopotamia and parts of Egypt.

**310-379** Reign of Shapur II of Persia.

**324** Constantine rebuilds Byzantium, renames it Constantinople, and makes it the Roman capital.

**325** First Council of the Christian Church meets at Nicaea in Anatolia (Turkey).

**484** The Persian empire is attacked by Huns and the emperor is killed.

*The Huns were armed horsemen from Central Asia. They used stirrups, then unknown to people farther west.*

## AFRICA

**AD44** Mauretania (Morocco) is conquered by Rome.

**70** Christianity reaches Alexandria. Starts spreading south from **c.180**.

**100-700** Civilization of Axum (Ethiopia): a trading state which derives its wealth from maritime trade and the export of ivory.

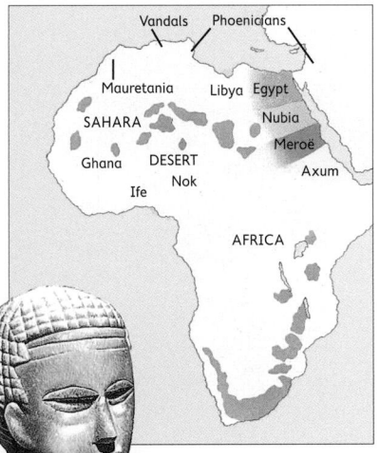


*Areas where rock paintings have been found*

*Sandstone sculpture from Meroë*

**193-211** A Libyan, Septimius Severus, becomes Roman emperor.

**238** Revolt begins in North Africa against Roman rule.

**c.285** Monastic life starts in Egypt.

**c.300-1200** Kingdom of Ghana.

**c.330-350** King Ezana rules Axum.

**c.333** The state of Axum converts to Christianity.

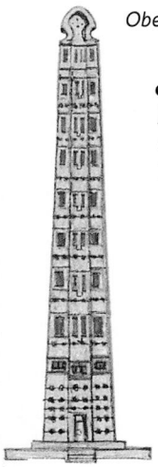

*Obelisk from Axum*

**c.350** Axum conquers Meroë and becomes the dominant power in the Red Sea area.

**c.350-600** The X-group culture flourishes in Nubia.

**c.400** The first towns appear south of the Sahara Desert.

**c.400** The use of iron spreads in East Africa.

**429-533** Vandal kingdom is set up in North Africa.

## ASIA

**AD1-100** Buddhism spreads from India throughout Asia.

**8-25** Hsin dynasty in China.

**25-222** Han dynasty is restored in China: a new age of Chinese culture.

**c.50** Nomadic tribes from Bactria, Central Asia, establish the Kushan empire in northern India.

**91** Chinese defeat the Huns in Mongolia.

**c.100** Paper is invented in China.

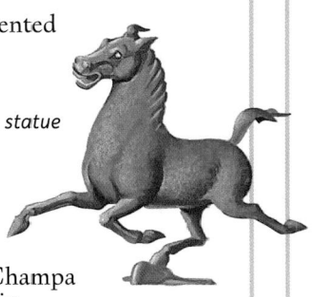

*Flying horse bronze statue from Kansu, China*

**c.100** Buddhism reaches China.

**c.100-1600** The Champa kingdom is set up in Southeast Asia.

**c.180** Tribes start to unite in Japan.

**c.195-405** Parthians control northern India.

**222-265** The Han dynasty in China is replaced by three separate states.

**265-316** China is divided into many small states.

**c.285** Traditional date for the introduction of writing to Japan.

**c.300-500** Yamato government in Japan. Society is organized into clans, who follow the Shinto religion.

**304** Huns break through the Great Wall in northern China.

**316** Japan invades Korea.

**316-589** Rival dynasties established in north and south China.

**320-535** Gupta empire in India is founded by Chandragupta II. Classical Age in India.

*Statue of the god Vishnu from the Gupta period*

**c.400** Settlers from Southeast Asia reach Easter island.

**430-470** Gupta empire breaks up after Huns invade.

**c.450** Writing comes to Japan from China.

## THE AMERICAS

**c.AD1-500** Basket makers culture in the southwest of North America.

**c.50** Central America: city of Teotihuacán is built, including the Great Pyramid of the Sun.

*Pyramid of the Sun, Teotihuacán*

**c.200-600** Growth of civilization around the city of Tiahuanaco, near Lake Titicaca in Bolivia.

**c.250-750** The Classical Period of the Zapotec culture in Mexico.

**c.500** Central America: Teotihuacán is rich and powerful.

*The powerful jaguar, native to South America*

### THE MAYA

One of the greatest early American civilizations was that of the Maya, which lasted from **c.2000BC-AD1460**. The Maya built cities deep in the Central American jungle, worshipped many gods and studied the stars. Mayan culture reached its peak in the Classical Period (**c.AD250-900**). They invented calendars, picture writing and number systems, and their astronomers developed advanced mathematical skills.

*The Maya played a ball game as part of a religious ceremony.*

OSIAS
IONAS

# THE MIDDLE AGES

500 - 1499

## SOUTHERN AND WESTERN EUROPE

**c.500-843** Frankish kingdom in France and Germany.

**507-711** Visigoth kingdom in Spain.

**529** St. Benedict founds the first monastery in Western Europe, at Monte Cassino, Italy.

**c.537** Death of King Arthur of the Britons, at the Battle of Camlan.

*Arthur, famous for his Knights of the Round Table, is shown here as a knight. He may have been a British chief who fought the invading Saxons.*

*Visigoth crown belonging to King Recceswinth*

**553** Emperor Justinian takes control of Ostrogoth kingdom in northern Italy.

**554** Emperor Justinian conquers part of the Visigoth kingdom in Spain.

**563** St. Columba, an Irish monk, founds a monastery on Iona, and sends missionaries to England and Scotland.

**568-774** Lombard kingdom in northern Italy.

**596** St. Augustine is sent to Britain by Pope Gregory to convert the Saxons to Christianity.

*Augustine preaching*

*An Anglo-Sazon helmet found in a ship grave in East Anglia*

**c.600** England is divided into seven kingdoms.

**664** Synod of Whitby: English Christians choose Roman rather than Celtic (Irish) branch of Christianity.

**c.695** Lindisfarne Gospels are produced: the first book of psalms in Anglo-Saxon.

## NORTHERN AND EASTERN EUROPE

**c.500-700** Slavs begin migrating from the Pripet region, west of the Dnieper river, to the forest areas of Russia and Eastern Europe.

### JUSTINIAN AND THE BYZANTINE EMPIRE

*Mosaic from Ravenna of Justinian's empress, Theodora*

The eastern Roman empire, usually known as the Byzantine empire, survived for a thousand years after the fall of Rome. Based in Constantinople (originally Byzantium, and now Istanbul), it was a major political power and helped to preserve classical learning and Christianity through the Eastern (Orthodox) Church. One of the greatest Byzantine emperors was Justinian (**527-565**). He rebuilt much of the city and organized the legal system into the Justinian code (**528-534**), the basis for modern European law. He also struggled to reconquer the old Roman empire, taking control of the Vandal kingdom in North Africa in **535**, the Ostrogoth kingdom in Italy in **553**, and part of the Spanish Visigoth kingdom in **554**. But these reconquests were lost after his death.

**540-561** War between Persia and the Byzantine empire.

**568** Lombards take northern Italy from the Byzantines.

**c.600** Avars, a nomadic people from the Steppes of Central Asia, establish a kingdom in the Balkans.

**603-629** Wars between Persia and the Byzantine empire.

**610-641** Reign of Byzantine Emperor Heraclius. The official language changes from Latin to Greek.

**611-616** Byzantines lose territory in the Middle East, North Africa, Spain and Sicily to the Persians.

**629** Emperor Heraclius wins back territory from Persia

**632-750** Arabs attack the Byzantine empire.

**674-678** Arabs unsuccessfully besiege Constantinople.

**c.680** Bulgars, a nomadic people from Central Asia, invade the Balkans and establish a Bulgar state.

*Church of St. Sophia, Constantinople, built in Justinian's reign*

## AFRICA AND THE MIDDLE EAST

**531** Justinian sends a group of monks, led by Julian, to the Christian kingdom of Axum, Ethiopia.

**531-579** Chosroes I rules the Persian Sassanid empire. The empire is at its greatest extent.

**533-697** Byzantines rule North Africa.

**543** Julian spreads Christianity to Nubia, which is divided into three Christian kingdoms - Nobatia, Makuria and Alodia. They are cut off from the rest of Christendom by the Arab conquest of Egypt (see below).

### MOHAMMED AND THE RISE OF ISLAM

The prophet Mohammed (**c.570-632**), founder of Islam, was born in Mecca, Arabia. In **610**, he began preaching that there was only one God, Allah, and won many converts. After local hostility, he was forced to flee to Medina (**622**), where he organized his followers. By his death, Islam had spread throughout most of Arabia - by means of conquest and conversion. He was succeeded by a series of elected caliphs, who created a vast Islamic empire between **632-850**.

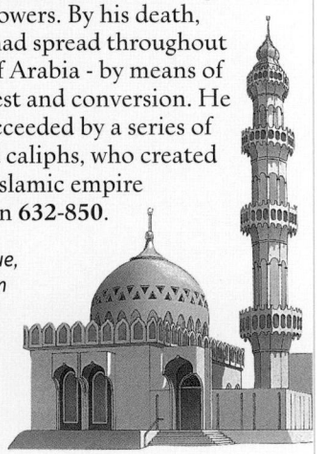

*A mosque, a Muslim place of worship*

**611-619** Persians conquer Byzantine territory in Middle East and North Africa: Antioch, Damascus, Jerusalem and Egypt.

**632** Mohammed is succeeded by Abu Bakr, who becomes first caliph.

**637-638** Arabs overrun Syria and Iraq and Jerusalem.

**639-642** Arabs occupy Egypt.

**642** Arabs overthrow Sassanids. Persia adopts Shi'ite branch of Islam.

**661-750** Omayyad dynasty rules from Damascus.

**697-700** Arabs conquer Carthage and Tunis. North African coast converts to Islam.

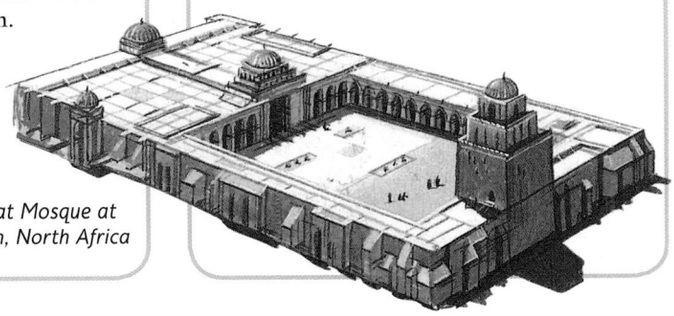

*The Great Mosque at Kairouan, North Africa*

## ASIA

**c.500** Yamato emperors control most of Japan.

**535** Gupta empire collapses. India divides into warring kingdoms.

**552** Buddhism is introduced into Japan from China.

**581** General Yang Chien founds the Sui dynasty. He unites China in **589**.

**594** Buddhism becomes the Japanese state religion.

**605-610** China: millions of people are drafted to build the Imperial Canal, linking the rivers Yangtze and Huang Ho.

**606** Written examinations are introduced in China for entry into the civil service.

**607** Tibet is politically unified.

**618-907** T'ang dynasty in China: one of China's most brilliant periods, in terms of the arts and military conquest.

**624** Buddhism becomes the official religion in China.

**627-649** Reign of T'ai tsung the Great, Emperor of China.

**c.628-645** Hsuan-tsang travels from China to northern India, returning home with manuscripts and statues.

**645** Buddhism reaches Tibet.

**657** Chinese defeat Turks and extend their power in Central Asia.

**668** Chinese take Pyongyang, capital of Korea.

**690-713** Empress Wu siezes the throne in China.

*Emperor T'ai tsung*

## THE AMERICAS

**c.500** North America: Hopewellian mound-builders begin to decline. Mississippi mound-builders start to appear at the lower end of the Mississippi River.

*Pottery bottles made by Mississippi mound-builders*

**c.500-900** Golden age of the Zapotec culture in Oaxaca, Mexico.

**c.500-1200** Culture of the Central Gulf coast of Mexico, also known as Totonac, based around El Tajín.

**c.600** Peak of Mayan civilization.

*A Mayan king with his servant*

**c.600** The Teotihuacán culture is at its peak, extending from the city to surrounding highlands. The city is about 20km (8 miles) square and laid out on a grid. Its wealth comes from agriculture, crafts and trade.

*A later Mexican city, Tenochtitlán, built* **c.1325**

**c.600-1000** The Middle Horizon Period in South America. Large towns are built. Local cultures are merged under two great empires, based around Tiahuanaco, an important religious base, and Huari, a military capital.

**c.650-850** Teotihuacán culture slowly declines.

**c.650-900** Huastecan culture in Mexico.

## SOUTHERN AND WESTERN EUROPE

700

**c.700s** Great age of art and literature in Ireland.

*The Ardagh cup, looted by Vikings in Ireland*

**711** North African Arabs, known as 'Moors', conquer Spain, except the northwestern kingdom of Asturias.

**732** Battle of Poitiers: Arabs advance into France and are defeated by Frankish leader Charles Martel and forced to retreat.

**756-1031** Arab Omayyad caliphate rules from Córdoba, southern Spain.

**751** Pepin III deposes the last Merovingian king of France and becomes first Carolingian king of France.

### CHARLEMAGNE

In **768**, the kingdom of Pepin III was inherited by his sons, Carloman and Charles. When Carloman died in **771**, Charles became sole ruler (**771-814**). A brilliant soldier, he built up the Frankish empire between **773-804** to include most of France, Germany and northern Italy, earning the title Charlemagne ('Charles the Great'). A committed Christian, he campaigned against non-Christian kingdoms and built churches and monasteries all over his empire. In **800**, the Pope crowned him 'Emperor of the Romans' in recognition of this.

*A golden bust of Charlemagne decorated with precious stones*

**751** Lombards conquer Ravenna, the last Byzantine possession in north Italy.

**757-796** Reign of Offa of Mercia. Builds a dyke to keep out the Welsh. Becomes ruler of all England by **779**.

**c.790-794** Vikings begin raiding Europe. They plunder Lindisfarne and Jarrow, England.

**806** Vikings raid a monastery on Iona, a Scottish island. Monks flee to Ireland.

**c.830-900** Frequent Viking raids on the British Isles and France.

**832-847** Vikings raid and settle in Ireland.

**843** Kenneth MacAlpin, King of the Scots tribe, becomes King of Scotland.

**843** Charlemagne's empire is split into three kingdoms.

**858** Rhodri Mawr is recognized as Prince of all Wales.

**867-874** Danes conquer Mercia, Northumbria and East Anglia.

**871-899** Reign of Alfred the Great of Wessex. He resists further conquests by the Danes. England is divided into Wessex and the Danelaw.

*Alfred fighting a Dane*

899

## NORTHERN AND EASTERN EUROPE

### THE VIKINGS

The Vikings were farmers, traders and warriors from Scandinavia. Increasing population and shortage of land at home drove some to raiding and looting. Between **c.800-1100**, they terrorized much of Europe. But the Vikings were also skilled shipbuilders and navigators, and they sailed as far as North America in search of new land. Many settled peacefully in Normandy in France (named after 'Northmen') and Russia, where they founded the first Russian state, named after a Viking tribe, the Rus.

**c.700** Vikings first arrive in Russia.

**716-1018** Bulgar state recognized by the Byzantine emperor.

**716-717** Arabs unsuccessfully besiege Constantinople.

**717** Byzantines ally with Bulgars and Khazars.

**726-843** Iconoclasm: Byzantine emperors prohibit the use of icons (religious pictures) and many are destroyed.

**787** Church Council of Nicaea orders the restoration of icons in churches.

**812** Battle of Adrianople: Khan Krum of Bulgaria defeats the Byzantines and kills their emperor.

**830** Slav kingdom of Moravia is established. It is destroyed by Magyars in **906**.

**c.860** Swedish Vikings settle in Russia.

**861** Vikings discover Iceland and settle there in **874**.

**862** St. Cyril and St. Methodius work as Christian missionaries in Moravia. Cyril adapts the Greek alphabet for the Slavs. It becomes known as the Cyrillic alphabet.

*Mosaic of Jesus Christ, from St. Sophia, Constantinople*

**c.862** Rurik of the Rus tribe of Vikings founds a Russian state, based in Novgorod.

**866** Conversion of Russia to Christianity begins.

**867-1056** Macedonian dynasty rules Byzantine empire.

**882** Russian ruler Oleg the Wise conquers Kiev.

**889** Magyars invade Hungary and set up a state under the Arpad dynasty (**896-1301**).

**c.890s-930s** Norway is first organized as a single kingdom, under Harald Fairhair.

## AFRICA AND THE MIDDLE EAST

**c.700s** Arab merchants develop a flourishing trade with rich Saharan trading cities. The Arabs bring horses, copper, tools and weapons in exchange for gold, ivory, skins and slaves. This encourages the growth of strong African kingdoms and trading empires.

*African king receiving Arab traders in Timbuktu*

**c.700-1200** Kingdom of Ghana: the first West African trading empire, rich in gold.

**750-1258** The Abbasid dynasty rules from Baghdad, Iraq: a golden age of Islamic culture.

*Arab astronomers from the Abbasid period, taken from an Islamic illustration*

**786-809** Reign of Abbasid caliph Harun al Rashid, known for the *Thousand and One Nights* stories.

**788** Shi'ite kingdom founded in Morocco.

**c.800** Three small, independent Arab kingdoms are set up in North Africa.

**c.800-1000** Kingdom of Igbo Ukwu in West Africa.

**c.800-1800** Kingdom of Kanem-Bornu, a great trading empire in West Africa.

**868-905** Tulunid dynasty rules Egypt and Syria.

## ASIA

**c.700-900** The Sailendra kingdom in Southeast Asia.

**c.700-1300** The Srivijaya kingdom in Southeast Asia.

**710-794** First permanent Japanese capital city is established at Nara.

**711** Arabs invade northern India.

**745-840** Uighur empire established in Mongolia.

**c.750-1000** Maoris from Pacific Polynesian islands reach New Zealand.

**c.750** Three empires in India wage war against each other: Rajputana (northwest), Rashtrakuta (south), and Bengal (northeast). Arabs begin invading the Indus region.

**751** Abbasids defeat Chinese armies at Talas River, ending China's influence in Central Asia.

**794-1185** Heian Period in Japan: the emperor rules from Heian (now Kyoto). Power is increasingly in the hands of the nobles.

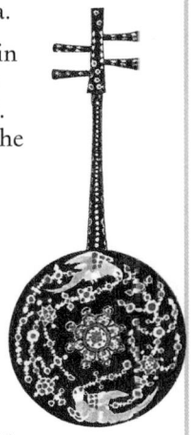

*A Heian lute, inlaid with mother-of-pearl*

*Phoenix Hall, Heian, Japan*

**c.800-1400** Khmer dynasty established kingdom in Cambodia, Southeast Asia, based at Angkor.

**842** Tibetan kingdom disintegrates.

**c.858-1160** Fujiwara clan controls the government in Japan.

**868** Earliest printed book, Buddhist *Diamond Sutra*, is produced in China.

**886-1267** Chola kings control most of southern India.

## THE AMERICAS

700

### MISSISSIPPI VALLEY CULTURE

From **c.700s**, the farmers of the Mississippi Valley began to build towns. In the middle of the towns were flat-topped mounds, on which they built temples or houses for the chief. The biggest town, Cahokia, had over a hundred mounds.

*Mississippi town showing flat top mounds*

**c.700-1000** North America: Hohokam farming communities in the southwest (Arizona) reach their most prosperous stage. They build platform mounds and play ball games, suggesting links with the Mayan people of Mexico.

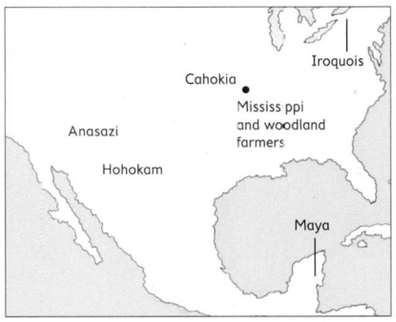


*Map of North and Central America c.700*

**c.700-1000** Anasazi farmers emerge in southwestern North America.

**c.750** Desert tribes in southwest of North America begin building villages, known as pueblos, with rooms stacked one above the other.

**c.750** Central America: the city of Teotihuacán is destroyed.

**c.750** Mayan civilization begins to decline.

**c.850** Mayan civilization collapses. Many cities abandoned.

899

## SOUTHERN AND WESTERN EUROPE

900

**c.900-911** Vikings settle in Normandy.

**910** Benedictine Abbey is founded at Cluny in Burgundy.

**911** Rollo, a Viking chief, is made Duke of Normandy. He is given Rouen and surrounding land by the Frankish king, Charles the Simple, on condition that he swears allegiance, and becomes a Christian. The land is known as terra *Normannorum* ('the land of the northmen' in Latin).

*Rollo being welcomed by the Archbishop of Rouen*

**912-961** Reign of Abd al-Rahman, Caliph of Córdoba in Spain: a period of prosperity and a flourishing of Arab culture.

**917-921** King Edward of Wessex conquers the southern half of the Danelaw (Danish-occupied part of Britain).

**924-939** Anglo-Saxon King Athelstan rules in England.

**926** Athelstan seizes the Danelaw.

**937** Athelstan repels an invasion by Vikings, Scots and Britons at the Battle of Brunanburh.

**979-1013** Reign of Anglo-Saxon King Ethelred the Unready.

**986-987** Reign of Louis V, last Carolingian king of France.

**987-996** Hugh Capet becomes first king of the French Capetian dynasty. The dynasty rules France until **1328**.

**991** Danes defeat the English at the Battle of Malden. The English are forced to pay Danegeld, a tax to prevent more Danish attacks.

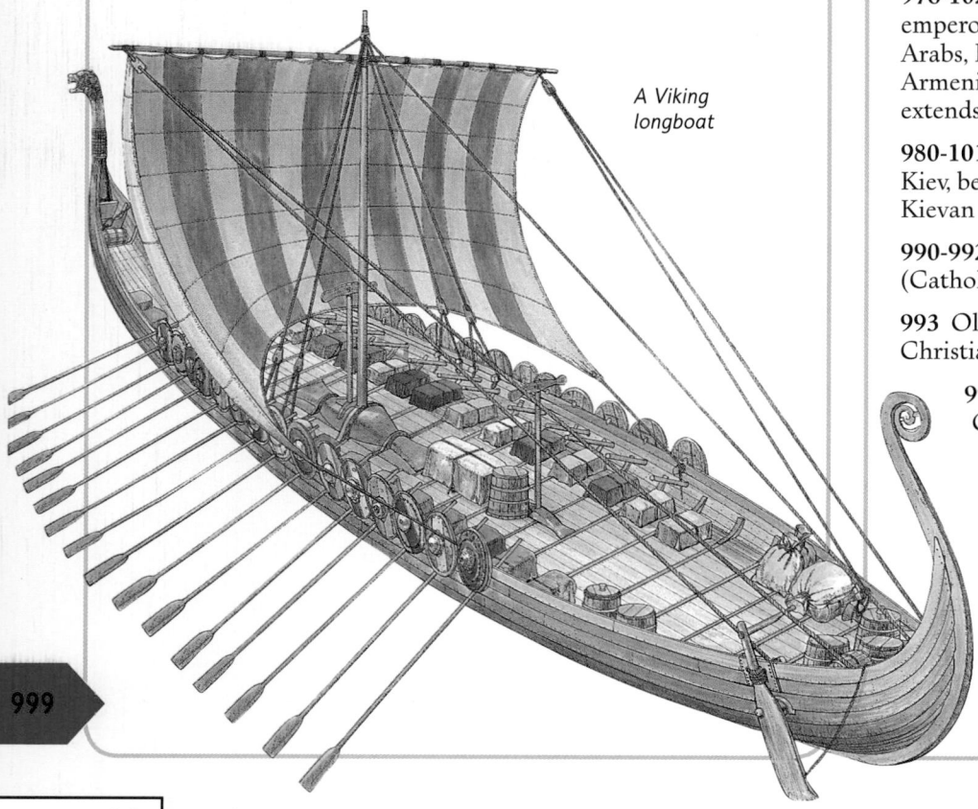

*A Viking longboat*

## NORTHERN AND EASTERN EUROPE

**911** Death of Louis III ('the child'), last Carolingian king of Germany. Conrad of Franconia becomes King of Germany.

**919-936** Reign of Henry I 'the Fowler' of Saxony, first king of the Saxon dynasty in Germany.

**929-967** Bohemia is united under Boleslav I, after he murders his brother Wenceslas.

**933** Henry I of Germany defeats the Magyars.

*Battle of Lechfeld*

**936-973** Reign of Otto I of Germany. He controls the German duchies and conquers Italy.

**955** Battle of Lechfeld: Otto I stops the westward advance of the Magyars, a nomadic people from Central Asia.

**960** Mieszko I (**960-992**) unites northern Poland and founds a Polish state.

**961** Byzantines take Crete from the Arabs.

**962** Otto I is crowned 'Holy Roman Emperor of the German nation' and rules until **973**.

*Harold Bluetooth's rune stone, the Jelling Stone, showing an image of Jesus Christ*

**965** Harald Bluetooth, King of Denmark, becomes a Christian.

**965** Russia destroys the Khazar empire.

**970-997** Geza I controls the Magyars and unites Hungary.

**976-1025** Reign of Basil II, Byzantine emperor. He wins victories against Arabs, Russians, Bulgarians, Armenians and Normans, and extends the Byzantine empire.

**980-1015** Vladimir, Grand Prince of Kiev, becomes sole ruler of Kievan Russia.

*Vladimir of Kiev*

**990-992** Poland adopts the Western (Catholic) Church.

**993** Olaf Skötkonung becomes the first Christian king of Sweden.

**995-1000** Reign of Olaf Tryggvason of Norway. Christianity is introduced.

**997-1038** Reign of Stephen I (St. Stephen), first Christian king of Hungary.

*Crown of Stephen I*

999

## AFRICA AND THE MIDDLE EAST

**c.900** West Africa: trade and prosperity grows in Hausaland, a region on the Lower Niger.

**902-1004** The Samanid dynasty rules in Persia. With their capital at Bukhara in Samarkand, their empire covers the region between the Caspian Sea and the Hindu Kush mountains. They develop important trading contacts, both with China and the far north.

*Samanid tomb at Bukhara, Central Asia*

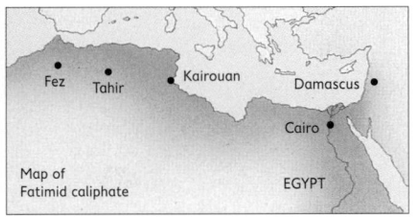


*Map of Fatimid caliphate*

**909-972** Fatimids take over the Arab kingdoms in North Africa.

**969-1171** Fatimids take control of Egypt. They build Cairo, which becomes the Egyptian capital.

**c.970** Cairo University established.

**997-1030** Reign of Mahmud, Sultan of Ghazni, who builds an empire in eastern Afghanistan and northern India. Ghazni becomes a base for Islamic culture.

*Islamic city*

## ASIA

**c.900** The Mataram dynasty is established in Java, Indonesia.

**907-960** Collapse of the T'ang dynasty in China is followed by the Epoch of the Five Dynasties. China is divided by civil wars.

**916** Khitan kingdom is founded in Mongolia.

**936** Three kingdoms in Korea are united under the state of Koryo.

**947-1125** Khitans overrun northern China and set up the Liao dynasty.

**960-1127** Northern Sung dynasty reunites central and southern China and rules from Kaifeng.

**985-1014** Reign of Rajara I, of the Chola kingdom, southern India. He conquers Kerala, South India (985) and Sri Lanka (1001).

*Bronze statue of the Hindu god Shiva*

**990** Yangtu (Beijing) becomes the capital of northern China.

## THE AMERICAS

**c.900** The heart of Mayan culture shifts to the Yucatán peninsula.

*Pyramid of Quetzalcoatl at Chichén Itzá on the Yucatán peninsula, Mexico*

**c.900** Anasazi people, from southwest of North America, begin building pueblos, clusters of buildings nestling in cliffs, reached only by ladders. They weave cotton cloth, make pots using a wheel, and work in turquoise and other stones.

**c.900-1200** Toltecs dominate much of Mexico. They destroy towns around Teotihuacán and invade Mayan territory.

*Statue of a Toltec warrior*

**c.900-1494** Mixtec culture in Mexico.

**947** Mexico: birth of Quetzalcoatl, revered by the Toltecs as a god.

**980** The Toltecs establish a capital at Tula.

**982** Eric the Red, a Viking, begins to colonize Greenland.

*In Greenland, the Vikings came across Inuit people, like this man.*

**c.990s** Quetzalcoatl flees from Tula after feuds between his followers and those of another man-god. He settles in the Mayan city Chichén, which is renamed Chichén Itzá. The city is rebuilt in a mixture of Mayan and Toltec styles.

## SOUTHERN AND WESTERN EUROPE

1000

**1004** Brian Boru is proclaimed 'High King' of Ireland.

**1008-1028** Moorish kingdom of Córdoba in Spain starts to weaken because of civil wars. Followed by the *reconquista*, the reconquest of the Muslim kingdoms of Spain and Portugal by the Christian Spanish kingdoms, which takes place between **1037-1492**.

*The Great Mosque at Córdoba*

**1014-1042** Danish kings rule England.

**1014** Brian Boru defeats the Vikings at Battle of Clontarf, but is killed in battle.

**1016** Normans, led by Robert and Roger Guiscard, invade southern Italy.

**1029** Spain: provinces of Castile and Aragon become independent of Moorish rule.

**1042-1066** Reign of St. Edward the Confessor, King of England.

**1054** Scotland: Macbeth, the Earl of Moray, is defeated and killed at Dunsinane by Malcolm Canmore, whose father, King Duncan, had been murdered by Macbeth.

**1054** The Pope makes Robert Guiscard Duke of Apulia and Calabria and invites him to take Sicily from the Arabs.

**1054** Eastern Orthodox Church splits from the Western Catholic Church.

**1060-1130** Normans conquer Sicily and southern Italy. Roger Guiscard is made Count of Sicily (**1061-1091**).

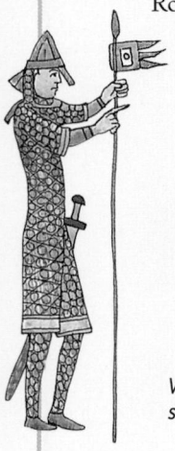

**1066** Battle of Hastings: William of Normandy conquers England, becoming King William I (**1066-1087**).

*William of Normandy (left) and part of the Bayeux tapestry showing the Norman cavalry attacking English footsoldiers*

**1071** Normans conquer Bari, last Byzantine city in Italy.

**1075-1122** Investiture Controversy: a quarrel between the Pope and the Holy Roman Emperor over who has the right to invest (or appoint) bishops and abbots. Settled at the Concordat of Worms (**1122**).

**1085** Castile conquers Moorish province of Toledo. Hero of the struggle is Rodrigo Diaz de Vivar, known as El Cid.

**1086** Domesday Book is compiled in England: a survey of all the property in the land.

1099

**1094** Portugal wins independence from Moorish Spain.

## NORTHERN AND EASTERN EUROPE

**1001** Pope recognizes the Christian kingdom of Hungary.

**1014-1035** Cnut, King of Denmark, rules an empire which covers Denmark, England and part of Sweden.

**1015-1028** Reign of Olaf II ('the Saint'), King of Norway.

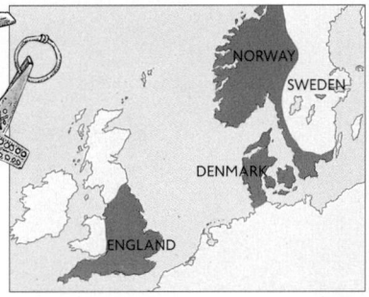


*Above left: Viking Christian symbols. In Cnut's reign, English missionaries converted the Danes to Christianity.*

*Left: map of Cnut's empire*

*A wooden church in Borgund, Norway*

**1019-1054** Yaroslav the Wise rules Kievan Russia.

**1028** Cnut conquers Norway and Olaf flees to Russia.

**1035** The kingdom of Norway is restored by Magnus the Good (**1035-1047**), after the death of Cnut.

**1035** Poland becomes a fief (subject state) of the Holy Roman Empire.

**1054** Schism (or split) between the Eastern Orthodox and Western Catholic Churches, after the Pope insists on supremacy over the whole Christian Church.

**1059-1078** Dukas dynasty rules Byzantine empire.

**1071** Battle of Manzikert: Byzantines are defeated by the Seljuk Turks and lose Asia Minor (Turkey).

*Seljuk Turks, nomadic people from Central Asia*

**1081-1085** Normans, led by Robert Guiscard, invade the Balkans.

**1081-1185** Comneni dynasty rules the Byzantine empire.

**1086** Holy Roman Emperor recognizes Bohemia as a kingdom under Vratislav.

**1093** Nomadic people called Polovtsy sack Russian capital, Kiev.

**1095** Byzantine emperor, Alexius Comnenus (**1081-1118**), calls on Pope Urban II for help against the Turks.

**c.1100** Viking raids end.

## AFRICA AND THE MIDDLE EAST

**c.1000-1200** Trading ports grow up on the east coast of Africa.

**c.1000-1450** Kingdom of Ife in West Africa.

**c.1000-1897** Kingdom of Benin in West Africa.

**c.1030** Seljuk Turks, nomadic people from Central Asia, extend their influence in Asia Minor.

**c.1050-1123** Life of Omar Khayyam, Persian mathematician, astronomer and philosopher, and author of the *Rubaiyat*, a famous series of poems.

**1052** Muslim Almoravids attack Ghana, which is destroyed by **1076**.

**1055** Seljuk Turks conquer Baghdad, the Abbasid capital.

**1056-1147** Almoravid kingdom in North Africa and Spain.

**1076** Seljuk Turks take Jerusalem and Damascus from the Fatimids. This provokes the Crusades.

### THE CRUSADES

The Crusades were military expeditions fought by European Christians to win back the Holy Land (Palestine) from the Seljuk Turks. As militant Muslims, they were far less tolerant than the previous Fatimid rulers, and posed a real threat to Christian pilgrims. After the First Crusade (**1096-1099**), the crusaders took back Jerusalem and set up states in Anatolia and Syria, but these were later lost. There were seven further crusades, but with limited success. By **1291** the last Christian stronghold had disappeared.

**c.1090** Assassins, a branch of Shi'ites who murder to destroy their opponents, are founded in Persia.

## ASIA

**c.1000** Chinese perfect the invention of gunpowder.

*Gunpowder was used in war and in firework displays.*

**c.1000** Maori people settle in New Zealand, after long sea voyages across the Pacific Ocean.

**c.1000-1300** Kingdom of Pagan in Burma, Southeast Asia.

**1001-1026** Mahmud of Ghazni leads raids on northern India and absorbs much of it into his empire.

**1002-1050** Angkor kingdom in Cambodia grows in importance under King Suryavarman.

**1020** Japan: *The Tale of Genji*, the first novel in any language, is written by Lady Murasaki Shikibu.

**1051-1062** Nine Years' Civil War in Japan: the beginning of the rise of the samurai.

### THE SAMURAI

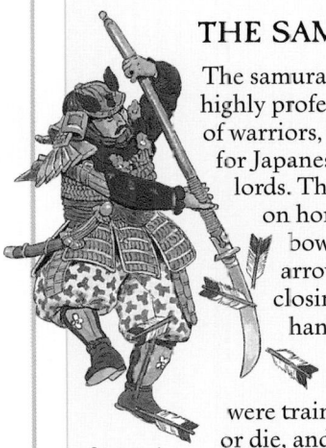

*Samurai warrior*

The samurai were a highly professional caste of warriors, who worked for Japanese feudal lords. They fought on horseback with bows and arrows, before closing in for hand-to-hand combat. Samurai were trained to win or die, and to give absolute loyalty to their lord, in return for gifts of land. They also helped to drive out foreign invaders. Running away from battle was seen as unforgivable, and samurai were sometimes even expected to commit ritual suicide, known as *seppuku*, or *harakiri*.

**1083-1087** Three Years' Civil War in Japan.

## THE AMERICAS

1000

**c.1000** Leif Ericsson, son of Eric the Red, travels along the North American coast, before returning to Greenland.

### THE VIKINGS IN AMERICA

Viking explorers appear to have been the first Europeans to set foot in North America - almost 500 years before Christopher Columbus landed in the Caribbean. Leif Ericsson landed in three places on the East Coast - which were probably Baffin Island, Labrador and Newfoundland. The remains of Viking-style buildings and other objects were dug up in Newfoundland in **1968**.

*Right: a statue of Leif Ericsson, in Iceland*

*Left: a Skraeling, the Viking name for Native Americans*

**c.1000** Hopewell people discover how to etch designs with acid.

**c.1000** Northern Iroquois people settle around eastern Great Lakes and St. Lawrence River.

**c.1000** Thule Eskimo people start to spread across the North American Arctic region.

**c.1000-1483** Late Intermediate Period in South America. Decline of the Huari-Tiahuanaco culture. Local styles and cultures re-emerge.

*Early Peruvian pot*

**c.1000-1600** The Easter Islanders, in the South Pacific, build huge stone heads.

1099

## SOUTHERN AND WESTERN EUROPE

1100

**1105** Roger Guiscard II is Count of Sicily. He acquires Calabria (**1122**), Apulia (**1127**) and is made King of Sicily (**1130-1154**). The Normans rule Sicily until **1204**.

**1128** Mathilda, heir to Henry I of England, marries Geoffrey of Anjou, nicknamed 'Plantagenet'.

**1135** Stephen of Boulogne seizes the English throne, on the death of his uncle, Henry I.

**1137-1144** St. Denis, Paris, first Gothic cathedral, is built by Abbot Suger.

*Stained glass window showing Abbot Suger at St. Denis*

**1139** Alfonso I is first King of Portugal.

**1139-1148** Civil war in England: Stephen and Mathilda struggle for the throne. Mathilda is defeated.

*Mathilda, though Queen of England, was never crowned.*

**c.1150** Paris University is founded.

**1152** Mathilda's son, Henry of Anjou, renews the struggle for the English throne.

*Tomb of Eleanor of Aquitaine (1102-1169), wife of Henry of Anjou*

**1153** Stephen recognizes Henry of Anjou as his heir.

**1154-1189** Henry of Anjou is Henry II of England and France.

**1157** Malcolm IV of Scotland cedes Northumberland, Cumbria and Westmoreland to Henry II.

**1159** Henry II introduces scutage, allowing knights to pay money instead of fighting in his wars.

**1170** English nobleman named 'Strongbow' seizes Dublin.

**1170** Thomas à Becket, Archbishop of Canterbury, is killed by Henry II's knights. Becket is made a saint in **1173**.

*15th century illustration of Becket's murder*

**1171** Henry II invades Ireland and proclaims himself Lord of Ireland.

**1184** Inquisition is formed to seek out and suppress heresy (opposition to the official teaching of the Church).

**1186** Constance, daughter of Roger II of Sicily, marries Emperor Henry VI.

*Mosaic showing Roger II of Sicily*

**1189-1199** Reign of Richard I 'the Lionheart' of England. He recognizes the independence of Scotland.

1199

## NORTHERN AND EASTERN EUROPE

**1105** West Germans begin colonizing East Germany.

**1122** Byzantines wipe out the Patzinaks in the Balkans.

**1122** Concordat at Worms, Germany, ends the power struggle between the Pope and the Holy Roman Emperor.

**1137-1268** Hohenstaufen dynasty rules the Holy Roman Empire.

**c.1147** Moscow is founded by Kievan Prince Yuri Dolgoruky.

**1147-1149** Second Crusade ends in complete failure, never reaching the Holy Land.

*A crusader's shield had a cross on it, the sign of his promise to go to Jerusalem.*

**1152-1190** Reign of Frederick I Barbarossa, Holy Roman Emperor. He fights six campaigns in Italy, putting down rebellions by the Normans in southern Italy, and helping the Pope fight rebellions by the Romans in Rome.

**c.1170s** Serbia becomes independent from the Byzantine empire.

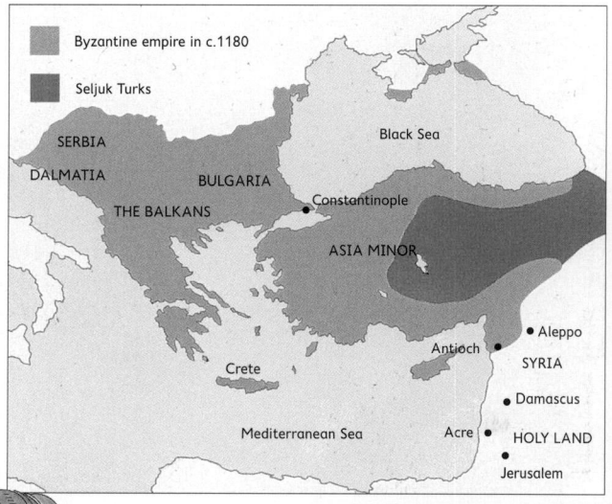


*Map showing territory of Byzantines and Seljuk Turks in the 12th century*

**1171** Emperor Manuel Comnenus arrests all Venetians on Byzantine territory, but loses the resulting war with Venice.

**1176** Byzantines are decisively defeated by the Seljuk Turks at Myriokephalon and lose more territory in Asia Minor.

**1185-1205** Angeli dynasty rules Byzantine empire.

**1186** Bulgarians rebel and establish independence from Byzantine empire.

**c.1190** Teutonic Knights, a military order of monks, are founded in Germany to defend the Christian states in the Holy Land.

## AFRICA AND THE MIDDLE EAST

**c.1100** Kingdom of Ife, West Africa, grows in importance.

*A bronze head of a ruler from Ife*

**1135-1269** Almohad kingdom rules much of North Africa.

**1147-1149** Second Crusade fails to reach the Holy Land.

**1171** Fatimids are thrown out of Egypt by Saladin, who founds the Ayyubid dynasty. He becomes ruler of Syria (**1174**) and Aleppo (**1183**).

*Portrait of Saladin, from an Arab illustration*

**1187** Saladin, Sultan of Egypt, defeats the Christians at the Battle of Hattin and takes control of Jerusalem.

**1189-1192** Third Crusade: Philippe II of France and Richard I 'the Lionheart' of England fail to retake Jerusalem.

**1190** A Christian named Lalibela becomes King of Ethiopia.

**1191** Crusaders capture kingdom of Acre in the Holy Land.

**1192** Peace of Ramlah: Saladin keeps Jerusalem, but recognizes the independence of the Christian kingdom of Acre.

*The castle of Krak des Chevaliers in Syria, rebuilt by crusaders in the 12th century on the site of an earlier Islamic castle*

## ASIA

**1126-1234** Chin dynasty overruns northern China.

**1127-1279** Southern Sung dynasty is established at Nanking, south China.

**c.1150** Suryavarman II of Cambodia (**1112-1152**) completes the temple of Angkor Wat.

*A procession at Angkor Wat*

**1156-1185** Civil wars in Japan between Taira, Fujiwara and Minamoto clans.

**1162** Temujin, later known as Ghengis Khan, is born in Mongolia.

**c.1170** Height of Srivijaya kingdom in Java under Indian Shailendra dynasty.

**c.1180** Angkor empire in Cambodia is at its greatest extent.

**1185** Japan: Yoshitsume Minamoto defeats the Taira clan. The Kamakura Period (**1185-1333**), named after the home district of the Minamoto.

**1192** Yoritomo Minamoto is given power under the title *shogun* (hereditary military dictator). His family rules Japan until **1219**.

**1193** Muhammud of Ghur conquers northern India.

## THE AMERICAS

1100

**c.1100** The Toltecs arrive in the Mayan city of Chichén Itzá.

**c.1100** Cahokia, at the junction of the Missouri and Mississippi rivers, is the largest town in North America.

**c.1100s** The Chimú peoples build large towns, including their capital Chanchan, on the north Peruvian coast. Ancestors of the Incas start to gather around Cuzco, Peru.

*Map of Early Central American peoples*

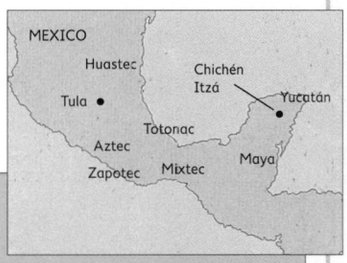


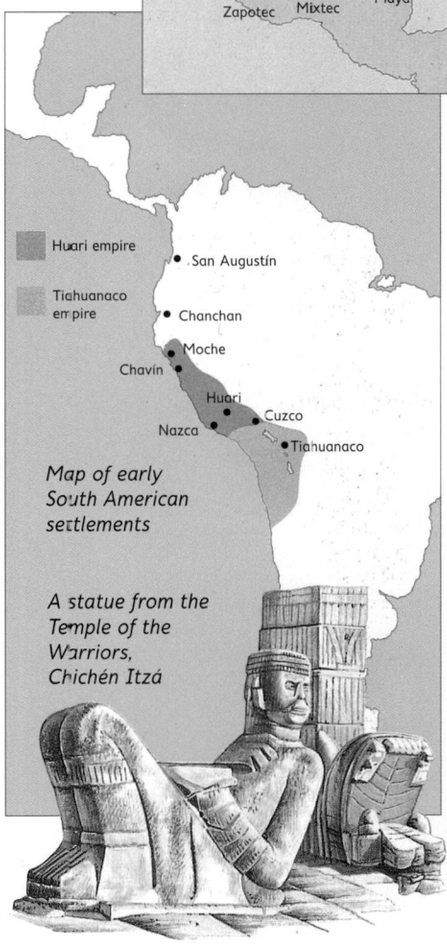


*Map of early South American settlements*

*A statue from the Temple of the Warriors, Chichén Itzá*

**c.1160** Chichén Itzá is invaded by tribes from the north and the Toltecs are scattered.

**c.1170** Chichimec people overrun the Toltec city of Tula. The Toltec civilization is destroyed.

**1179** Chichén Itzá is burned and destroyed.

**c.1190** Second era of Mayan civilization begins.

1199

## SOUTHERN AND WESTERN EUROPE

1200

**c.1200s** Rise of Gothic architecture in Europe.

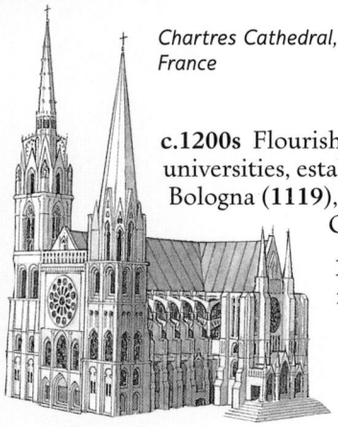

*Chartres Cathedral, France*

*Gothic window*

**c.1200s** Flourishing of the first universities, established in Bologna (**1119**), Paris (**1150**) and Oxford (**c.1170**).

**1202** Arabic numerals are introduced into Europe.

**1204** Philippe II of France conquers English territory in northern France: Normandy, Maine, Anjou and Touraine.

**1210-1229** Albigensian Crusade, led by Simon de Montfort the elder, against the Albigensians, an heretical sect.

**1212** Battle of Las Navas de Tolosa: Christian kings of Castile, Aragon and Navarre defeat the Muslim kingdoms. Starts the break-up of the Muslim kingdoms in Spain.

**1214** Battle of Bouvines: Philippe II takes all remaining English land in France, except Guyenne and Gascony.

**1214-1294** Life of Roger Bacon, English monk, scholar and scientist. He carries out research into optics and is one of the first to suggest the use of lenses as spectacles.

**1215** English nobles force King John to sign the *Magna Carta* ('Great Charter'), giving them the right to a Council to discuss problems. Their meetings grow to form the basis for Parliament.

*An early English court meeting*

### HERETICS

*Heretics burning at the stake*

The medieval Church became more and more powerful and corrupt, which led to criticism and movements for reform. Some complaints about abuses ended in attacks on the Church's authority, or official teaching. The Church condemned this as heresy. The Inquisition was set up to find and suppress heresy. People found guilty were tortured or burned. One popular heretical sect was the Cathars, known as 'Albigensians' in southern France, after Albi, where they began.

**1225-1274** Life of Thomas Aquinas, Italian theologian and philosopher.

**c.1230** Popes begin to use inquisitors to stamp out heresy.

**1244** Albigensians are virtually wiped out after the conquest of their stronghold at Montségur, southern France.

1249

## NORTHERN AND EASTERN EUROPE

**1204** During the 4th Crusade (**1202-1204**), Crusaders sack Constantinople, depose the Byzantine emperor and set up a Latin empire, ruled by Western Roman emperors until **1258**.

**1218** The ruling family in Switzerland dies out. Small independent states, called cantons, are formed.

### FREDERICK II

In **1220**, Frederick II of Hohenstaufen (**1194-1250**), King of Sicily and Germany, became Holy Roman Emperor. Frederick was well-educated and lived in Sicily at the heart of a brilliant court. He reorganized the Sicilian government, making it one of the most advanced European states at the time. But his conduct and attitudes offended many. His conflict with Pope Gregory IX led to a feud between the Ghibellines (Frederick's allies) and the Guelphs (the Pope's supporters), which continued after Frederick's death, causing political chaos in Germany.

**1222** Andreas II of Hungary issues the Golden Bull, giving power to the nobles and rights to the national assembly.

**1224-1239** Teutonic Knights are sent by Frederick II to convert Prussians to Christianity.

**1227** Denmark is defeated at Bornhöved by north German princes, who increase trade with the Baltic.

**1231** German secular princes are given the same rights over territory as ecclesiastical princes.

**1237-1242** Mongols invade Russia, Hungary and Poland and set up the Khanate of the Golden Horde.

*Treasure taken from Russia by the invading Mongols*

**1240** Battle of Neva: Russians defeat Swedes. Their general, Alexander, becomes known as 'Nevsky', because of his part in the victory.

**1242** Alexander Nevsky defeats Teutonic Knights at Battle of Lake Peipus.

**1249** Birger Jarl of Sweden conquers Finland and gives trading privileges to the Hanseatic League, an association of German and Scandinavian trading cities, led by Lübeck.

*Nevsky's father's helmet*

## AFRICA AND THE MIDDLE EAST

**1200s** Trans-Saharan trade continues. Ghana is in decline.

*Saharan traders*

**1200s** East Africa: trading cities, such as Kilwa, continue to flourish.

**c.1200** King Lalibela of Ethiopia builds 11 churches and chapels cut into rock in the Lasta mountains, including the Church of St. George.

*One of King Lalibela's churches*

**c.1200-1300** Mongols invade Seljuk lands.

**1202-1204** Fourth Crusade.

**1217-1219** Fifth Crusade.

**1218** The Egyptian Ayyubid empire breaks up.

**1228** Civil war in Egypt between Saladin's heirs.

**1228-1229** Sixth Crusade: crusaders capture Jerusalem and Emperor Frederick II is crowned King of Jerusalem.

**c.1235** Sun Diata Keita establishes kingdom of Mali, West Africa, which lasts until **c.1500**.

**1240** Kumbi, former capital of Ghana, is destroyed.

**1244** Egyptian Muslims retake Jerusalem.

**1248-1254** Seventh Crusade, led by Louis IX of France against Egypt.

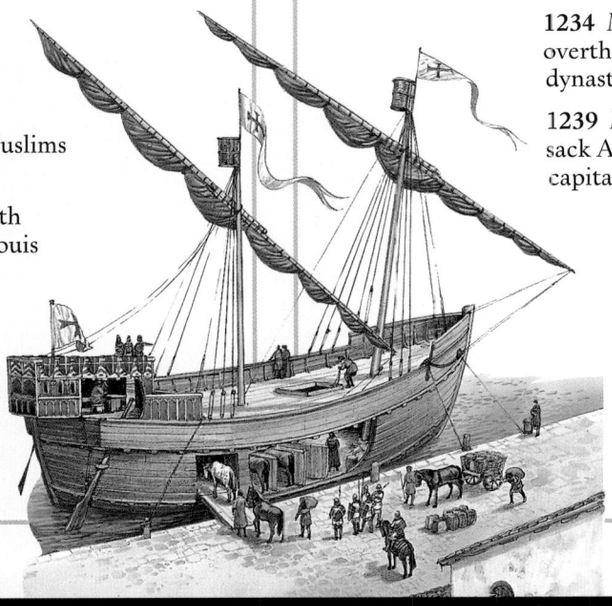

*Crusader galleon cut away to show cargo inside*

## ASIA

**c.1200-1500** First Thai kingdom, Sukhothai, is established.

**1206-1526** Rule of Islamic Sultanate of Delhi, known as the Slave Dynasty: it rules most of northern India.

**1211** Mongols invade China.

**1218-1224** Mongols attack the empire of Khwarizm.

**1221** Mongols attack Delhi.

*Mongol soldiers were trained to fight on horseback*

### THE MONGOLS

The Mongols were warlike nomadic tribes who roamed the plains of Central Asia. In **1206**, a young Mongol warrior named Temujin was given the name Genghis Khan (meaning 'supreme ruler') after uniting the tribes. Under his leadership, the Mongols began a conquest of Asia and built up a vast empire.

**1227** Genghis Khan dies. His son, Ogadei is elected Great Khan (**1229-1241**).

**1234** Mongols overthrow Chin dynasty in China.

**1239** Mongols sack Ani, the capital of Armenia.

## THE AMERICAS

**c.1200** North America: the Mississippians dominate a wide area. They develop a remarkable culture, influenced by Mexico, building large cities on flat-topped mounds.

### THE PUEBLO BUILDERS

By **c.1200**, the Pueblo builders were at their peak in the southwest of North America. They made ornaments from polished stone, pottery jugs and pots and wove clothes from brightly dyed cotton. Towns grew up in places where the Pueblo people met to trade with each other. One of the largest known was Pueblo Bonito, built deep inside a valley, surrounded by a network of roads. It housed around 1200 people in 800 rooms.

**c.1200** The Aztecs begin to found small states in Mexico.

**c.1200** The Mayan capital, Chichén Itzá, is abandoned and a new capital built at Mayapán, defended by 8 km (5 miles) of wall.

**c.1200-1300** Chimú kingdom continues in Peru.

*Chimú gold mummy burial mask*

**c.1200-1300** Beginning of the early Inca period in Peru.

## SOUTHERN AND WESTERN EUROPE

1250

**1250** The Pope gives Sicily to Charles of Anjou (in France).

**1258-1282** Llewelyn of Gruffydd is Prince of Wales.

**c.1258-1265** Uprising of English barons against Henry III, led by Simon de Montfort the younger. Defeated at Evesham.

*Henry III of England (1207-72) being crowned at Gloucester Cathedral*

**1265-1321** Life of Dante Alighieri, Florentine poet and writer, famous for *La Divina Commedia* (the Divine Comedy).

**1275** The English Parliament begins to meet regularly.

**1282** Sicilian Vespers: Sicilians rise against their French rulers and massacre them.

**1282** The death in battle of Prince Llewelyn of Wales marks the end of Welsh independence from England.

**1290** Jews are expelled from England.

**1290** Margaret, child Queen of Scotland, dies. Edward I of England claims the throne.

*A Welsh army attacking an English castle*

**1295** Mateo Visconti seizes control in Milan. His dynasty rules Milan until **1447**.

**1295** Edward I of England calls the Model Parliament, which forms the basis for the House of Commons.

**1297** French occupy Flanders (now part of Belgium).

**1297** Scots, led by William Wallace, defeat the English at the Battle of Stirling Bridge.

*Statue of William Wallace*

1299

## NORTHERN AND EASTERN EUROPE

**c.1250-1480** Mongols withdraw to southern Russia and rule the Khanate of the Golden Horde.

*A Tartar soldier*

**1250** Collapse of imperial power in Germany and Italy, followed by the Great Interregnum (**1254-1273**).

**1253-1278** Rule of Ottokar II of Bohemia.

**1258-1282** Michael Paleologus deposes the Latin emperor in Constantinople and restores Byzantine rule.

*Arabs attacking Constantinople in the 13th century, based on an early drawing*

**1261** Greenland is conquered by Norway.

**1262-1264** Iceland comes under Norwegian rule.

**1263** Norway is defeated by Scots and gives up the Hebrides islands to Scotland.

**1266** Norway gives up Isle of Man to Scotland.

**1273-1291** Rudolf of Habsburg is elected Holy Roman Emperor.

**1278** Ottokar II of Bohemia is killed at Marchfeld. Bohemia and Moravia become estates of the Holy Roman Empire.

**1280-1303** Reign of Daniel, Prince of Moscow, son of Alexander Nevsky. Under his dynasty, Moscow slowly expands in size and importance to become state of Muscovy.

**1282** Rudolf of Habsburg makes his son, Albert, Duke of Austria.

**1291** Three Swiss cantons (Unterwalden, Schwyz and Uri) sign the Pact of Rutli forming the Swiss Confederation.

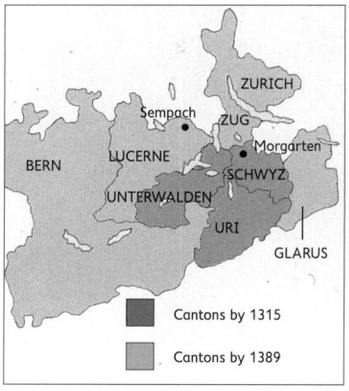


*Map showing Swiss cantons in the 13th and 14th centuries*

**1293** Sweden conquers Karelia (Finland).

**1298-1308** Reign of Albert I Habsburg as Holy Roman Emperor.

## AFRICA AND THE MIDDLE EAST

**c.1250** Ottomans (Muslims from Turkestan) settle in northwest Turkey, working for the Seljuk Turks.

**c.1250** North Africa: Berber states flourish for over 200 years. Europeans call North Africa the Barbary Coast.

**1250** Mamelukes seize power and found their own military state in Egypt and remain in power until **1517**.

**1258** Baghdad destroyed by Mongols.

**1260-1277** Reign of Mameluke Sultan Baibars of Egypt.

**1260** Battle of Ain Jalut, Palestine: the Mongol advance is halted by the Egyptians, led by Sultan Baibars.

*13th-century water clock, built for an Arab sultan. Every hour the bird whistled.*

**1262-1263** Baibars conquers the Ayyubid lands in Syria.

**1265-1271** Baibars takes most of the Christian kingdom of Outremer in the Holy Land.

**1268** Baibars captures Antioch, Anatolia.

**1270-1291** Eighth and last Crusade, led by Louis IX of France, who dies in Tunis, North Africa.

**1281-1326** Reign of Osman I, *emir* (chief) of a small Turkish princedom. In **1301**, he declares himself Sultan of the Turks and becomes the founder of the Ottoman empire.

*Osman I*

**1291** Egyptian Mamelukes take Acre, the last stronghold of Outremer. The end of the Crusades.

## ASIA

**1251-1265** Hulagu, grandson of Genghis Khan, conquers Persia and sets up the Il-Khan empire, which survives until **1336**.

**1259-1294** Kublai Khan takes over as Great Khan, ruling the Eastern Khanate.

**1271-1295** Marco Polo of Venice travels overland to China. From **1275-1292**, he works for Mongol ruler Kublai Khan.

**1274-1281** Unsuccessful Mongol invasion of Japan.

*Kublai Khan*

**1279** Kublai Khan founds the Yuan dynasty in China. Mongol empire is now at its largest.

**1280** Kublai Khan overthrows the Sung dynasty. Yuan dynasty rules all China until **1368**.

**1281** Second attempted invasion of Japan by Mongols. The Japanese attack the Mongol fleet and capture several ships. The rest of the fleet is scattered by *kamikaze* ('divine winds').

*Japanese woodcut showing a Mongol ship under attack*

**1290-1325** Firuz, a Turkish Muslim, founds the Khalij dynasty in Delhi, India. Islam starts to spread south to the Deccan.

**1293** The first Christian missionaries reach China.

## THE AMERICAS

1250

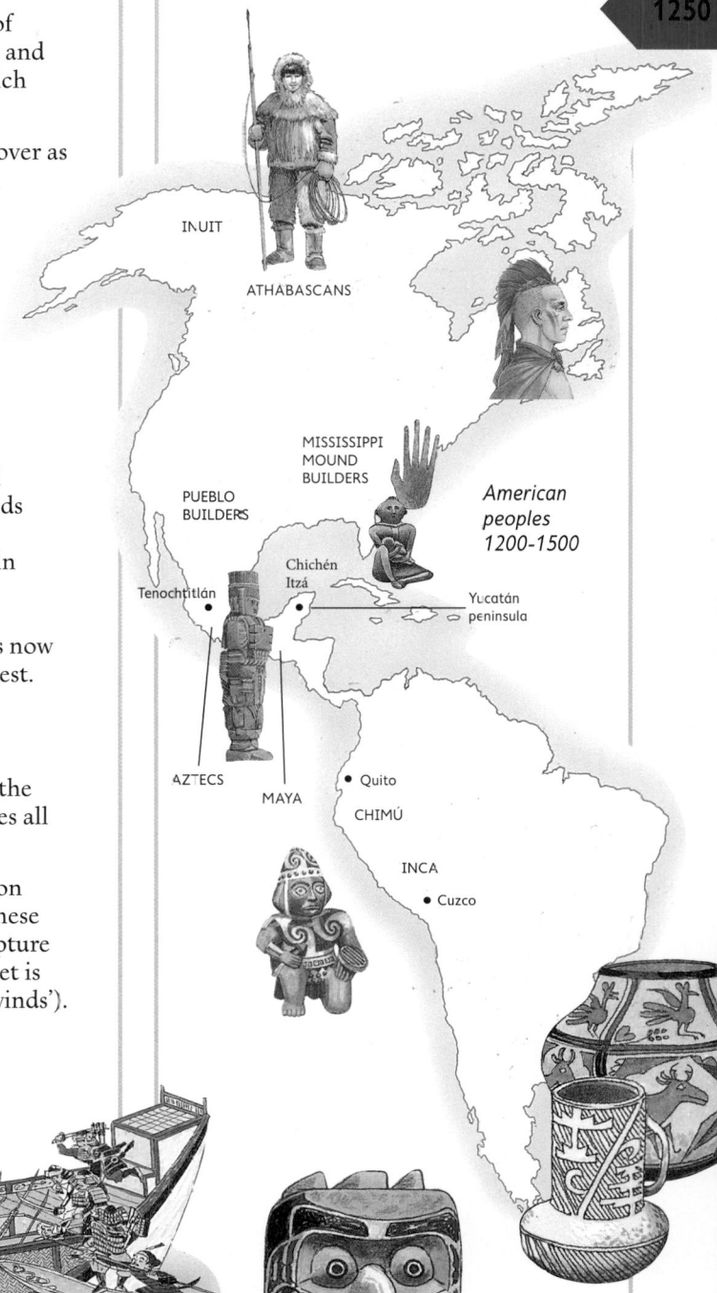


*American peoples 1200-1500*

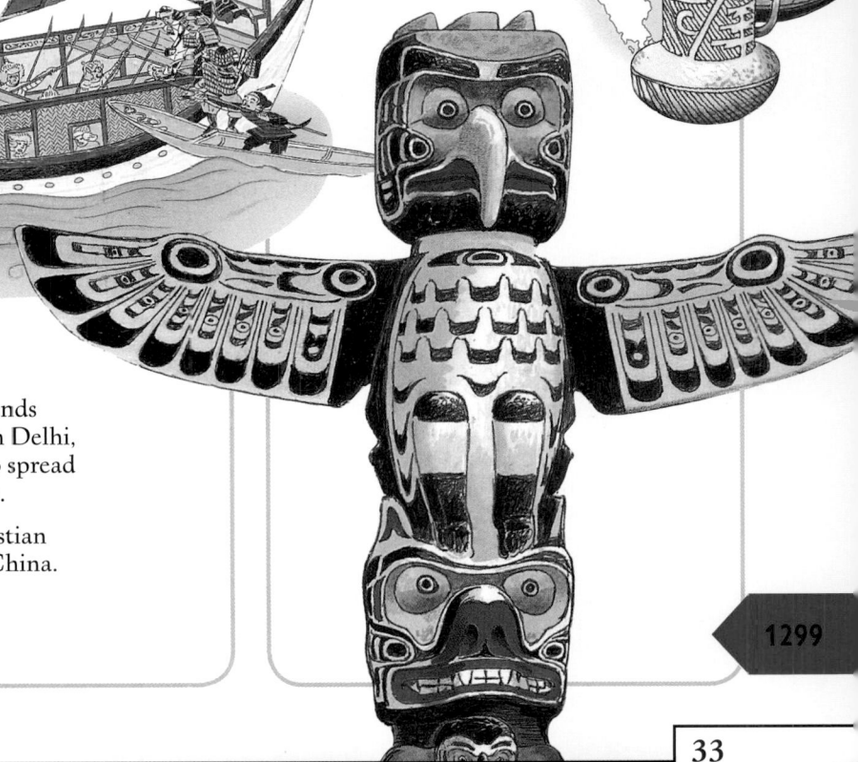

1299

## SOUTHERN AND WESTERN EUROPE

1300

**1301** Wales becomes the principality of the heir to the English throne.

**1302** Flemish craftsmen seize power from wealthy pro-French merchant guilds. They fight and defeat the French army at the Battle of Courtrai, but are beaten at Cassel.

**1306** Jews are expelled from France.

**1307-1314** Knights Templar, a military religious order, are investigated for heresy.

**1309-1378** Pope's court moves to Avignon, France.

**1314** Robert Bruce, King of Scotland (**1306-1329**) defeats the English at the Battle of Bannockburn.

**1317** Salic Law in France bans women from inheriting the throne.

**1323** The Declaration of Arbroath sets the wishes of Scotland's people above those of the Scottish kings.

**1328** Valois dynasty begins in France.

**1328** Edward II accepts Scotland's independence.

### THE HUNDRED YEARS' WAR

The Hundred Years' War is the name given to the struggle between England and France, which lasted from **1337-1453**. Ever since **1066**, there had been wars between them over land held in France by the English kings. This time, war broke out when the English king, Edward III, claimed the French throne itself. The English made early gains, winning battles at Sluys (**1340**), Crécy (**1346**), Calais (**1347**) and Poitiers (**1356**), when they took the French king captive. By the Treaty of Brétigny (**1360**), they won large areas of France, but hostilities soon broke out again. By the end of the war in **1453**, the English kept only Calais and the Channel islands.

*Edward III of England and his coat of arms, which included the fleur-de-lis, symbol of the French kings*

### THE BLACK DEATH

**1347-1353** The Black Death, a bubonic plague carried by fleas on black rats, reaches Genoa, Italy from the East via the Crimea. It sweeps through Europe, killing as many as 20 million people - one person in three.

*Trying to stop the spread of infection by burning the clothes of plague victims*

1349

## NORTHERN AND EASTERN EUROPE

*Hungarian coat-of-arms*

**1301** The Arpad dynasty comes to an end in Hungary.

**1306** King Wenceslas III of Hungary and Bohemia is murdered. The Premsyl dynasty dies out.

**1308** Henry VII of Luxembourg becomes Holy Roman Emperor until **1313**.

**1310** John of Luxembourg inherits Bohemia.

**1315** Battle of Morgarten: Swiss peasants repulse an attack by the army of Leopold I of Austria.

**1320** Vladislav Lokiekek becomes King of Poland and restores Polish unity.

**1328-1340** Moscow grows under Duke Ivan I. It becomes the residence of the Metropolitan, the head of the Orthodox Church in Russia.

*Muscovite artists painted religious pictures, called icons, usually on wooden panels. This one is of St. Michael.*

**1333-1370** Casimir III 'the Great' strengthens Poland.

**1342-1382** Reign of Louis the Great of Hungary. He conquers Croatia, Serbia, Bosnia, Wallachia, Bulgaria, Transylvania and Moldavia.

**1343** Teutonic Knights acquire Estonia from Denmark.

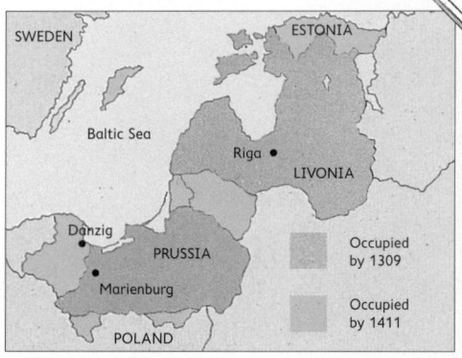


*Territory held by the Teutonic Knights*

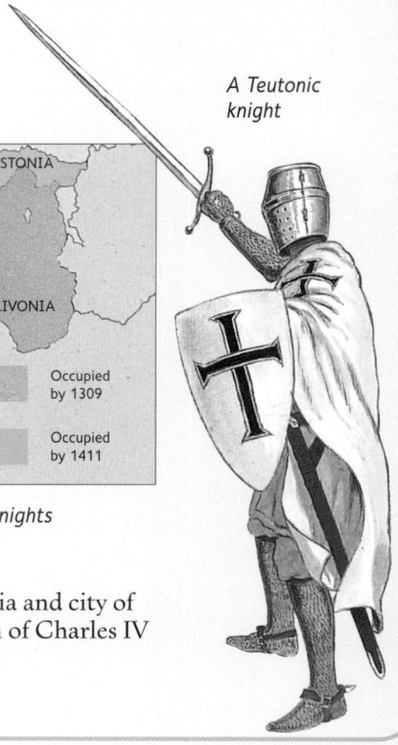

*A Teutonic knight*

**1346** Golden age of Bohemia and city of Prague begins with the reign of Charles IV of the Luxembourg dynasty.

## AFRICA AND THE MIDDLE EAST

**c.1300** The empire of Benin emerges in Nigeria.

**c.1312-1337** Mansa Musa rules Mali.

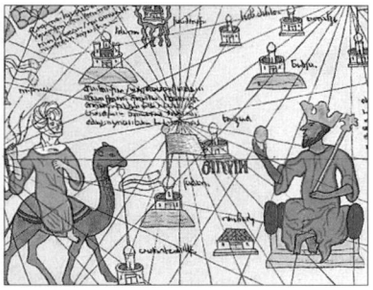

*Mansa Musa, from a 14th-century map*

**1324** Mansa Musa, King of Mali, goes on pilgrimage to Mecca. He visits Cairo and impresses everyone with his wealth.

*Cairo city gates, built during the rule of the Fatimid Dynasty*

**1325** Ibn Batutta, a Moroccan Muslim, travels to Mecca, Arabia, via Egypt, Jerusalem and Damascus.

*Ibn Battuta used Arabic script and probably had writing materials like these.*

## ASIA

**c.1300** Ghazan, Mongol ruler of Persia, declares Islam the state religion.

**1307** The first Catholic archbishop is established in Beijing, China.

**c.1325** No plays develop in Japan: classic Japanese drama, using music and dancing.

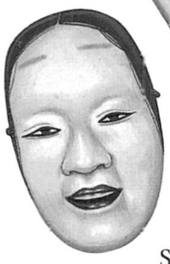

*No masks of a young girl and the devil*

**1325-1351** Reign of Mohammed Ibn Tughluk, Sultan of Delhi. He expands his territories and briefly conquers the Deccan (South India).

*Tower built by the first Sultan of Delhi, to celebrate his victories*

**1333** China suffers drought, famine, floods, and plague. Five million die.

**1333** Kamakura shogunate ends in Japan. Emperor Go-daigo rules without a shogun (1333-1336).

**1336** The Il-Khan empire is replaced by a Turcoman dynasty.

**1336-1565** India: the Hindu empire of Vijayanagar becomes a base for resistance to Islam. It is dominant in southern India by **c.1370**.

**1349** Earliest Chinese settlement in Singapore.

## THE AMERICAS

1300

**c.1300** Constant warfare among the Maya people in Yucatán contributes to the decline of their civilization.

**c.1300** North America: Pueblo building ends abruptly, possibly as a result of drought and the arrival of Athabascan Indians migrating from the northwest. By **c.1500**, they have completely taken over the southwest.

*The quetzal bird, sacred to the Aztecs*

**c.1300** The Inca people settle around Cuzco in Peru.

**c.1300** The Aztec people arrive in the Valley of Mexico.

### THE RISE OF THE AZTECS

From **c.1325**, the Aztecs built up a large, well-organized empire in Mexico. They were a great warrior people, but their culture was also highly sophisticated in many areas, especially science, art, architecture and agriculture. The Aztecs had strict laws and complex religious beliefs and ceremonies. The city of Tenochtitlán, built by a group led by Chief Tenoch, on islands in Lake Texcoco, became the residence of the major tribe.

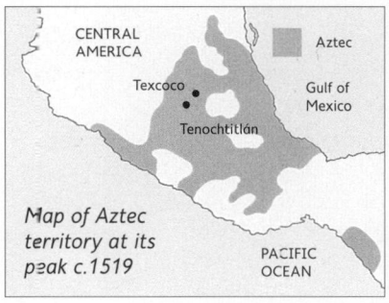


*Map of Aztec territory at its peak c.1519*

*Aztec warrior*

**c.1335** Tenochtitlán is increased in size by the building of floating gardens in the lake.

*This is what an Aztec temple might have looked like.*

1349

## SOUTHERN AND WESTERN EUROPE

1350

**c.1350** The Renaissance begins in Italy.

**c.1350** The first firearms, muzzle-loading cannon, are used in Europe.

**1355** Revolt against taxes in Paris, led by cloth merchant Etienne Marcel.

**1358** The Jacquerie: French peasants rebel against harsh conditions, but are defeated by nobles and merchants.

**1363-1404** Philippe the Good, son of King Jean II of France, is made Duke of Burgundy.

**1367** Civil war in Castile, Spain. France and England back opposite sides.

**1371** House of Stewart rules in Scotland.

**1373** Treaty of Anglo-Portuguese friendship.

### THE GREAT SCHISM

In **1296** and **1302**, Pope Boniface VIII issued two documents, called bulls, banning churchmen from paying taxes to kings and declaring the authority of the Catholic Church. This led to conflict. Philippe IV of France imprisoned Boniface and set up a papal court in Avignon, France, electing a French pope. In **1378**, Urban VI was also elected pope and established a rival court in Rome. This period, known as the Great Schism, lasted until **1417**.

*Bishop's staff*

**1378** Unsuccessful uprising of ciompi (clothworkers) in Florence, Italy.

**c.1380** In England, John Wycliffe preaches that the Bible alone is the authority for Christian belief. The Church condemns his teachings and his followers, the Lollards, are persecuted.

**1381** Jack Straw and Wat Tyler lead English peasants in a march to London to protest against living and working conditions. They disperse after the King agrees to some of their demands.

**1381** Venice defeats Genoa after a hundred years of war.

**1382** Uprising in Paris, France, against taxes.

**1387** Geoffrey Chaucer (**c.1345-1400**), the first great poet to write in English, writes *The Canterbury Tales*.

*Peasants revolt*

1399

## NORTHERN AND EASTERN EUROPE

**1354** Turks acquire Gallipoli, their first European possession.

**1355** Charles IV of Bohemia becomes Holy Roman Emperor and reigns until **1378**.

*Charles IV's crown*

*15th-century Prague*

**1361** Denmark is defeated by the Hanseatic League.

**1370** Lithuanians are defeated at the Battle of Rudan by the Teutonic Knights.

**1370** Hungary and Poland are unified under the Hungarian king, Louis of Anjou.

**1370** Peace of Stralsund between Denmark and the Hanseatic League. The League's power is at its height.

**1373** The Byzantine emperor becomes an Ottoman vassal (subordinate to the Ottoman empire).

**1380** Muscovites defeat Mongols at the Battle of Kulikova.

*Prince Dimitri of Moscow and his army at the Battle of Kulikova*

**1386** Union of Poland and Lithuania.

**1389** Battle of Kosovo: Turks gain control of the Balkans.

**1397** The Union of Kalmar unites Scandinavia under Margaret, Queen of Denmark and Norway (**1387-1412**).

## AFRICA AND THE MIDDLE EAST

**c.1350** Fortress at Great Zimbabwe, southern Africa, is at its largest.

*Fortress of Great Zimbabwe*

**c.1350-1600** Kingdom of Songhai in West Africa.

**1352-1355** Ibn Battuta travels in West Africa and visits Mali and writes an account of all he sees. He reaches Timbuktu in **1353**. From the writings of other Arab scholars, and archaeology, other African states from this period are known: Kanem-Bornu, Kongo and Benin.

*Ibn Batutta welcomed by an Indian prince*

**1375** Mamelukes conquer Sis, Armenia: the end of Armenian independence.

**c.1380-1662** Kongo kingdom in Central Africa.

**1397** Portuguese explorers reach the Canary Islands.

## ASIA

**c.1350** Cultural peak of the Majapahit empire in Java.

### TAMERLANE

From **1369-1405**, a Mongol chief named Tamerlane began to build a new empire, from his base at Samarkand. He seized land in Persia, Russia and India, conquering Herat in **1381**, destroying Delhi in **1398-1399** and annexing the Punjab. But the empire did not last long after his death.

*Tamerlane*

**1368** The Yuan dynasty in China is overthrown and replaced by the native Chinese Ming dynasty, founded by a Buddhist monk named Chu Yuan-chang, also known as Hung Wu.

*Ming porcelain*

**1369** Thais invade Cambodia.

**1392-1636** Great age of the Choson dynasty in Korea.

**1394** Temple of the Golden Pavilion is built, near Kyoto, Japan.

*Chinese boat, known as a junk*

## THE AMERICAS

**c.1352** Acamapitzin is elected first King of the Aztecs in Mexico.

*Illustration of an Aztec god protecting a corn plant, taken from a 16th-century book painted by an Aztec artist*

*An Aztec warrior*

## SOUTHERN AND WESTERN EUROPE

1400

**1400-1415** Rebellion of Owen Glendower in Wales.

**1407** Casi di San Georgio, the first European public bank, is established in Genoa, Italy.

**1410-1411** Civil war in France.

**1415** Henry V of England defeats French at Agincourt.

*Henry the Navigator*

**1416** Henry the Navigator, Prince of Portugal, founds a school of navigation. He encourages expeditions **c.1420-1460**.

**1422-1461** Henry VI is King of England.

**1429** Jeanne d'Arc, a French peasant girl, drives the English out of Orléans, France. Burned as a witch in **1431**.

**1434** Cosimo de' Medici takes control of Florence, Italy. The Medici dynasty rules Florence until **1737**.

**1442** Alfonso of Aragon conquers Naples.

**1447** French Orléans family claims Milan by inheritance.

### THE RENAISSANCE

The Renaissance means 'rebirth'. It is the name given to the renewed interest in the art, architecture and learning of Classical Greece and Rome, which inspired people to try out new ideas, and marked the end of the Middle Ages and the beginning of modern times. The movement began in Italy in the 14th century, and eventually influenced all of Europe, reaching its height in the 15th and 16th centuries. The most powerful patrons of the Renaissance were the Medici, a family of Florentine bankers, who encouraged artists and scholars to work in their city. Florence was the home of great artists such as Leonardo da Vinci (**1452-1519**) and Michelangelo Buonarroti (**1475-1564**), architects such as Filippo Brunelleschi (**1377-1446**) and writers such as Dante Alighieri (**1265-1321**).

*Lorenzo de' Medici leading a procession through the city of Florence*

## NORTHERN AND EASTERN EUROPE

**1410** Poles defeat the Teutonic Knights at Tannenberg.

**1415** John Hus (**1372-1415**), a Bohemian religious reformer, is condemned by the Church Council of Constance and burned as a heretic.

**1415** Frederick VI of Hohenzollern becomes Frederick I, Elector of Brandenburg.

**1416** Venetians defeat the Turks off Gallipoli, Turkey.

**1419-1436** Hussite wars between Bohemia and Moravia and the Holy Roman Empire triggered by the death of John Hus.

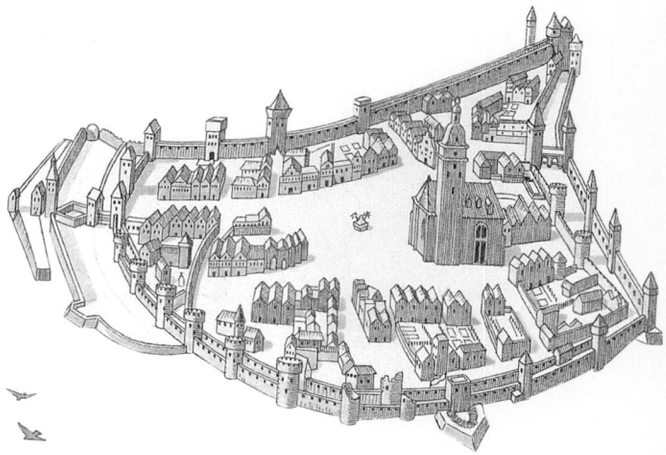

*Mount Tabor castle, a Hussite stronghold*

**1422** First siege of Constantinople by the Ottoman Turks. Sultan Murat I invades Greece.

**1430** Murat I of Turkey conquers Thessalonika, Greece.

**1437** Albert II Habsburg of Austria becomes King of Hungary and Bohemia, and is elected King of Germany in **1438-1439**. The Habsburgs are king-emperors until **1918**.

**1439** Russian and Greek Orthodox Churches are formally separated.

1449

## AFRICA AND THE MIDDLE EAST

**c.1400s** Chinese traders join Arab and Indian merchants trading in East Africa.

**1401** Tamerlane conquers Damascus (in Syria) and Baghdad (in Iraq).

*East African traders*

**1415** Portuguese conquer Ceuta, North Africa.

**1419** Portuguese reach Madeira.

**c.1420** Chinese are believed to have rounded Cape of Good Hope (South Africa).

**c.1430** Massive stone buildings are erected at Great Zimbabwe.

*15th-century Chinese map showing Cape of Good Hope*

**1431** Portuguese reach the Azores.

**1434** Portuguese explorer Gil Eannes sails around Cape of Bojador, near Canary Islands, after several failed Portuguese attempts.

*Portuguese ship*

## ASIA

**1403-1424** Reign of Yung-Lo, one of the greatest Ming emperors of China.

*Emperor Yung-Lo*

**1405-1433** Chinese admiral, Cheng Ho, with a fleet of 317 ships and 27,000 men, makes seven great voyages. He visits Indochina, Indonesia, Siam (Thailand), the Maldives, Borneo, the Persian Gulf, Arabia and East Africa.

**1421** Beijing becomes the capital of China.

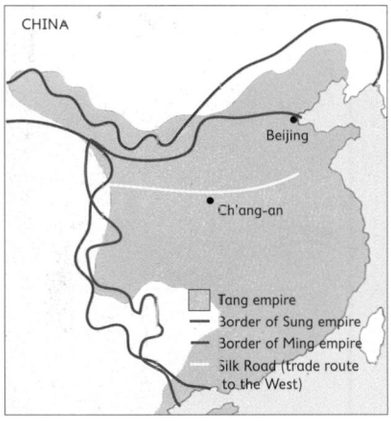


*Map of China in the Middle Ages*

**1424** King of Siam dies. His two eldest sons fight each other for the throne on elephants and both die.

*Battling on elephants*

**1428** Chinese are expelled from Vietnam.

## THE AMERICAS

**c.1400s** Peru: Viracocha Inca (8th emperor) takes the title Sapa Inca, meaning 'Supreme Inca'.

**c.1420s** Mexico: a causeway is built from the Aztec island city of Tenochtitlán to the mainland. Emperor Itzcoatl adopts an aggressive policy toward local tribes. He forces them to pay tribute and establishes a three-city league with Texcoco and Tlacopán, to gain political control of the region.

**c.1436-1464** Rule of Emperor Montezuma I of the Aztecs.

### THE INCA EMPIRE

The Late Inca (or Empire) Period in Peru began with the reign of Pachacuti Inca (**1438-1471**), who started conquering an empire from his capital Cuzco. He was regarded as half-god, half-human. The Incas had a well-developed social system. Everyone had to work in accordance with their rank and ability. In return, orphans, the sick and elderly were looked after. The Incas were also expert stonemasons and farmers, and built good roads across very difficult, rough land.

*An Inca knife*

*Inca warriors*

## SOUTHERN AND WESTERN EUROPE

1450

**1450** Francesco Sforza becomes Duke of Milan.

**1452-1519** Life of Leonardo da Vinci, Florentine artist.

### THE WARS OF THE ROSES

The Wars of the Roses (**1455-1485**) is the name given to the struggle between two rival families for the English crown: York, whose emblem was a white rose, and Lancaster, whose emblem was a red rose. Henry VI of Lancaster (**1422-1461**), was only a child when he became king and proved incompetent when he came of age. Richard, Duke of York, was made Protector in **1454**, but in **1455** he was excluded from the Royal Council and fighting broke out. The wars ended in **1485**, with the victory of Henry Tudor, who became Henry VII (**1485-1603**) first king of the Tudor dynasty.

*Henry Tudor's army*

**1461-1483** Edward IV is King of England.

**1462-1492** Lorenzo de' Medici ('the Magnificent') rules Florence.

**1469** Ferdinand of Aragon marries Isabella of Castile.

**1477** Charles the Bold, Duke of Burgundy, is killed. His daughter Marie marries Maximilian Habsburg of Austria.

**1477-1493** France and Austria fight over Burgundian lands.

**1479** Ferdinand of Aragon succeeds his father as King of Aragon and unites the kingdom with Castile.

**1483** Charles VIII of France claims Naples.

**1483** Edward V is King of England, but not crowned.

**1483-1485** Richard III is King of England.

**1485** The Battle of Bosworth ends the Wars of the Roses in England. Henry Tudor becomes Henry VII, first king of Tudor dynasty.

**1487** Rebellion in England by Lambert Simnel, who claims to be the nephew of Edward IV.

**1492** Ferdinand and Isabella conquer Granada, the last Muslim kingdom in Spain.

**1493** Maximilian Habsburg becomes Holy Roman Emperor. Peace of Senlis: Burgundy is divided between France and the Empire.

**1494-1495** France invades Italy and is driven back. Start of a struggle for power between France and the Habsburgs.

**1497** Rebellion in England by Perkin Warbeck who claims to be the son of Edward IV.

1499

**1498** Louis XII of France invades Italy and takes Milan.

## NORTHERN AND EASTERN EUROPE

**1453** Ottoman Turks capture Constantinople: the Byzantine empire finally comes to an end.

*Mehmet II, the Ottoman sultan, marching his troops through the city of Constantinople after their victory*

**1455** Johann Gutenberg develops printing presses and publishes the Gutenberg Bible, the first printed book in Europe.

*Gutenberg and a page from his Bible*

### THE FIRST TSARS

Ivan III ('the Great') of Moscow (**1462-1505**) extended his territory and in **1478** conquered Novgorod, the old Russian capital. In **1480**, he liberated Moscow from Mongol rule and declared himself first Tsar (sole ruler) of Russia. Ivan married a Byzantine princess and adopted many Byzantine customs. Russia continued to grow under his son, Vassily, and grandson, Ivan IV 'the Terrible'.

*St. Basil's Cathedral, Moscow, built by Ivan IV*

**1456-1467** Ottoman Turks take over Balkan states.

**1468-1469** Denmark pawns Orkney and Shetland to Scotland.

**1471-1480** Ottoman Turks raid Styria (in Austria).

**1488** South German cities, knights and princes establish the Swabian League, to preserve peace within the Empire.

**1499** Swiss independence is recognized at the Peace of Basle.

## AFRICA AND THE MIDDLE EAST

**c.1450** Portuguese start trading in West Africa.

**1451-1481** Reign of Ottoman Turkish Sultan Mehmet II, known as 'the Conqueror', after his conquest of Constantinople in **1453**.

*Mehmet II*

**1461** Portuguese reach Sierra Leone, West Africa.

**1463-1479** Ottoman Turks are at war with Venice.

**1464-1492** Reign of Sunni Ali, ruler of Songhai in West Africa, who conquers Timbuktu and expands his empire at the expense of Mali.

**1471** Portuguese conquer Tangier, Morocco.

**1482** Portuguese establish a fort at El Mina on the Gold Coast (Ghana).

**1487-1488** Portuguese navigator, Bartholomeu Dias, rounds the Cape of Good Hope, South Africa.

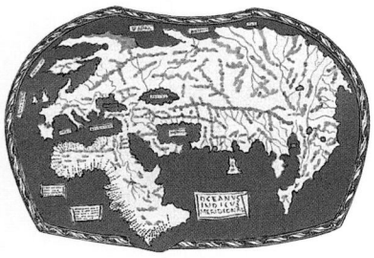

*This European map of 1489 shows a little knowledge of the West African coast.*

**1490** King Nzinga Nkuwu of the Kongo becomes a Christian.

**1493** Songhai empire in West Africa reaches its peak.

*The city of Timbuktu*

## ASIA

**1451-1489** Rule of Bahlol Lodi, the first Pathan king of Delhi.

**1467-1477** Onin War in Japan between rival clans.

**1469-1539** Life of Guru Nanak, who founds the Sikh religion in **c.1500**.

*The Sikh flag* *Guru Nanak*

**1471** Vietnamese expand south.

**1477-1568** Provincial wars in Japan, ending with the victory of Oda Nobunaga.

**1494** Babar, a descendent of Genghis Khan and Tamerlane, becomes Prince of Ferghana, Central Asia.

*Babar*

**1497-1499** Vasco da Gama, a Portuguese navigator in search of trade, makes the first sea voyage by a European to India and back. Da Gama met hostility on the East African coast, where trade was controlled by Arabs.

*Da Gama's ship being attacked*

## THE AMERICAS

1450

**1460** Mayapan is destroyed: the Mayan civilization comes to an end.

**1471-1493** Reign of Emperor Topa Inca, who extends the empire south.

**c.1476** Incas conquer the Chimú kingdom in Peru.

**1492-1493** Christopher Columbus reaches Bahamas and West Indies, while sailing west in search of a route to the East Indies.

*Columbus setting off in search of the East Indies*

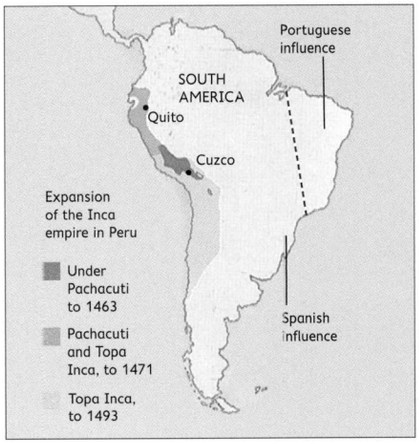


**1493-1525** Reign of Huayna Capac, the greatest Inca conqueror. He founds a second capital at Quito.

**1494** Treaty of Tordesillas: Pope Alexander VI fixes a line to divide spheres of influence in America between Spain and Portugal.

**1497** John Cabot, an Italian explorer employed by Henry VII of England, reaches Newfoundland, Canada.

**1498** Christopher Columbus reaches Trinidad and the coast of Venezuela.

**1499-1502** Amerigo Vespucci, a Florentine navigator, explores the South American coast.

*Amerigo Vespucci*

1499

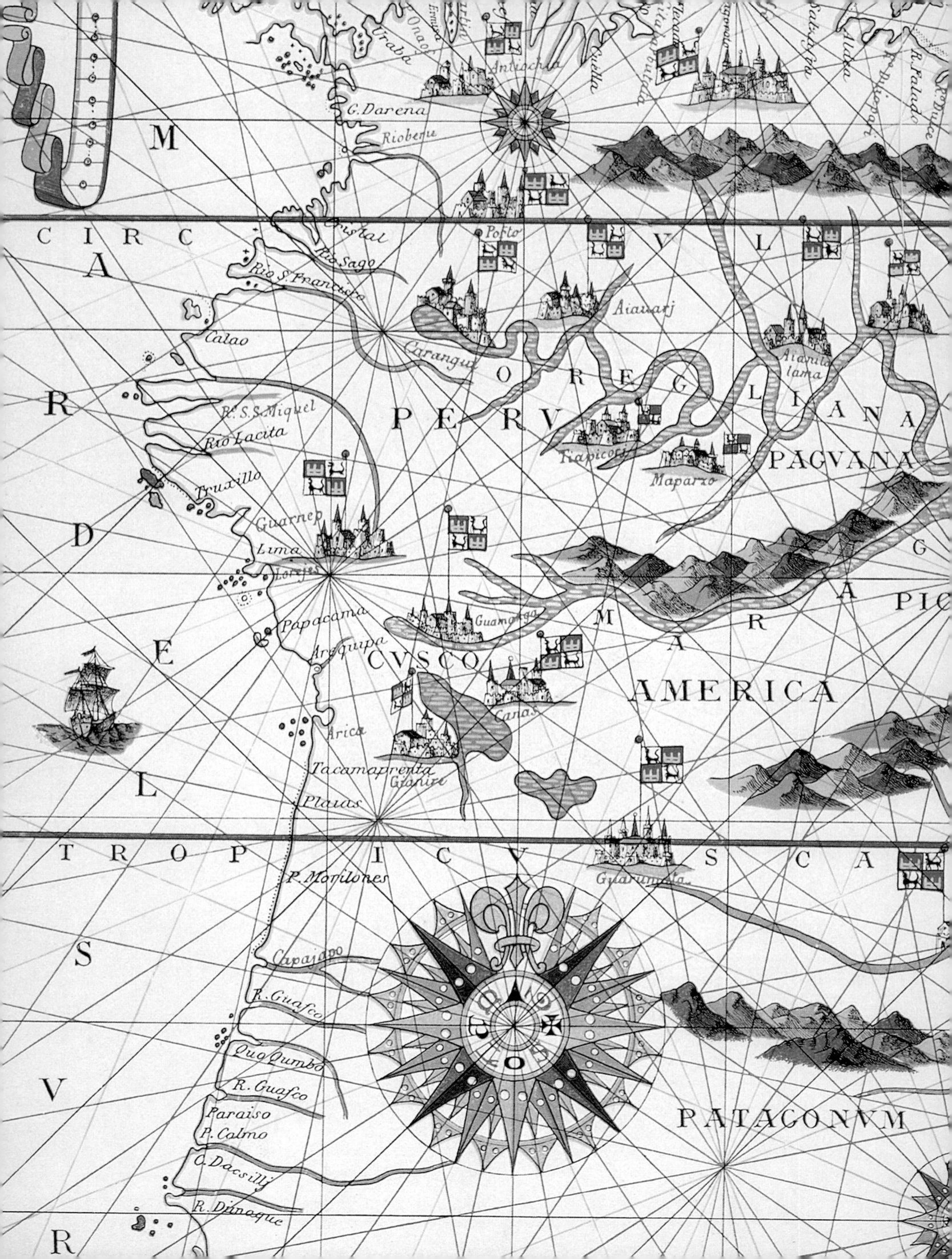
Urabe
Onaqo
Antiochia
Quella
R. Falado
G. Darena
Riobeju
M
CIRC
A
Cristal
Rio Sago
Rio S. Francisco
Calao
Aiauarj
Carangui
O R E G L I A N A
R
R. S. S. Miquel
Rio Lacita
P E R V
Tapicori
Maparro
PAGVANA
Truxillo
Guarnep
D
Lima
Lorejas
G
A
PIC
Papacama
Guamanga
M
R
A
Arequipa
E
CVSCO
AMERICA
Canas
Arica
Tacamapreuta
Glanire
L
Plaias
T R O P I C V S C A
P. Morilones
Guarumata
S
Capajapo
R. Guafco
Quo Qumbo
R. Guafco
V
Paraiso
P. Calmo
PATAGONVM
C. Dacsilly
R. Dinaque
R

# THE 16th CENTURY

## 1500 - 1599

## SOUTHERN AND WESTERN EUROPE

1500

**1501** Louis XII of France conquers Naples, Italy.

**1509-1547** Reign of King Henry VIII of England.

**1510** Holy League formed to drive France from Italy.

**1512** French invade Milan, but are defeated and expelled from Italy.

**1512** Ferdinand II of Castile annexes Navarre.

*Henry VIII's coat-of-arms*

**1513** Battle of Flodden between England and Scotland. James IV of Scotland is killed.

**1513** Niccolò Machiavelli (**1469-1527**), a Florentine statesman, writes *The Prince*, advocating ruthlessness and cunning in order to achieve political success.

### THE EMPIRE OF CHARLES V

In the early 16th century, Europe was dominated by the vast empire of Charles V (**1500-1558**), of the Austrian Habsburg family. He became King of Spain in **1516** and was elected Holy Roman Emperor in **1519**, making him the most powerful monarch in Europe. He defeated his great rival, François I of France, after five wars in Italy, and stopped the advance of the Ottoman Turks. Spain prospered, because of the riches discovered in the New World (America). But there were social and economic difficulties in Germany, as well as religious turmoil caused by the Reformation (see next column). In **1521**, Charles divided his empire, giving Austria to his brother Ferdinand. In **1556**, Charles abdicated, splitting the empire between his brother Ferdinand and his son, Philip II.

*Charles V*

**1515-1547** Reign of François I of France. He defeats the Swiss at the Battle of Marignano (**1515**) and conquers Milan, Italy.

*Coffee beans*

**1516** Coffee is first imported from America.

**1520** Field of the Cloth of Gold: peace talks between Henry VIII and François I.

**1520** Chocolate is imported from America.

**1521** Silk-making begins in France.

**1521-1544** Four wars between Charles V and the French in Italy.

1524

## NORTHERN AND EASTERN EUROPE

**1513** Scandinavia: the Union of Kalmar ends.

**1516** The Netherlands comes under Spanish control, with the accession of Charles I of Spain.

### THE REFORMATION

The Reformation began as an attempt to reform the Catholic Church, but it provoked a religious upheaval that led to the creation of Protestant churches and a split in Christian Europe. It was triggered by Martin Luther (**1483-1546**), a monk and professor of theology at Wittenburg in Germany, who believed that religious beliefs should be based on the Bible, rather than the teachings of the Church. In **1517**, he nailed his 95 theses (proposals for change) to a church door. As a result, he was declared a heretic at the Diet of Worms (a council held by the Emperor), in **1521**. Luther went into hiding, and developed his ideas for a Lutheran Church. Lutheranism won followers in several German states, provoking quarrels and wars between them and German Catholic states.

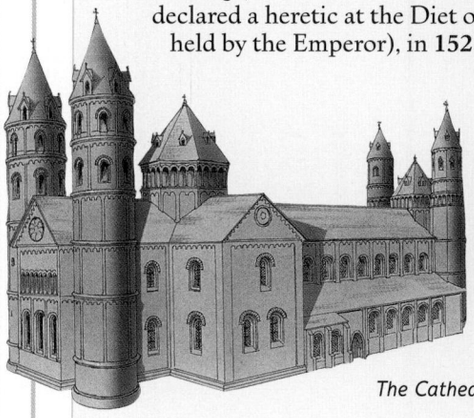

*The Cathedral at Worms*

**1519** Inspired by Luther, Ulrich Zwingli (**1484-1531**) begins preaching church reform in Zurich. In **1523** he writes 67 theses, suggesting changes in religious belief, and church organization. These are accepted by the city council. His ideas spread through South Germany and Switzerland.

**1519** Charles I, King of Spain, is elected Holy Roman Emperor, Charles V.

**1521** Belgrade, Serbia, falls to the Ottoman Turks.

**1522-1523** The imperial knights rebel against their overlord, the Archbishop of Trier, in protest against their declining economic and social position.

**1523** Sweden gains independence from Denmark. Vasa dynasty begins with the reign of Gustav I (**1523-1560**).

**1523** German imperial knights are defeated by an alliance of princes at the Battle of Landstuhl.

**1524-1525** Peasants rise up against their landlords in South and Central Germany.

*Mercenary soldier, or landsknecht, employed by the Emperor*

## AFRICA AND THE MIDDLE EAST

**1500** Mohammed Turre (**1494-1528**) of Songhai expands his territory in West Africa.

**1502** Safavid dynasty is established in Persia (now Iran) by Ismail I.

**1504** Nubians destroy the Christian kingdom of Meroë (now Sudan).

**1504-1546** Reign of the Christian King Afonso of the Kongo.

**1505** Songhai people invade Mali.

**1505-1507** Portuguese establish forts on the East African coast.

**1508** Portuguese set up a factory in Mozambique.

**1509** Spain takes Oran, North Africa.

**1513** Portuguese establish posts at Sena and Tete on the Zambezi river.

**1514** Turks fight the Persians.

**1516-1518** Selim of Turkey conquers North Iraq, Syria and Palestine.

**1517** Turks conquer Egypt.

**1518** First full cargo of slaves sails from Guinea to the New World.

### THE OTTOMAN TURKS

The great age of the Ottoman Turks was in the 16th century, especially during the reign of Suleiman 'the Magnificent' (**1520-1566**). Under him the Turkish empire took control of Egypt, parts of North Africa, and most of the Middle East. They also held land in the Balkans, in Eastern Europe.

*When they captured Constantinople, the Ottomans added minarets (towers) to the Church of St. Sophia, converting it into a mosque.*

## ASIA

**1504** Babar becomes Master of Kabul, Afghanistan.

*Babar, the first Mogul*

**1510** Portuguese annex Goa, on the west coast of India.

**1511** Portuguese take control in Malacca, Malaya.

**1514** Portuguese reach China. By **1516**, they are trading from Canton.

**1519-1522** The first circumnavigation of the world is led by Ferdinand Magellan, a Portuguese navigator, sponsored by Emperor Charles V. Magellan was heading for the Molucca islands in the East Indies, which were rich in spices, by sailing west around the tip of South America.

**1521** Magellan reaches the Molucca islands, but is killed in the Philippines: one of his captains continues to sail west back to Europe.

**1523** European traders are expelled from Chinese ports.

*Chinese boat called a junk*

## THE AMERICAS

1500

**1500** Aztec empire reaches its greatest extent under Ahuizotl.

**1501** Anglo-Portuguese expedition to Newfoundland.

**1504** Amerigo Vespucci, a Florentine navigator, describes his voyages to South America. His discoveries are known as the New World.

**c.1507** The New World becomes known as America, after Amerigo Vespucci.

**1510** The first African slaves are brought to America.

**1513** Ponce de León, a Spanish explorer, discovers Florida.

**1513** Nuñez de Balboa, a Spanish explorer, crosses the Isthmus of Panama and finds the Pacific Ocean.

### THE CONQUEST OF MEXICO AND PERU

The early explorers of the New World returned with stories of the great wealth to be found. Spanish fortune-hunters, known as conquistadors, followed in search of gold and land. The most famous were Hernando Cortés, who conquered Mexico between **1519-1521**, and Francisco Pizarro, who conquered Peru between **1532-1534**. The Spanish conquerors came into conflict with two great native warrior civilizations - the Aztecs of Mexico and the Incas of Peru. But the Spaniards had the advantage of horses and cannons and these civilizations were soon destroyed.

*Aztec carving showing stars and planets*

**1520** Ferdinand Magellan, Portuguese navigator, finds the Magellan Straits.

**1521-1549** Spaniards colonize Venezuela.

1524

## SOUTHERN AND WESTERN EUROPE

1525

**1525** Battle of Pavia: Spain defeats France and François I is taken prisoner. England and France make peace with Spain.

**1527** Charles V's troops sack Rome and capture Pope Clement VII.

**1527-1530** The Medici family is expelled from Florence.

**1529** Peace of Cambrai: France renounces claim to Italy and Charles V renounces his claim to the lost Burgundian lands.

**1530** The Knights Hospitaller, a military religious order founded during the Crusades, establish a base in Malta.

**1531** The Inquisition is established in Portugal.

*King Henry VIII*

**1534** Henry VIII of England declares himself supreme head of the English Church.

**1536** The English and Welsh governments are unified.

**1541** John Knox starts the Reformation in Scotland.

**1542** Mary Stuart (**1542-1587**) becomes Queen of Scotland, at the age of one week.

**1543** Andreas Vesalius, a pharmacist from Brussels, is the first scholar to make a detailed study of the human body.

**1543** Alliance of Henry VIII of England and Charles V of Spain against France and Scotland.

**1544** Peace of Crespi ends wars between France and Spain in Italy.

**1547** English invade Scotland and defeat Scots at the Battle of Pinkie. Mary, Queen of Scots, is sent to France to marry the Dauphin (the heir to the throne).

**1547-1559** Reign of Henri II of France.

### THE COUNTER REFORMATION

To fight the Reformation, the Catholic Church set up colleges to train priests to win back Protestants and make new converts. The Jesuits, founded by Ignatius Loyola in **1534**, acted as teachers and missionaries, as far away as India and Japan. In **1545**, the Council of the Catholic Church met at Trent, North Italy, launching an energetic campaign. They reinstated the Inquisition, and Protestants were condemned and burned as heretics. The Baroque movement in the arts also helped to attract converts, with its flamboyant style of painting, music and architecture.

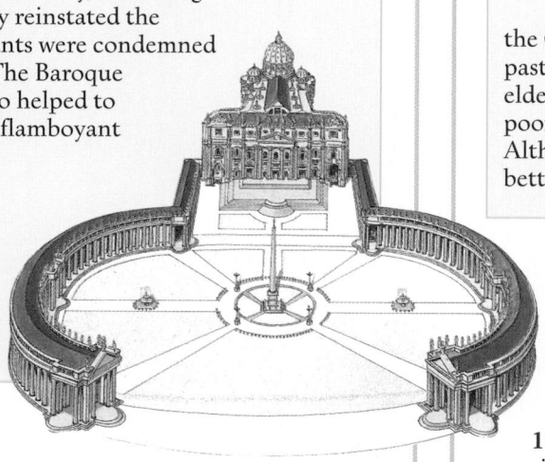

*The piazza of St. Peter's, Rome, built in the Baroque style in 1656-1667 by Bernini*

**1547-1553** Reign of Edward VI of England.

1549

## NORTHERN AND EASTERN EUROPE

**1525** Albert of Hohenzollern, ruler of Prussia, becomes a Lutheran and secularizes the state.

**1526** Battle of Mohacs: Louis II of Hungary is defeated and killed by the Ottoman Turks. Charles V's brother, Ferdinand, and John Zapolya are both elected kings of Hungary.

**1529** Ottoman Turks besiege Vienna, Austria.

**1529** Second Diet of Speyer, Germany.

**1529** War between Swiss Catholics and Protestants.

**1530** Charles V is crowned Holy Roman Emperor by the Pope: the last imperial coronation by a pope.

**1531** The Protestant League of Schmalkalden is formed.

**1531** Copernicus (**1473-1543**), a Polish astronomer, circulates his revolutionary theory, demonstrating that the planets move around the Sun, not around the Earth as the Church had taught.

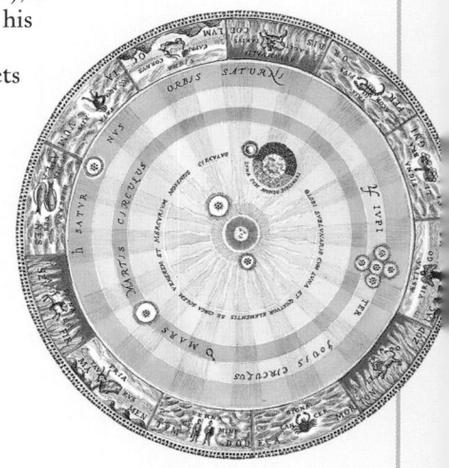

*Diagram showing Copernicus's idea of the universe*

**1532** Peace of Nuremburg: Protestants in the Holy Roman Empire are allowed to follow their religion.

**1532-1533** War between Turkey and Austria over Hungary.

**1533-1584** Reign of Ivan IV ('the Terrible') in Russia.

**1534-1535** Münster in northern Germany is taken over by Anabaptists, religious sects who deny the need for government.

### JOHN CALVIN

Jean Cauvin (**1509-1564**), usually known as John Calvin, was another leading figure of the Reformation. Based in Geneva, Switzerland, he published *Institutes* in **1536**, containing his ideas for reform, which became the basis for a new religion: Calvinism. In **1541**, Calvin began organizing the Church in Geneva. It was to be self-governing, electing pastors (to preach), doctors (to decide on matters of faith), elders (to enforce discipline) and deacons (to care for the poor). A committee, called a synod, arranged elections. Although Calvinism was stricter than Lutheranism, it was better organized and won many converts.

**1541-1688** Hungary becomes a province of the Ottomans.

**1547** Charles V defeats League of Schmalkalden at Battle of Muhlberg.

**1547** Ivan IV (right) takes the title 'Tsar of all the Russias'.

## AFRICA AND THE MIDDLE EAST

**1535** Charles V of Spain conquers Tunis, North Africa.

**1538** Ottoman Turks capture Aden.

**1543** Ethiopian Christians, helped by Portugal, repel the Muslim advance into Ethiopia.

*Ethiopian Christian crosses*

**1545** Ottoman Turks occupy Ethiopian city of Massawa and complete their occupation of the rest of Ethiopia.

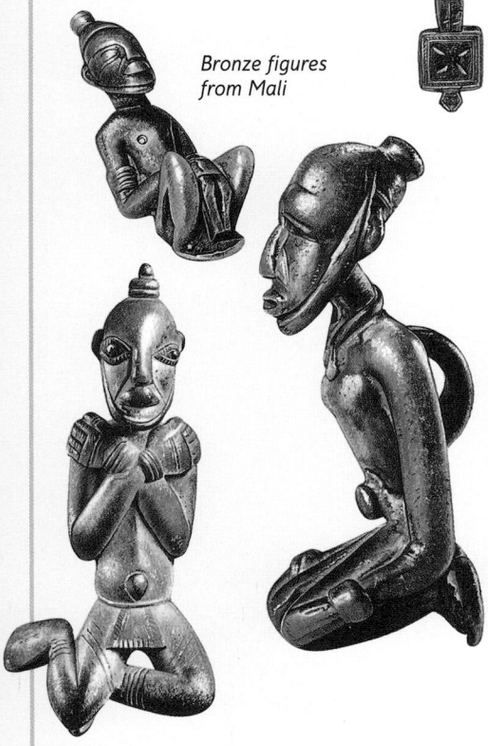

*Bronze figures from Mali*

**1546** The Songhai people destroy the Mali empire in West Africa.

**1549-1582** Reign of Askia David, King of Songhai.

## ASIA

### THE MOGUL EMPIRE

*The Qur'an*

The Muslim Mogul empire was founded by Babar, Prince of Ferghana in Afghanistan, a descendent of the Mongol Tamerlane. He invaded the Punjab in **1526** and defeated the Sultan of Delhi at the Battle of Panipat, and gradually established control, winning battles at Kanwaha in **1527** and Gogra in **1529**. Babar's grandson, Akbar **(1556-1605)** extended Mogul control over most of central and northern India. Akbar was a wise ruler, who attempted to unite his subjects culturally, as well as by conquest, by allowing religious toleration. Indian culture flourished during his reign, producing great works of art, architecture and poetry.

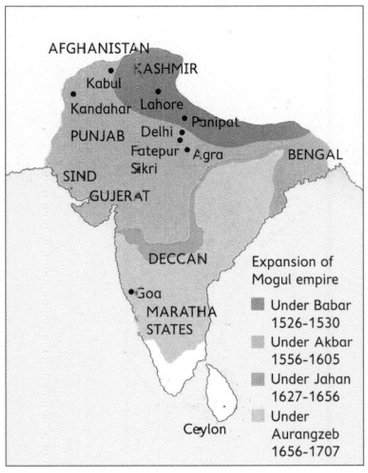


**1533** North Vietnam splits into Tongking and Annam.

**1539** Burmese kingdom of Toungoo conquers Mons kingdom of Pegu.

**1540** Babar's son, Humayun, is driven out of India by the Afghan Sher Shah.

**1542** Francis Xavier, a Portuguese Jesuit missionary, arrives in Goa, on the west coast of India.

**1545** Humayun captures Kabul, Afghanistan.

**1549-1551** Francis Xavier and his missionaries spread Christianity in Japan and participate in trade.

## THE AMERICAS

1525

**1526** John Cabot, Italian explorer, sails to the River Plate, Argentina.

**1528** Germans attempt to colonize Venezuela.

**1530** Portuguese begin to colonize Brazil.

**1531** Rio de Janeiro, Brazil, is founded.

**1534** French expedition, led by Jacques Cartier, reaches Labrador, Canada.

**1535** Buenos Aires, Argentina, and Lima, Peru, are founded.

*Jacques Cartier*

**1535** Jacques Cartier discovers the St. Lawrence River, and sails to the site of Montreal, Canada.

**1535-1538** Gonzalo Jiminez de Quesada, a Spanish conquistador, conquers Colombia.

**1536** Jesuits found Asunción, Paraguay.

**1536** Inca rebellion in Peru, led by Manco Inca. He rules from Vilcabamba until **1544**, when the Inca Empire comes to an end.

**1540-1544** Pedro de Valdivia, a Spanish conquistador, explores Chile.

*North American moose*

**1541** Native American revolt in Mexico.

**1542** Spanish explorer Francisco de Orellana sails along the Amazon river.

**1542** Charles V's New Laws abolish native slavery in Spanish colonies and limit the colonists' control.

**1545** Silver discovered in Peru.

**1548** Silver discovered in Mexico.

*Silver llamas made of Peruvian silver*

1549

## SOUTHERN AND WESTERN EUROPE

1550

**1552-1556** War between Henri II of France and Charles V of Spain.

**1553** Tobacco first introduced into Europe, from America via Spain.

**1553-1558** Reign of Mary I of England. She marries Philip II of Spain and England returns to Catholicism. 300 Protestants are burned.

*Mary I*

**1555** Charles V abdicates. His son becomes Philip II of Spain, and inherits Habsburg land in Italy, Netherlands and America.

**1558** England loses Calais to France.

**1558-1603** Reign of Elizabeth I of England. She reinstates the Anglican Church.

**1559** Jean Nicot first imports tobacco into France from America. The word nicotine is named after him.

**1559** Treaty of Cateau-Cambresis: peace between France and Spain.

**1560** Francis II of France dies. His widow, Mary, Queen of Scots, returns to Scotland from France.

### THE FRENCH WARS OF RELIGION

By the mid-16th century, rival factions of French Protestants (called Huguenots) and Catholics had emerged at the French Court. A succession of weak kings failed to keep their rivalry in check and the result was a series of bloody civil wars, which lasted from **1562-1589**. These wars came to an end when Henri of Navarre, a Huguenot leader, became King Henri IV of France. Henri succeeded in uniting the country by converting to Catholicism, while allowing toleration for the Huguenots with the Edict of Nantes (**1598**).

*Henri IV*

**1560-1574** Reign of Charles IX of France.

**1563** English Poor Law: Justices of the Peace are entitled to raise a poor rate to look after the poor in each parish.

**1564-1616** Life of William Shakespeare, English playwright and poet.

*The Globe Theatre, London, where Shakespeare's plays were performed*

**1567-1625** Reign of James VI of Scotland, later James I of England.

**1572** St. Bartholomew's Day Massacre: 20,000 Huguenots are murdered by troops acting on behalf of the French regent, Queen Catherine de' Medici.

1574

## NORTHERN AND EASTERN EUROPE

**1553-1555** Richard Chancellor, an English navigator, goes on expeditions to Russia.

**1555** Peace of Augsburg: Emperor Charles V allows the Protestant princes freedom of worship.

**1555** English Muscovy Company is given a charter to explore and trade with Russia.

*Muscovy Company coat-of-arms*

**1556** Ferdinand, the brother of Charles V, becomes Holy Roman Emperor. Habsburg empire is divided between him and Charles V's son, who becomes Philip II of Spain.

**1557-1582** Russia, Poland, Sweden and Denmark fight over territories in the Baltic.

**1563-1570** War between Sweden and Denmark, which ends with the Peace of Stettin. Livonia is partitioned between Poland and Denmark.

**1564-1576** Reign of Maximilian II, Holy Roman Emperor.

### THE DUTCH REVOLT

When Philip II of Spain inherited the Netherlands in **1555**, much of the population had already converted to Calvinism. So when Philip tried to impose Catholicism, he met with opposition. By **1566**, Calvinist worship had become public, and there were attacks on Catholic churches. In **1568**, the Spanish governor executed Calvinist counts Hoorn and Egmont, and rebels, known as Sea Beggars, escaped to sea to attack Spanish ships. This marked the start of a long struggle, known as the Dutch Revolt. It finally came to an end when the Spanish recognized Dutch independence, at the Peace of the Hague in **1648**.

**1571** Battle of Lepanto (off the Greek coast): Turks defeated by Spain and Venice. The end of Turkish sea power in Europe.

**1571** Tartars (Mongols) from the Crimea destroy Moscow.

**1572** Poland introduces a system of electing kings.

**1572** Dutch Sea Beggars capture towns of Briel (Brill) and Vlissingen (Flushing) in the Netherlands.

**1573** Henri of Valois (later Henri III of France) becomes the first elected King of Poland.

## AFRICA AND THE MIDDLE EAST

**c.1550s** England starts trading with West Africa.

**1551** Ottoman Turks take Tripoli, Libya. War between Turkey and Hungary.

**1554-1555** War between the Turks and the Persian Safavids.

*Safavid warriors*

**1562** England joins the slave trade, shipping slaves from West Africa to the Caribbean. John Hawkins, a navigator, allies with two kings in Sierra Leone and attacks local tribes, taking captives as slaves.

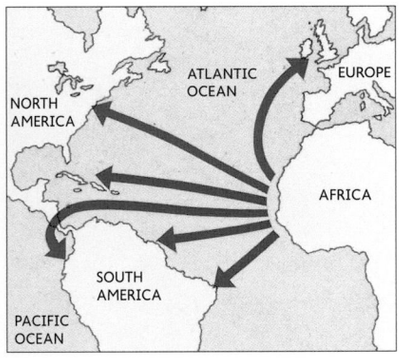


*Map showing the slave routes*

**1566** The Ottoman empire is now at its greatest extent.

**1566-1574** Reign of Sultan Selim II of Turkey.

**1573** Don John of Austria captures Tunis, North Africa, and Turkey goes to war with Austria.

**1574-1595** Reign of Sultan Murad III of Turkey.

**1574** Portuguese colonize Angola.

**1574-1575** Ottoman Turks retake Tunis and conquer the rest of Tunisia.

*Ottoman ceramics*

## ASIA

**1550** The Mongol leader, Altan-Khan, invades northern China. Japanese pirates raid China.

**1555** Humayun regains his Indian empire from Sher Shah.

**1555** The King of Toungoo captures the northern Burmese kingdom of Ava. This results in a unified Burmese state, which grows at the expense of the Thai kingdom.

**1556-1605** Reign of Akbar the Great, greatest of the Mogul rulers. A new phase of conquest begins.

*Akbar (on the second elephant) pursuing his enemies*

**1556** Astrakhan is annexed by Russia.

**1557** Portuguese establish a settlement at Macao. Trade with China is restricted to Macao.

**1560** Oda Nobunaga becomes leading daimyo (landowner) in Japan.

**1564** Spaniards occupy the Philippines and build Manila.

**1565** Akbar extends the Mogul empire to the Deccan.

**1567** Oda Nobunaga becomes *shogun* (military dictator) of Japan.

**1570** Nagasaki, Japan, is opened to foreign traders. Traders come via Macao, China, bringing silk.

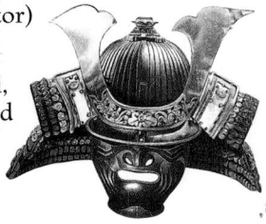

*Japanese samurai helmet*

**1573-1577** Akbar conquers Gujerat and Bengal and unifies northern India.

*Map of Japan*

## THE AMERICAS

**1554** São Paulo, Brazil, is founded.

*Golden conure (left) and macaws from the Amazon rainforest in Brazil*

**c.1560** Silver from Mexico and Peru is established as the chief export from the Americas to Spain.

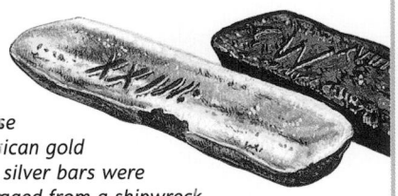

*These Mexican gold and silver bars were salvaged from a shipwreck.*

**1562-1565** French colony in Florida is destroyed by the Spaniards.

**1562** John Hawkins makes his first slave trade voyage to Hispaniola (Haiti). Second and third voyages follow: **1564-1565** and **1567-1568**.

**1563-1571** Titu Cusi Inca rules at Vilcabamba, Peru.

**1572** Sir Francis Drake, an English navigator, attacks Spanish ports in America.

**1572** Topa Amaru, the last Inca ruler, is captured and executed.

*Inca soldiers like these were no match for the Spaniards.*

## SOUTHERN AND WESTERN EUROPE

1575

**1577-1580** Sir Francis Drake, English navigator, sails around the world.

**1580-1640** Union of Spain and Portugal.

**1581** First known ballet, *Le Ballet Comique de la Reine*, is performed at the marriage of the Queen of France's sister.

*A viol, used for early ballet music*

*Dancing shoes were worn, as there were no special ballet shoes.*

**1582** Gregorian Calendar (the one we use today) is devised by Pope Gregory XIII, and introduced in Catholic countries.

**1586** The War of the Three Henris in France: Henri III, Henri of Guise and Henri of Navarre.

**1587** Mary, Queen of Scots, is executed by Elizabeth I for plotting against her. Elizabeth accepts Mary's son, the Protestant James VI of Scotland, as her heir.

**1588** The defeat of the Spanish Armada, a fleet of ships sent by Philip II to conquer England.

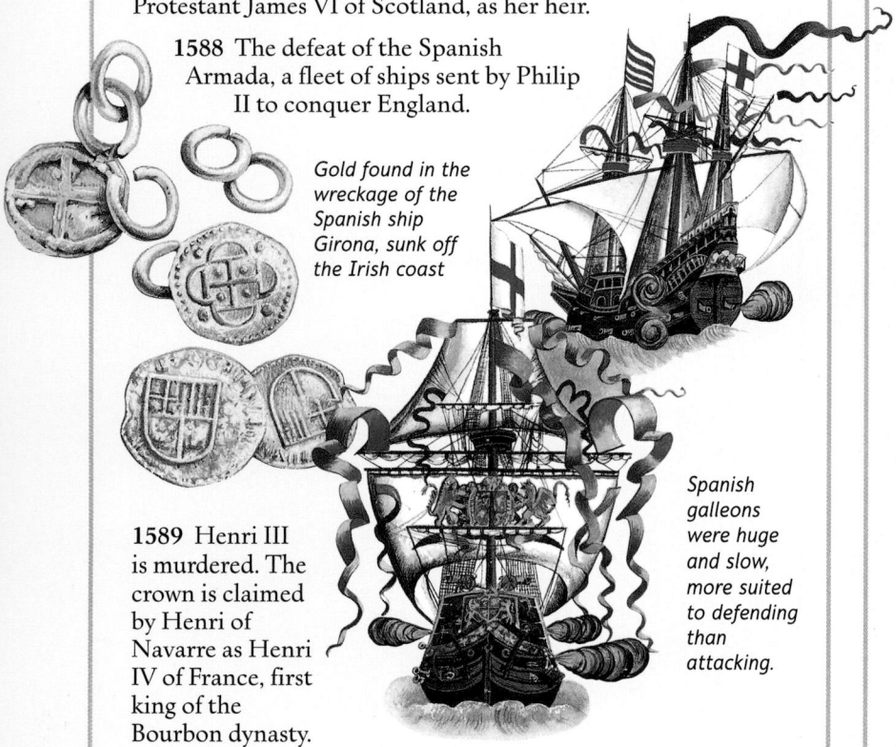

*Gold found in the wreckage of the Spanish ship Girona, sunk off the Irish coast*

*Spanish galleons were huge and slow, more suited to defending than attacking.*

**1589** Henri III is murdered. The crown is claimed by Henri of Navarre as Henri IV of France, first king of the Bourbon dynasty.

**1590** Henri IV defeats French Catholics at the Battle of Ivry.

**1592** Presbyterianism (a form of Calvinism) is adopted in Scotland, influenced by the teachings of John Knox.

**1593** Henri IV of France becomes a Catholic.

**1594** Henri IV of France enters Paris and begins his reign.

**1596** Galileo Galilei (**1564-1642**), an Italian astronomer, mathematician and physicist, invents the thermometer.

**1596** English attack Cadiz, on the southwest coast of Spain, and upset the preparation of a second Armada.

**1597** Irish rebellion against the English, led by Hugh O'Neill, Earl of Tyrone.

**1598** Henri IV of France issues the Edict of Nantes, allowing religious toleration to Huguenots (French Protestants).

1599

## NORTHERN AND EASTERN EUROPE

**1576** Spanish soldiers sack Antwerp. Pacification of Ghent: 17 Netherlands provinces unite to drive out the Spaniards.

**1576** Russia begins expanding across the Ural mountains.

**1578** Peace of Arras: 10 southern provinces of the Netherlands unite with Spain.

**1579** Union of Utrecht: the seven northern provinces of the Netherlands unite against Spain.

**1581** Russians begin the conquest of Siberia.

*Russian aristocrats known as boyars*

**1581** Seven northern provinces of the Netherlands proclaim independence as the United Provinces and elect William, Prince of Orange, as their ruler.

**1582** Peace between Russia and Poland. Russia is cut off from the Baltic Sea.

**1584** William of Orange, ruler of the United Provinces, is assassinated.

**1585** Gerardus Mercator (**1512-1594**), a Flemish geographer and map-maker, introduces a more accurate way of drawing maps than had previously been used.

**1587-1688** Catholic Vasa dynasty rules Poland.

**1596** France, England and the United Provinces unite against Spain.

**1598** Death of Tsar Theodor, last of the Rurik dynasty: the start of a period known as 'the time of troubles' in Russia.

*Early print of the city of Moscow*

## AFRICA AND THE MIDDLE EAST

**1578** King Sebastian of Portugal invades Morocco, but is defeated at the Battle of al-Ksar al-Kabir. Ahmed al Mansur of Fez establishes the Sharifian dynasty and Morocco expands in power.

**1580-1617** Reign of Idris Alooma, greatest of the kings of the Kanem-Bornu.

**1581** Moroccans begin penetrating the Sahara Desert.

*Dromedary camel found in the Sahara*

**1581** Peace between Turkey and Spain.

**1585** Ottoman empire begins to decline.

**1586-1622** Reign of Shah Abbas the Great in Persia.

**1590** Moroccans reach the Niger and take Timbuktu.

**1590** Shah Abbas of Persia makes peace with Turkey.

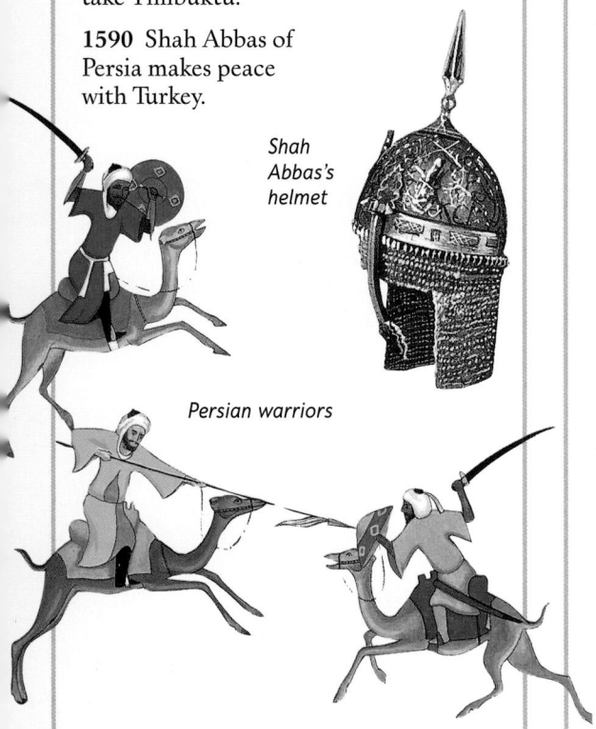

*Shah Abbas's helmet*

*Persian warriors*

**1591** Battle of Tondibi: Moroccans invade and defeat Songhai and cause the kingdom to collapse.

**1592** Portuguese capture Mombasa, on the East African coast.

**1598** Dutch capture Mauritius.

**1598** Shah Abbas makes Isfahan the capital of Persia.

## ASIA

**1579** Portuguese trading station is established in Bengal, India.

**1581** Akbar subdues Afghanistan, formally annexing it in **1585**.

**1581** Russians conquer Siberia.

**1582-1598** Toyotomi Hideyoshi succeeds as leader in Japan.

**1584** Phra Narai creates an independent kingdom of Siam.

**1587** Akbar takes Kashmir, northern India.

**1591** First English voyage to the East Indies.

*Hindu statue from Java, Indonesia, East Indies*

**1592** Annamese take Hanoi and unite North Vietnam.

**1592** Akbar conquers Sind, India.

**1593** Japanese leave Korea under pressure from the Chinese.

**1594** English begin trading in India.

**1594** Mogul emperor Akbar conquers Kandahar, India.

**1595** Dutch start to establish colonies in the East Indies.

**1597** Japanese invade Korea, but the Chinese help the Koreans to expel them.

**1598** Death of Toyotomi Hideyoshi, ruler of Japan. He is succeeded by a child, and five regents compete for power.

*Japanese building called a pagoda, often built next to Buddhist temples*

**1599** Mogul emperor Akbar begins to conquer the Deccan, India.

## THE AMERICAS

1575

**1576-1577** Martin Frobisher, an English navigator, explores North Atlantic and discovers Baffin Island.

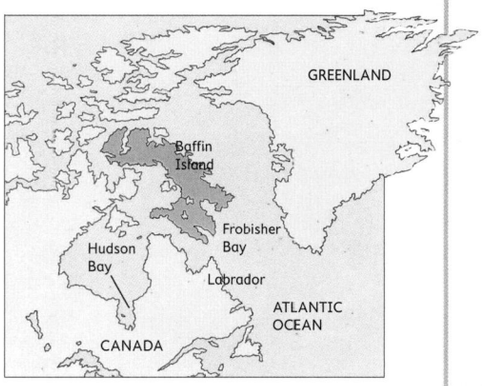


*Frobisher met local people, the Inuits, paddling in one-manned canoes called kayaks.*

**1577** Humphrey Gilbert, an English navigator, is granted a patent to found colonies in North America.

**1579** Sir Francis Drake claims New Albion (California) during his voyage around the world (**1577-1580**).

*Sir Francis Drake*

**1583** Humphrey Gilbert establishes the first English colony in Newfoundland.

**1584** Walter Raleigh (English) discovers and annexes Virginia. He founds a colony in **1585**, but it is abandoned by settlers in **1586**. A second colony is set up in **1587-1591**.

**1585-1587** John Davis, English explorer, searches for a northwest passage to Asia and explores the Davis Strait.

1599

# THE 17th CENTURY

## 1600 - 1699

## SOUTHERN AND WESTERN EUROPE

1600

**1600** English East India Company is founded.

**1602** Dutch East India Company is founded.

**1603** Tudor dynasty ends with death of Elizabeth I. James VI of Scotland becomes James I of England and Scotland (**1603-1625**). The start of the Stuart dynasty.

*Funeral procession for Elizabeth I*

**1604-1616** 12-year truce in the Netherlands between the Spanish and the Dutch, supported by the English and French.

**1605** Gunpowder Plot: a failed attempt by a group of English Catholics, including Guy Fawkes, to blow up the Houses of Parliament. They are caught and executed.

**1605** Miguel Cervantes (**1547-1616**) writes *Don Quixote de la Mancha*, the first modern novel.

**1608** The first practical telescope is invented by Hans Lippershey, a Dutch lens maker.

**1609** Moors (North African Arabs) are expelled from Portugal.

**1610** Galileo Galilei, an Italian astronomer and mathematician, publishes *The Starry Messenger*, about his discoveries with the use of a telescope.

**1610** Assassination of Henri IV of France. Start of reign of Louis XIII (**1610-1643**).

**1611** King James Bible published in England.

**1614** John Napier, a Scottish mathematician, invents his logarithm tables.

**1614-1616** Civil war in France.

**1616** William Harvey, an English doctor, introduces the idea of the circulation of the blood around the body.

*Two of Galileo's telescopes mounted on a stand*

## NORTHERN AND EASTERN EUROPE

**1603** Grigoriy Otrepieff, a monk, claims to be Dimitri, youngest son of the late Ivan IV, and heir to the Russian throne. (Dimitri had in fact been murdered in **1591**.) Grigoriy invades Russia and is crowned Tsar, but becomes unpopular.

**1604** Russians expand across Siberia and found Tomsk.

**1606** Russia: the false Dimitri is defeated and murdered in a revolt led by Boris Gudunov.

**1607-1611** Reign of Charles IX of Sweden.

**1608** Formation of a Protestant Union in Germany.

*Tsarevich Dimitri (top) and Grigoriy Otrepieff, the false Dimitri (bottom)*

**1609** Maximilian of Bavaria forms a Catholic league.

**1609** Johannes Kepler (**1571-1630**), a German astronomer, announces his laws of planetary motion. Kepler developed Copernicus's idea that planets revolve around the Sun, but suggested that they did so in ellipses rather than circles.

*Diagram of Kepler's idea of planetary motion*

**1611-1613** War between Sweden and Denmark.

**1611-1632** Reign of Gustavus Adolphus II of Sweden, great soldier and statesman. Sweden acquires land on the Baltic and becomes a major power.

*Gustavus Adolphus II*

**1613** Russia: Romanov dynasty (**1613-1917**) is founded by Tsar Michael.

**1613** Turks conquer Hungary.

**1617** Treaty of Stolbovo: Russia gives up Ingria and Karelia to Sweden.

## THE THIRTY YEARS' WAR

The Thirty Years' War (**1618-1648**) began as a revolt by the Bohemian provinces of the Holy Roman Empire, but it soon merged with several other conflicts. Fought mainly in Germany, the war devastated the land, killing thousands. The two sides were divided mainly on religious lines, with Spain and Catholic German states supporting the Empire, and Denmark and Protestant German states supporting Bohemia. Later, political factors grew more important. In **1630**, the Protestants were joined by Sweden, whose brilliant commander, Gustavus Adolphus, wanted to expand his own power in the Baltic. Catholic France, already at war with Spain, joined the Protestant side in **1635**. The peace treaty in **1648** ended the threat of Habsburg domination.

1619

*The city of Magdeburg, Germany, under seige in 1631, from an early print*

## AFRICA TO INDIA

**c.1600** Oyo kingdom in West Africa is at its height.

**1602-1627** Wars between the Persian Safavids and the Ottoman Turks. Turks lose Baghdad (Iraq) in **1603**, Tabriz (northwest Persia) in **1604** and Georgia in **1618**.

**1605** India: Emperor Akbar dies. Succeeded by Jahangir (**1605-1627**).

*An Oyo carving*

*Jahangir, Mogul emperor*

**1609** Dutch take Ceylon from Portugal.

**1610** English East India Company sets up its first factory in India.

*The Blue Mosque, Isfahan, Persia*

**1611** English East India Company establishes first trading post in India, at Surat.

**1612** Persians take Baghdad (Iraq) from the Ottoman Turks.

**1616** Dutch and French establish trading posts in Senegal and the Gold Coast (Ghana), West Africa.

**1616** English East India Company trades with Persia.

## THE FAR EAST

**c.1600** Dutch trading bases established in Java and Sumatra.

**1600** Civil war in Burma: Burmese empire breaks up.

### JAPAN UNDER THE TOKUGAWAS

In **1600**, Ieyasu Tokugawa won the Battle of Sekigahara, ending civil war, and in **1603** assumed the title of *shogun* (military ruler), founding the Tokugawa dynasty. The Tokugawa ruled Japan from their new capital, Edo (Tokyo), until **1867**. They organized Japanese society into rigid classes, with *daimyo* (warlords) and *han* (fiefs) closely regulated by the shogun.

*Ieyasu Tokugawa*

**1602** First Dutch traders arrive in Cambodia and Siam.

*Dutch tile*

**1605** Hidetada Tokugawa becomes ruler in Japan.

**1606** Willem Janszoon, Dutch navigator, is first European to reach Australia.

**1613-1646** Reign of Sultan Agung of Mataram, who tries to rule Java.

**1614-1636** Europeans begin to explore Australia.

**1616** Manchu Tartars invade China.

**1618-1629** Dutch expel Portuguese from East Indies. Set up base at Batavia (Jakarta), Sumatra in **1619**.

*Puppets from Java, East Indies*

## THE AMERICAS

**1602** Spaniards explore the coast of California.

**1603** French start to colonize North America: Newfoundland, Nova Scotia and New France.

**1605** Spaniards found Santa Fé, New Mexico.

**1605** James I of England is proclaimed King of Barbados.

**1606** First permanent English settlement in North America, at Jamestown, Virginia.

*Early settlers*

**1608** French found Quebec, Canada.

**1608** Paraguay founded by Jesuits.

**1609** English settlers on Bermuda.

**1609** Dutch found Manhattan.

**1610-1611** Henry Hudson, English navigator, explores Hudson Bay, in search of Northwest Passage to East.

*Native North Americans traded furs for guns, knives and blankets.*

**1610** Etienne Brulé, French explorer, discovers Lake Huron.

**1612** Tobacco cultivated in Virginia.

**1613** Samuel de Champlain, French explorer, explores Ottawa river, Canada.

**1613** English destroy French settlement at Port Royal, Jamaica.

**1616** Willem Schouten, Dutch navigator, rounds Cape Horn.

**1619** First slaves imported into Virginia from West Africa.

**1619** First colonial assembly is held at Jamestown, Virginia.

## SOUTHERN AND WESTERN EUROPE

1620

**1620** Uprising of Huguenots (Protestants) in France.

**1620s** Johannes Kepler (**1571-1630**), a German astronomer, studies the movement of the planets.

**1621-1625** Philip IV of Spain resumes war against the Dutch.

**1622-1673** Life of Molière (born Jean-Baptiste Poquelin), great French comedy playwright.

**1624-1629** France and England at war.

**1624-1642** Cardinal Richelieu is first minister to Louis XIII of France.

**1625-1649** Reign of Charles I of England.

**1628** Cardinal Richelieu captures Huguenot stronghold of La Rochelle, ending Huguenot threat to French unity.

*Cardinal Richelieu*

*Siege tower at La Rochelle, on the west coast of France*

**1629-1640** England: King Charles I dissolves Parliament after disagreements with the House of Commons over customs and excise duties and Catholicism. He does not recall Parliament until **1640**. Charles builds up his navy to rival that of the Dutch, levying an old tax called Ship Money to cover the cost.

*Charles I*

**1632** Galileo Galilei (**1564-1642**), an Italian astronomer and mathematician, publishes his *Dialogues*, which revolutionizes scientific thinking.

**1635** France declares war on Spain and joins the Thirty Years' War.

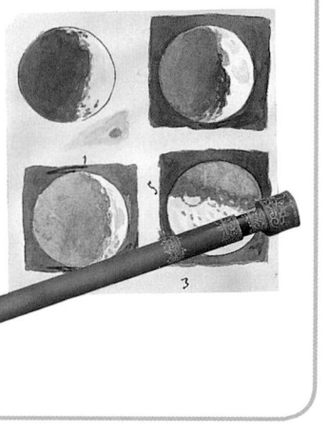

*Galileo's telescope and his sketches of the moon*

**1637** René Descartes, French mathematician, does important work on analytical geometry.

1639

## NORTHERN AND EASTERN EUROPE

**1620** Battle of the White Mountain outside Prague: victory for the imperial forces in the Thirty Years' War.

**1621** Gustavus Adolphus gains Livonia from Poland.

**1622** England sends first ambassador to Turkey.

**1623** Protestant worship is forbidden in Bohemia.

**1625** Denmark joins the Thirty Years' War.

**1628** Swedish royal flagship, the *Vasa*, sinks in Stockholm shortly after being launched.

**1629** Peace of Lübeck between Denmark and the Holy Roman Empire.

*The Vasa*

**1630** Sweden joins the Thirty Years' War.

**1631** Battle of Breitenfeld: imperial forces are defeated.

**1632** Battle of Lützen: Swedes defeat imperial forces, but King Gustavus Adolphus is killed.

**1632** Russians continue to expand in Siberia: Irkutsk is founded.

*Russian fur traders in Siberia, from an old print*

**1632-1654** Reign of Queen Christina of Sweden, guided by the great statesman, Axel Oxenstierna.

**1634** Battle of Nördlingen: Sweden loses South Germany.

*Map showing the growth of the Swedish empire*

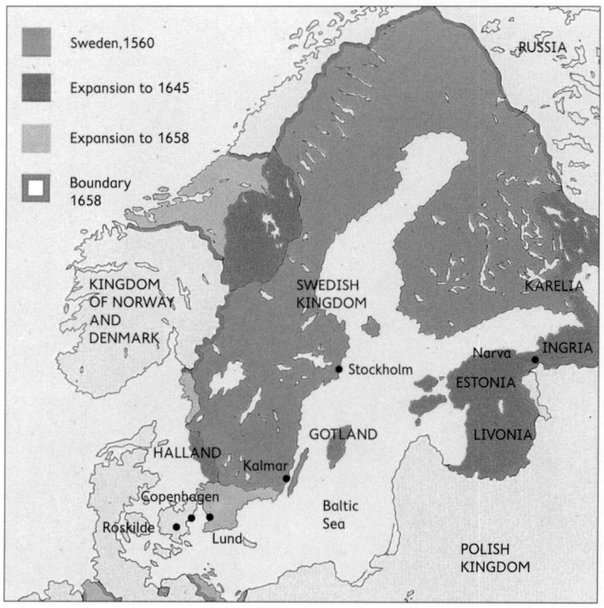

## AFRICA TO INDIA

**1627-1656** Rule of Mogul emperor, Shah Jahan, who adds territories to the empire. From **1632-1653**, he builds the white marble Taj Mahal, a tomb for his beloved wife Mumtaz Mahal.

*Shah Jahan and the Taj Mahal*

**1628** Portuguese destroy the Mwenemutapa kingdom in southern Africa.

**1629** Death of Shah Abbas the Great of Persia.

**1631-1642** Dutch West India Company ousts the Portuguese from the Gold Coast (Ghana).

**1636** Sultans of the Deccan, India, become subject princes of the Moguls.

**1637** Dutch take El Mina, West Africa, from the Portuguese.

**1637** French establish trading posts in Senegal, West Africa.

**1639** Ottoman Turks make peace with the Persians after capturing Iraq from them.

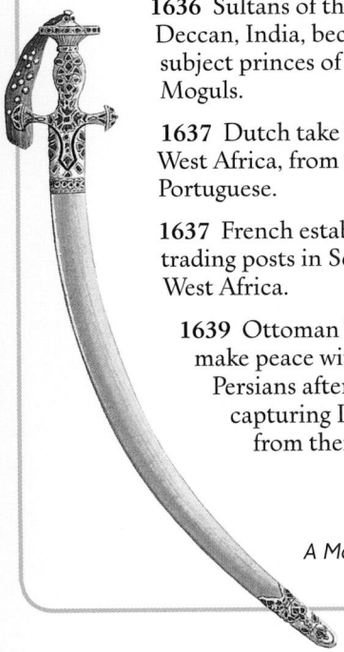

*A Mogul sword*

## THE FAR EAST

**1622-1624** Christian missionaries are executed in Japan.

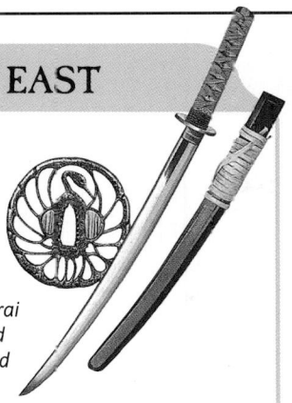

*Japanese Samurai sword, scabbard and sword guard*

**1623** Amboyna Massacre: Dutch destroy the English East Indies base.

**1623-1651** Rule of the powerful shogun Iemitsu Tokugawa in Japan. Fearing foreign influence or invasion, he forbids all Japanese to travel abroad and almost all existing foreign merchants are expelled: only the Dutch are allowed to remain on an island off Nagasaki.

**1626-1662** Dutch trade with China from Formosa (Taiwan).

**1627** Manchu people from Manchuria, northern China, begin expanding into other parts of China and Korea.

**1636** Manchus proclaim a new Chinese dynasty, the Ch'ing, at Mukden, Manchuria.

*Manchu armies attacking*

**1637** Korea becomes a subject state of China.

**1637** English establish a trading post in Canton, China.

**1639-1850s** Japan enforces isolationist policies. Japanese are forbidden to go abroad and foreigners banned from entering Japan. Japan becomes virtually isolated from European contact. During this period, towns grow and trade flourishes.

*Illustration of wealthy Japanese woman*

## THE AMERICAS

**1620** The *Mayflower* sails from Plymouth, England, to Massachusetts, carrying the Pilgrims (English Puritans).

*Wild North American turkey*

*Pilgrims at Thanksgiving meal*

**1625** French establish a port at Cayenne, Guiana.

**1625** Dutch found New Amsterdam (now New York).

**1627** French Cardinal Richelieu sets up a company to colonize all land between Florida and the Arctic.

**1629** English capture Quebec from France (restored to France **1632**).

**1630-1642** 16,000 settlers join the Massachusetts Bay Colony.

**1634** Maryland is founded for Catholic colonists.

**1634** Dutch establish a base at Curaçao, West Indies.

**1634** Jean Nicolet, French explorer, explores Lake Michigan and St. Lawrence and Mississippi rivers.

**1636** Founding of Dutch Guiana. (Becomes British Guiana in **1814**).

**1636-1637** Pequot War between settlers and native North Americans in New England.

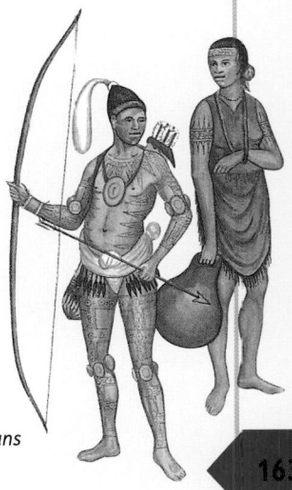

*Native American Indians from the East coast*

1620

1639

## SOUTHERN AND WESTERN EUROPE

1640

**1640** England: Charles I summons Parliament to raise money to fight the Scots.

**1640** Portugal becomes independent under the House of Braganza (until **1910**).

**1642** Blaise Pascal, a French mathematician, designs a mechanical adding machine.

### THE ENGLISH CIVIL WAR

The English Civil War (**1642-1649**) was the result of a rift between Parliament and the early Stuart kings, James I (**1603-1625**), and Charles I (**1625-1649**). MPs felt the kings were claiming too much power, and attempting to rule without them. Many of them were Puritans (strict Protestants) and they suspected the kings of Catholic sympathies. War began in **1642**. By **1646**, the Roundheads (the Parliamentary side), led by Oliver Cromwell and his New Model Army, had defeated the Cavaliers (the King's side). Fighting broke out again between **1648-1649**, ending with the defeat and execution of Charles I.

*Helmet*

*Charles I*

**1643** Evangelista Torricelli (**1608-1647**), a Florentine, invents the barometer.

**1643** French beat the Spaniards at the Battle of Rocroi: the start of French military superiority in Europe.

**1643-1715** Louis XIV of France comes to the throne, aged 5. His mother reigns for him until **1651**, and policy is controlled by first minister Cardinal Mazarin until **1661**.

**1644** René Descartes, a French mathematician and philosopher, publishes his *Principles of Philosophy*.

**1648** Peace of the Hague ends the Dutch Revolt. Spain recognizes independent United Provinces (Dutch Republic).

**1648-1653** Riots in Paris: period of civil disorder in France known as the Fronde.

**1649-1660** England is ruled by the Commonwealth (**1649-1653**), then the Protectorate (**1653-1658**), under Oliver Cromwell.

**1649** Oliver Cromwell puts down Scottish and Irish rebellions.

**1652-1654** First Anglo-Dutch Trade War.

**c.1658** Robert Boyle, Irish scientist, and Robert Hooke, English scientist, design and build a new air pump to create a vacuum in a glass tube.

*Hooke and Boyle's air pump*

**1659** Peace of the Pyrenees between France and Spain.

1659

## NORTHERN AND EASTERN EUROPE

**1640-1688** The state of Brandenburg-Prussia grows in importance under Frederick William, 'the Great Elector'.

*Frederick William I*

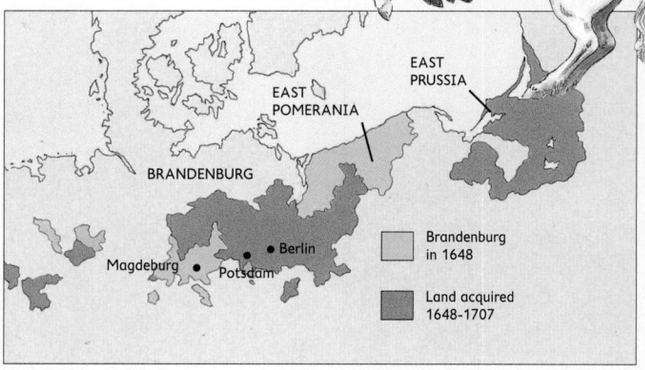


*Map showing Brandenburg-Prussia 1648-1707*

**1643-1645** War between Sweden and Denmark. Sweden becomes the major power in the Baltic.

**1645-1659** War between Venice and the Turks leads to the conquest of Crete by the Turks.

**1646** Swedes take Prague and invade Bavaria.

**1648** Peace of Westphalia ends the Thirty Years' War.

**1649** The Code of Laws marks the establishment of serfdom in Russia. (Serfs are peasants with no land of their own.)

**1649** Russians reach the Pacific Ocean and found Okhotsk in eastern Siberia.

**1654** Queen Christina of Sweden abdicates and becomes a Catholic.

*Queen Christina of Sweden*

**1654-1657** War between Russia and Poland. Russia acquires Smolensk and eastern Ukraine.

**1654-1660** War between Sweden and Poland.

**1657** Elector of Brandenburg wins the sovereignty of Prussia.

**1658** Peace of Roskilde: the Danes give up all claims to southern Sweden.

## AFRICA TO INDIA

**1640** English acquire the port of Madras, India.

**1643** French establish Fort Dauphin, Madagascar.

**1644** Dutch settle in Mauritius.

**1648** Arabs recapture Muscat from Portugal.

**1650** Ali Bey makes himself hereditary governor of Tunis, North Africa.

**1651** English occupy St. Helena, in the Atlantic Ocean.

**1652** Dutch found the Cape of Good Hope, South Africa.

*Cape Dutch farmhouse*

**1656-1661** Grand Vizier Mohammed Koprülü saves the Ottoman empire from decline.

**1656** Dutch displace the Portuguese in Ceylon (Sri Lanka).

**1656-1707** Rule of Aurangzeb, the last great Mogul emperor. He defeats and deposes his father, Jahan, and conquers Kandahar, Kabul and the Deccan. The empire reaches its greatest extent, but decay sets in.

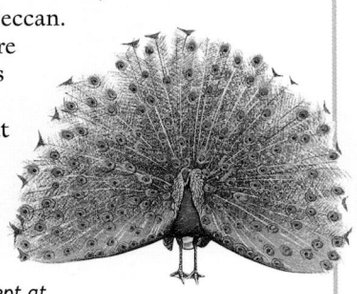

*Peacock kept at Emperor's palace*

*Elephants dressed for Mogul celebration*

**1659** French found trading posts on coast of Senegal.

## THE FAR EAST

**1641** Dutch seize Malacca from Portugal and dominate trade in East Indies.

**1641** Japan cuts itself off from the rest of the world. Dutch keep a trading post on an island off Nagasaki.

*Nagasaki Bay*

**1642** Abel Tasman, Dutch explorer, discovers Van Diemen's Land (Tasmania) and New Zealand.

**1643** Tasman discovers Fiji islands.

**1644** Abel Tasman explores the north and west coasts of Australia.

### THE CH'ING DYNASTY

In **1627**, the Manchu people began expanding into other parts of China, from their base at Mukden, Manchuria in northern China. In **1636**, they proclaimed a new Chinese dynasty, the Ch'ing. Meanwhile, rebellions broke out against the Chinese Ming dynasty. In **1644**, bandits occupied Beijing and the dynasty was deposed. The Chinese people then invited the Manchus to overthrow the bandits. By **1652** most of the country was under Ch'ing control. They ruled China from Beijing until **1911/1912**.

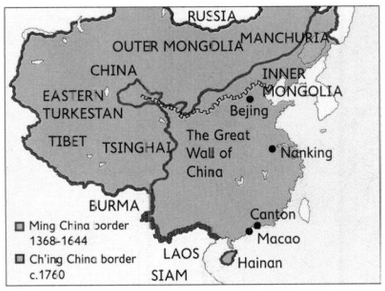


*The boundaries of China under the Ming and Ch'ing dynasties*

**1648** Bering Strait is discovered by Russian Cossack explorer, Dezhnev.

## THE AMERICAS

1640

**1642** French found Montreal, Canada.

*The Canadian fur trade continues to grow. These are some of the animals hunted for their fur.*

*Stoat*

*Beaver*

*Otter*

*Inuit bow*

**1643** New Hampshire is founded.

**1644** Rhode Island separates from the Massachusetts Bay Colony.

**1648** French establish settlements in the Caribbean islands of St. Martin, St. Bartholomew, St. Croix, The Saints, Maria Galante, St. Lucia and Grenada.

**1648-1653** War between the Iroquois and the Huron and Algonquin tribes in North America.

**c.1650** Settler population in the 13 North American colonies reaches about 60,000.

**1651** Maine becomes part of the Massachusetts Bay Colony.

**1654** First sugar cane plantations set up in the Caribbean by the English and French. Slaves are imported from West Africa to work on them.

**1655** England acquires Jamaica from Spain.

**1655** French acquire Haiti.

1659

## SOUTHERN AND WESTERN EUROPE

1660

**1660** The Restoration: Charles II is restored to the thrones of England, Scotland and Ireland.

### LOUIS XIV - THE SUN KING

In **1661**, at the age of 22, Louis XIV took control of the government in France. During his reign, France became the dominant power in Europe, and literature, art, drama and music flourished at his court. In a series of brilliant military victories, he extended France's boundaries, provoking hostility and fear abroad. Under his minister, Colbert (**1619-1683**), the economy was modernized and Louis was able to control his nobles, ruling with absolute power. His absolutism - the idea that the power of the state should be embodied in one person (the monarch), who does not have to answer to anyone - became the model for other European rulers.

*Louis XIV*

*Louis XIV was nicknamed the 'Sun King'. This image is taken from his palace at Versailles.*

**1661** Robert Boyle, Irish scientist, defines chemical elements.

**1664** French East India Company is founded.

**1665-1667** Second Anglo-Dutch Trade War ends in the Peace of Breda.

**1665** Portugal wins independence from Spain, with English help. Recognized at the Treaty of Lisbon (**1668**).

**1665** Isaac Newton (**1642-1727**), English scientist, discovers gravity.

**1665** The Great Plague in London.

*The Fire of London*

**1666** The Great Fire of London.

**1668** Isaac Newton invents the reflecting telescope.

**1670** Treaty of Dover: a secret treaty between Charles II and Louis XIV, supplying Charles with funds to fight the Dutch and restore Catholicism in England.

**1672-1674** Third Anglo-Dutch Trade War.

**1672-1678** War between France and Netherlands ends in the Peace of Nijmegen.

**1672-1702** William III of Orange is hereditary stadtholder (ruler) of the Netherlands.

**1679** Exclusion Crisis in England: parliamentary bill prevents James, the Catholic Duke of York, from succeeding his brother as King of England. Charles II dismisses Parliament.

1679

## NORTHERN AND EASTERN EUROPE

**1660** Treaty of Oliva ends war between Sweden, Poland, Brandenburg and the Holy Roman Empire.

**1660** Brandenburg acquires sovereignty over Prussia.

*Prussian foot soldier*

**1660-1697** Reign of Charles XI of Sweden.

**1661** First European banknote is issued by the Bank of Stockholm, Sweden.

*Early Swedish banknote*

**1663-1699** Ottoman Turks attack Central Europe.

**1664** Ottoman Turks invade and occupy Hungary.

**1667** End of a 13-year truce between Russia and Poland. Kiev is ceded to Russia.

**1669** Venice cedes Crete to the Turks, marking the end of Venice's colonial empire.

**1670** Rebellion of Ukrainian Cossacks and peasants subject to Poland is crushed by the Polish leader, Jan Sobieski.

**1671** Turks declare war on Poland, in support of Cossacks.

*Cossack soldiers dancing*

**1672** Turks and Cossacks invade Poland. Poles give up Podolia and Ukraine.

**1673** Poles defeat the Turks at the Battle of Khorzim.

**1674** Jan Sobieski is elected King of Poland.

**1675** Elector of Brandenburg defeats the Swedes at the Battle of Fehrbellin.

**1676** Peace of Zuravno ends the war between Poland and Turkey. Turkey gains the Polish Ukraine.

**1676** Swedes defeat the Danes at the Battle of Lund.

**1677** Swedes defeat Danes at Rostock and Landström.

**1677-1979** War between Russia and Turkey. At the Treaty of Radzin, Russia gains most of Ukraine from Turks.

**1678** War between Russia and Sweden.

**1679** Peace between Sweden and Brandenburg.

## AFRICA TO INDIA

**c.1660-1670** Rise of the Bambara kingdoms of the Upper Niger, West Africa.

*Carving from the Kongo kingdom*

**1661** Portuguese cede Tangier, North Africa to England.

**1665** Battle of Ambuila: Portuguese destroy the Kongo kingdom, Central Africa.

**1666-1668** Civil wars in India.

**1668** English East India Company obtains control of Bombay, India.

**1669** Aurangzeb bans Hinduism in India and persecutes Hindus.

**1672** English Royal Africa Company merges with the Guinea Company. West African trade increases.

**1674** French establish a trading station at Pondicherry, India.

**1674** Sivaji Bhonsla, leader of the Marathas, breaks away from Moguls and founds a Maratha state in India.

**1676** Uprising of Sikhs, a reformed Hindu sect, in India.

*The Sikh Golden Temple, Amritsar, rebuilt in 1766 after attacks by the Moguls*

## THE FAR EAST

**1661** Two Jesuit priests, John Grueber and Albert d'Orville, travel from Beijing, China to Agra, India and become the first Europeans to visit the city of Lhasa, in Tibet.

*The Palace of Potala at Lhasa in Tibet, the residence of the dalai lamas, the political and religious rulers of Tibet*

**1661-1688** Rule of King Narai of Siam. He tries to resist Dutch attempts to monopolize trade by enlisting French help. This proves unpopular and his dynasty is overthrown, and the French soldiers expelled.

**1662-1722** Reign of the powerful Chinese emperor, K'ang Hsi.

*K'ang Hsi, Emperor of China*

**1663** French missionaries enter Vietnam.

**1667** Dutch increase their territory in Java.

**1679** War between Vietnam and Cambodia. Cambodia loses the Mekong river delta.

## THE AMERICAS

1660

**1663** European settlers in the Carolinas.

**1665** England gains New Netherlands (New York and New Jersey) and Caribbean islands from the Dutch.

**1670** Hudson's Bay Company is founded in England to explore and acquire territory in the Hudson Bay area of Canada. They claim the fur trading area of Rupert's Land.

**1673** Jacques Marquette and Louis Jolliet, French explorers, reach the headwaters of the Mississippi river.

**1674** Plantations in Quebec, Canada, become French royal colonies.

**1675-1676** War between settlers and Native Americans in New England. Settlers win control of the North American seaboard.

**1679** Robert de la Salle, French explorer, explores the Great Lakes.

*Map of the Great Lakes*

*Niagara Falls, explored by de la Salle*

1679

## SOUTHERN AND WESTERN EUROPE

1680

**1685** The revocation of the Edict of Nantes forces half a million Huguenots to flee France.

**1685** Catholic James II becomes King of England. A Protestant uprising on behalf of Charles's illegitimate son, the Duke of Monmouth, is defeated.

**1686** League of Augsburg: Holy Roman Empire, Spain, Sweden, Saxony, Bavaria and the Palatinate ally against France.

**1687** Isaac Newton publishes the *Principia*, containing his three Laws of Motion and theory of gravitation.

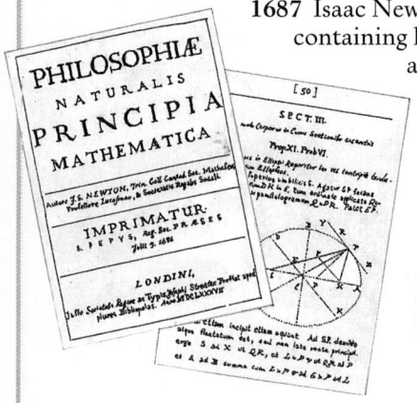


*Pages from Newton's book, the Principia*

*A device designed to demonstrate Newton's Third Law of Motion*

**1688-1689** Glorious Revolution in England: The House of Lords invites William of Orange to save England from Catholicism. James II flees to France. William becomes King of England and reigns with his wife Mary (daughter of James II) as William III and Mary II (**1689-1702**).

*William III of Orange and his wife Mary II of England*

**1688-1697** War of the League of Augsburg.

**1689** Parliament confirms the abdication of James II. Declaration of Rights safeguards Parliament and bars Catholics from throne.

**1690** Battle of the Boyne: Irish Catholic supporters of the exiled James II are defeated by English forces.

**1692** Scotland: massacre at Glencoe of members of the MacDonald clan (supporters of the Catholic James II) by the Campbells (supporters of the Protestant English throne).

**1694-1778** Life of Voltaire, French writer and philosopher, author of *Candide*.

**1697** Treaty of Rijswick ends the War of the League of Augsburg. France recognizes William III as the King of England and the Protestant succession of Queen Anne.

**1698** England, France, United Provinces and HRE agree on the Spanish succession. Charles II of Spain makes a will, leaving his possessions to the Elector Prince of Bavaria.

1699

**1699** The Elector of Bavaria dies.

## NORTHERN AND EASTERN EUROPE

**1682** Sighting of Great Comet (named Halley's Comet) by Edmund Halley. The comet had also appeared in **1066**, before the Battle of Hastings, and in **1531** and **1607**.

*Halley's Comet shown in the Bayeaux tapestry, made after the Battle of Hastings*

**1682** Princess Sophia becomes regent of Russia, on the accession of the 10-year-old Peter (see below).

**1683** Ottomans besiege Vienna for the last time and fail. Turkish threat in Europe declines and Austrian power grows.

**1684** The Holy League (Holy Roman Empire, Poland and Venice) is formed by Pope Innocent XI to fight the Turks.

**1687** Battle of Mohacs: Turks are defeated and Hungary becomes a hereditary Habsburg possession.

### PETER THE GREAT

Peter the Great (**1689-1725**) was one of the greatest rulers in Russian history. Coming to the throne in **1682**, at the age of 10, Peter took sole control in **1689** when he was just 17. Under his leadership, Russia developed into a major European power. Peter founded the Russian navy, strengthened the army and extended Russia's boundaries. To give himself a 'window on the west', he built a new capital city, St. Petersburg, on the Baltic Sea. Peter's reforms strengthened and modernized the country: he improved education and introduced new industries and crafts. But, despite this, most people continued to live as serfs (landless peasants) and benefitted little from Russia's development.

*Peter the Great*

*The Winter Palace at St. Petersburg*

**1690** Turks take Belgrade, Serbia, in a counterattack against the Austrian empire.

**1691** War continues between Turks and Austrians. Turks are defeated at Zelankemen. Habsburgs conquer Transylvania.

**1695-1706** Russo-Turkish War: Russia captures Azov, a fort on the Black Sea, and Kamchatka, a peninsula at the eastern end of the continent.

**1697** Battle of Zenta, Serbia: Prince Eugene of Savoy defeats the Turks.

**1699** Treaty of Karlowitz: the Austrians recover Hungary, Croatia and Transylvania from the Turks. Poland takes the Turkish Ukraine. Venice gains Peloponnese and Podolia.

## AFRICA TO INDIA

**1680** Death of Sivaji Bhonsla, great leader of the Hindu Marathas in India.

*Sivaji Bhonsla*

**1680-1708** French increase their trading activities in Madagascar and Nigeria.

**1681** India: Prince Akbar leads an unsuccessful revolt against his father, Aurangzeb, and flees to the Deccan.

**1686** Madagascar is annexed by the French East India Company.

**1687** English East India Company transfers its headquarters from Surat to Bombay.

**c.1690** Mogul empire reaches its greatest extent.

**1690** English establish a trading base in Calcutta, India.

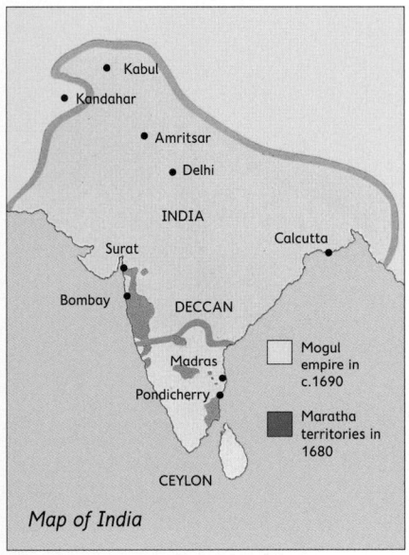


*Map of India*

**1697-1712** Expansion of the Ashanti kingdom in West Africa.

*The Ashanti were famous for their carving in gold.*

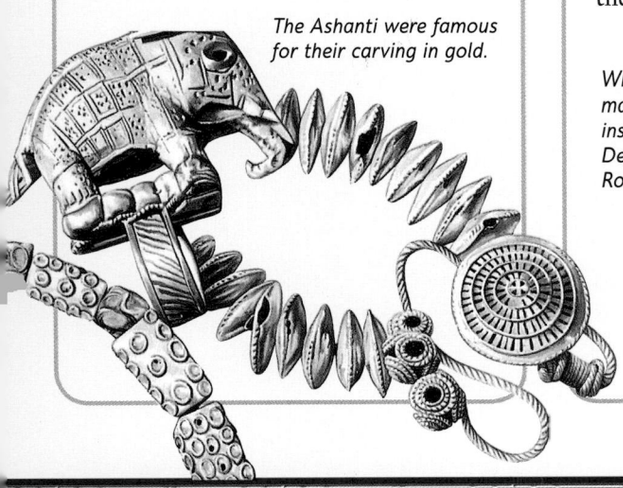

## THE FAR EAST

**1680** Dutch territories in the East Indies are joined together.

**1683** Manchus conquer Formosa (Taiwan).

**1683** Dutch traders are admitted to Canton, China.

**1684** Dutch take control in Java.

**1685** Chinese ports are opened to foreign trade.

*Chinese woodcut of a flat-bottomed boat, called a junk*

**1688** King Narai of Siam dies. Siamese policies become isolationist until the **1850s**.

*King Narai on an elephant*

**1688** William Dampier, English adventurer, explores Australia.

**1697** Chinese conquer western Mongolia.

**1698** First French legation to China.

**1699** Dampier leads expedition to the Pacific, increasing European knowledge of the South Seas.

*William Dampier, who may have been the inspiration for Daniel Defoe's novel, Robinson Crusoe*

## THE AMERICAS

1680

**1680** Portuguese establish the colony of Sacramento, Uruguay.

**1681** William Penn, an English Quaker, is granted a charter to found colony of Pennsylvania.

**1682** Robert de la Salle, French explorer, founds St. Louis and takes the Mississippi Valley.

*De la Salle exploring the Mississippi river*

**1683** William Penn founds Philadelphia and Quaker colony of Pennsylvania. Penn makes a treaty with the Native Americans, which keeps Pennsylvania at peace.

*Native North Americans often smoked a peace pipe, like this one, after peace was made.*

**1684** Bermuda becomes an English Crown Colony.

**1688** German Quakers make first anti-slavery protests in North America.

**1691** Massachusetts absorbs the Plymouth colony.

**1691** The Carolinas are divided into North and South.

**1691** English found Kingston, Jamaica.

**1699** French found Louisiana.

*Early settlers and explorers were often powerless when attacked by bears.*

1699

# THE 18th CENTURY

## 1700 - 1799

## SOUTHERN AND WESTERN EUROPE

1700

### WAR OF THE SPANISH SUCCESSION

*Shields of claimants to the throne*

The War of the Spanish Succession (**1701-1714**) was fought by major European countries to determine who would inherit the kingdom of the childless Charles II of Spain. With land in Italy and the Spanish Netherlands, and rich colonies in America, it was a valuable prize. There were claims both by the French Bourbons and the Austrian Habsburgs: Philip, grandson of Louis XIV of France, and Charles, son of Emperor Leopold, both claimed the throne. Fearing French supremacy, the English and Dutch formed an alliance to support Austria, later joined by Portugal and Savoy, and they won a series of brilliant victories. But in **1711**, Charles became emperor, altering the balance of power, and the English and Dutch swapped sides to support Philip. In the Peace of Utrecht (**1713-1714**), Philip became Philip V of Spain, but on the condition that Spain and France should never unite.

**1702-1714** Reign of Queen Anne, the last of the Stuart monarchs of England.

**1704** England seizes Gibraltar from Spain.

**1704** Battle of Blenheim: Anglo-Austrians, led by the Duke of Marlborough and Prince Eugene of Savoy, save Vienna from French and Bavarians.

*The Duke of Marlborough*

**1706** Thomas Newcomen, an English engineer, invents the first practical working steam engine for use in coal mining.

*Union Jack*

**1707** Union of England and Scotland. The British Isles become known as Great Britain.

**1709** Bartolomeo Cristofori (Italian) builds the first piano.

**1710** St. Paul's Cathedral in London is completed.

*St. Paul's Cathedral*

**1712-1778** Life of Jean-Jacques Rousseau, French writer and philosopher.

**1714-1727** Reign of George I of Great Britain, first king of the German house of Hanover.

**1715** Uprising in Scotland by Jacobites, supporters of James Edward, son of James II and pretender to the throne.

**1718** Quadruple alliance is formed by Austria, Britain, France and Netherlands against Spain.

1719

## NORTHERN AND EASTERN EUROPE

**c.1700** Great age of Baroque music in Europe: J.S. Bach (**1685-1750**), Handel (**1685-1759**) and Vivaldi (**1675-1741**).

*A violin, a popular Baroque instrument*

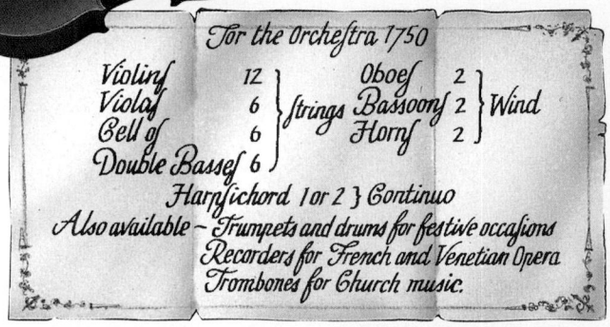

For the Orchestra 1750

| | | | | | |
|---|---|---|---|---|---|
| Violins | 12 | Strings | Oboes | 2 | Wind |
| Violas | 6 | | Bassoons | 2 | |
| Cells of | 6 | | Horns | 2 | |
| Double Basses | 6 | | | | |

Harpsichord 1 or 2 } Continuo

Also available – Trumpets and drums for festive occasions
Recorders for French and Venetian Opera
Trombones for Church music.

*List of instruments in a Baroque orchestra*

**1700-1721** Great Northern War: a struggle for supremacy in the Baltic between Russia and Sweden. Swedes defeat Russians at Narva (**1700**) and invade Poland (**1701-1702**).

**1701** Elector Frederick III of Brandenburg crowns himself Frederick I, 'King in Prussia' (**1701-1713**).

**1703** Peter the Great of Russia founds St. Petersburg.

*An engraving of St. Petersburg*

**1703-1711** Hungarians revolt against Austria.

**1706** Treaty of Altranstadt: Augustus II renounces the Polish throne and is replaced by Stanislaus Leszczynski.

**1708-1709** Charles XII of Sweden invades Russia and is defeated at the Battle of Poltava (**1709**).

**1709** Augustus II regains the Polish throne.

**1710-1711** War between Russia and Turkey.

**1710** Russia conquers Swedish Baltic provinces.

**1712** St. Petersburg becomes capital of Russia.

**1713-1740** Reign of Frederick William I of Prussia: Prussia develops as a strong military state.

**1716-1718** War between Turkey and Austria ends with Peace of Passarowitz: Turkey cedes Belgrade to Austria and Hungary is liberated from Austria.

**1718** Gabriel Fahrenheit, German scientist, invents the mercury thermometer.

**1719** Russians invade Sweden. A coalition of Denmark, Sweden, Prussia and Britain is formed to oppose Russia.

## AFRICA TO INDIA

**c.1700** West Africa: kingdoms of Ashanti, Benin and Oyo flourish. The Ashanti are known for their work in gold. Yoruba kingdom declines.

*Ashanti leather and brass shield*

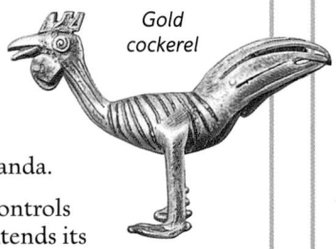

*Gold cockerel*

**c.1700** East Africa: rise of the Bantu kingdom of Buganda.

**c.1700** Oman controls Zanzibar and extends its influence along the East African coast. Portuguese influence declines.

**1705** Turkish rule is overthrown in Tunis and Hussain Ibn Ali establishes the Hussainid dynasty.

**1707** Mogul empire disintegrates after the death of Aurangzeb.

**1708** English East India Company territories in India are divided between Bengal, Madras and Bombay.

**1708** Revolution in Ethiopia.

**1709-1711** Afghans rise against their Persian overlords and set up an independent Afghan state.

**1711** Tripoli, Libya, becomes independent from Turkey.

**1712-1755** Bambara kingdoms grow in the Upper Niger, West Africa.

**1714** Ahmed Bey sets up Karamanli dynasty in Tripoli, Libya.

**1714-1720** Hindu Maratha princes from central India increase their territory in northern India.

**1715** French take control in Mauritius.

*Maratha soldier*

## THE FAR EAST

**1700** English East India Company establishes a base in Borneo.

**1700** William Dampier, English navigator, discovers the north coast of New Guinea.

**1707** Last eruption of Mount Fuji in Japan.

**1714-1733** Reign of King Taninganway Min of Burma. Flourishing period of Burmese culture and power.

**1715** China conquers Mongolia and East Turkestan.

**1715** English East India Company builds its first factory at Canton, China.

*Port of Canton in the 18th century*

**1716** Emperor K'ang Hsi prohibits the teaching of Christianity in China.

**1716-1745** Rule of Shogun Yoshimune of Japan.

**1717** Bugis people from Selangor, Malaya, extend their influence in Johore.

## AMERICA AND THE PACIFIC

1700

**1701** French set up base at Detroit to control the trade in Illinois.

**1701** Yale College is founded in New Haven, Connecticut.

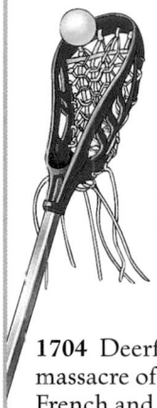

*Stick and ball used in lacrosse, a game played by Native Americans*

**1701** Peace treaty between French and Native Americans in New France (Canada).

**1703** Delaware becomes a colony.

**1704** Deerfield, Massachusetts: massacre of British colonists by French and Native North Americans.

**1709** First German settlers arrive in North America.

**1713** Britain acquires Nova Scotia, Hudson Bay and Newfoundland from France.

**1714-1716** War between French and Native Americans in New France.

**1718** French found New Orleans.

### THE SLAVE TRADE

From the early 18th century until the early 19th century, millions of slaves were shipped from West Africa to work on sugar and cotton plantations in America and the Caribbean. Conditions on board ship were cramped, unhealthy and hot, and more than a million died en route.

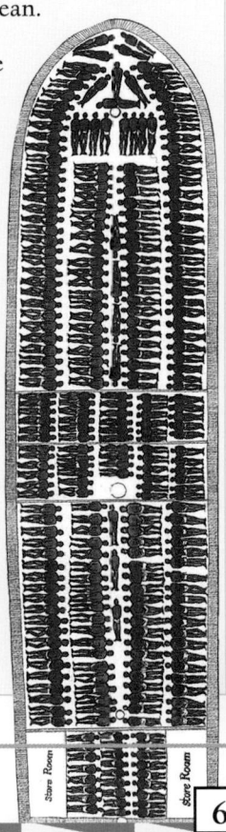

*Diagram showing the cramped conditions of slaves on board ship*

*Head of cotton*

1719

## SOUTHERN AND WESTERN EUROPE

1720

**1720** South Sea Bubble: South Sea Company fails in Britain, causing financial panic.

**1720** John Law's Mississippi Company collapses in France. This leads to national bankruptcy.

**1721-1742** Robert Walpole becomes the first Prime Minister of Great Britain.

*Robert Walpole*

**1725** Treaty of Vienna between Philip V of Spain and Charles VI of Austria. Philip guarantees the Pragmatic Sanction, allowing the succession of Charles VI's daughter, Maria Theresa.

**1726** Russia allies with Austria.

**1727-1729** War between Spain and Britain over Gibraltar.

**c.1730** Rococo, a highly decorative style applied to architecture and interiors, often including scrolls and shells, reaches the height of its popularity.

*Examples of Rococo furniture and ornaments*

**1733** Pact between French and Spanish Bourbons.

**1733** John Kay, British inventor, invents the flying shuttle loom, which improves weaving.

**1734** France invades Lorraine.

**1734** Spain takes the kingdom of Naples.

**1737** Death of the Grand Duke of Tuscany marks the end of the rule of the Medici in Florence.

**1739** John and Charles Wesley found the Methodist movement in Oxford, England. John travels all over the country preaching, especially to the poor.

**1739** War of Jenkins' Ear between Britain and Spain, named after a Captain Jenkins who claimed that Spaniards had boarded his ship and cut off his ear.

*Centurion, a British battleship used in the war against Spain*

1739

## NORTHERN AND EASTERN EUROPE

**1720** Treaty of Stockholm between Sweden, Prussia, Hanover, Denmark, Savoy and Poland.

**1721** Peace of Nystadt ends war between Russia and Sweden. Russia makes great gains (Estonia, Livonia and part of Karelia) and ends Swedish domination of the Baltic. Peter the Great is proclaimed Emperor of all the Russias.

*Dragoon officer in Peter's army*

**1722-1723** War between Russia and Turkey. Russia makes gains on the Caspian Sea.

**1725** Treaty of Hanover: alliance between Britain, France, Prussia, Sweden, Denmark and the Netherlands.

**1725-1727** Empress Catherine I rules Russia, after the death of her husband, Peter the Great.

*Catherine I of Russia*

**1732** Frederick William I of Prussia introduces military and administrative reforms.

**1733** Death of Augustus II, Elector of Saxony and King of Poland.

**1733-1738** War of the Polish Succession. France and Sweden support Stanislaw Leszczynski. Austria and Russia support Augustus II's son. Treaty of Vienna ends the war and Augustus III succeeds to the throne.

**1735-1739** War between Russia and Turkey. Russia obtains the Black Sea port of Azov, so expanding Russian territory as far as the Black Sea.

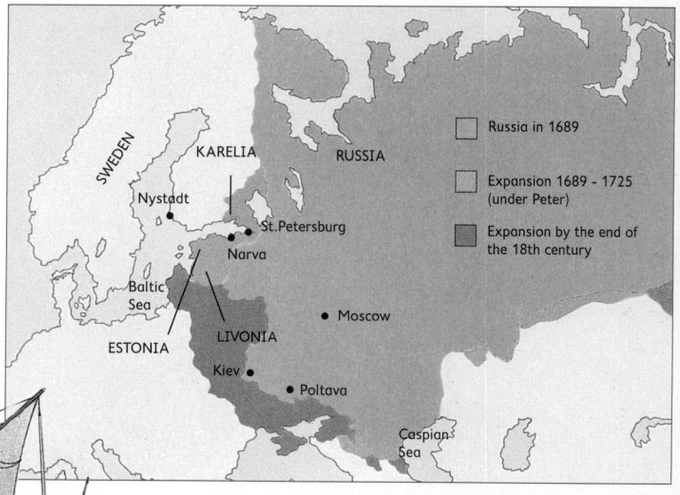


*Map showing the expansion of Russian territory*

## AFRICA TO INDIA

**1721** French annex Mauritius.

**1722-1730** Afghans invade Persia, bringing an end to Safavid rule. The Afghans are expelled in **1730**.

**1723** British Africa Company acquires land in Gambia.

**1724** Hyderabad, India, wins independence from the Moguls.

**1727** Morocco: death of ruler Mulai Ismail is followed by a period of anarchy.

**1729** Portugal loses Mombasa to the Arabs.

**1731-1743** West Africa: war between Kano and Bornu. Sultan of Bornu becomes overlord of Kano.

*Bornu horsemen*

**1735** French East India Company sets up sugar industry on Mauritius.

*Sugar cane*

**1736-1747** Nadir Khan rules Persia.

**1737** Marathas extend their power in northern India.

**1737-1739** Nadir Khan of Persia occupies northern and western India and Afghanistan and attacks Delhi. He takes Mogul Emperor Jahan's peacock throne back to Persia.

**1739** Anglo-Maratha Treaty allows the British to trade in the Deccan.

## THE FAR EAST

**1720** China conquers Tibet.

*Pandas, native to northwest China and Tibet*

**1721** China suppresses a revolt in Formosa (Taiwan).

**1726** France establishes a settlement on the Seychelle Islands.

**1727** Treaty between Russia and China settles borders.

### THE CHINA TRADE

In the 17th and 18th centuries, China had a flourishing export trade through the port of Canton, exporting tea, silk, porcelain and crafts to Europe. Chinese style became increasingly fashionable in Europe, although the Chinese had no interest in western goods and asked to be paid only in silver. From **1736-1796**, China was ruled by the powerful emperor, Ch'ien Lung. During his reign, the country prospered and the population increased. But there was increasing hostility to European missionaries and to imports of opium from India. This provoked tensions and led to the outbreak of the Opium Wars (see page 81).

*Tea, silk and jade were some of China's main exports to Europe*

## AMERICA AND THE PACIFIC

1720

**1721-1722** Jacob Roggeveen, Dutch explorer, discovers Pacific islands of Samoa, Solomons and Easter Island.

*Statues on Easter Island*

**1726** Spanish first settle in Montevideo, Uruguay.

**1727** Coffee is planted in Brazil.

**1727** Quakers demand the abolition of slavery.

**1728** Vitus Bering, a Danish navigator, discovers the Bering Straits between Russia and America.

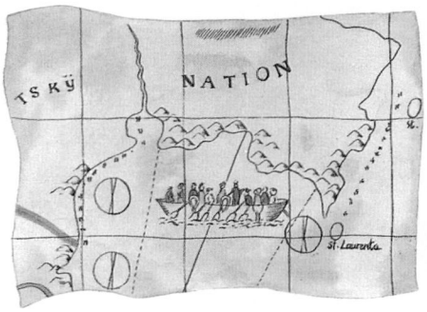


*Detail of the map drawn by Bering*

**1729** North and South Carolina become British crown colonies.

**1730** First sugar cane refinery is established in New York. The success of sugar cane plantations in the Caribbean, worked by slaves imported from Africa, leads to the expansion of the trade in sugar.

**1733** Georgia, the last of the 13 Colonies, is founded.

**1737** Richmond, Virginia, is founded.

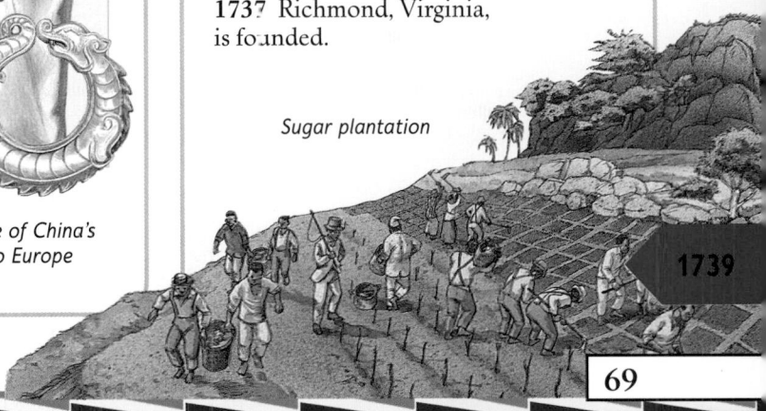

*Sugar plantation*

1739

## SOUTHERN AND WESTERN EUROPE

1740

### MARIA THERESA

In **1740**, Maria Theresa became Archduchess of Austria and Queen of Bohemia and Hungary on the death of her father, Charles VI. Although the empire she inherited was decaying and bankrupt, and her land and titles were coveted by other countries, she emerged as one of the greatest rulers in modern history. She successfully fought the War of Austrian Succession (**1740-1748**) and the Seven Years' War (**1756-1763**) and built Austria into a strong, stable power. During her long reign, Vienna became one of the cultural capitals of Europe: painting, music and architecture thrived and great palaces were built. Among the musicians who played at her court was the six-year-old Wolfgang Amadeus Mozart.

*Maria Theresa*

**1744** War between France and Britain in Europe, India and the West Indies. Lasts intermittently until **1815**.

**1744** Sighting of the most-tailed comet on record, the De Cheseaux comet. It had at least six bright tails.

**1745** Second Jacobite uprising in Scotland attempts to put Charles Edward Stewart (Bonnie Prince Charlie) on the throne. English defeat the Jacobites at Culloden (**1746**).

*Bonnie Prince Charlie*

**1746** France seizes the Austrian Netherlands (Belgium). They are restored to Austria in **1748**.

**1748** Georges de Buffon, French naturalist, publishes 36 volume survey of natural history. He suggests fossils provide evidence of extinct species.

**1748** Peace of Aix-la-Chapelle ends War of the Austrian Succession.

**1750-1777** Reign of José I of Portugal. The chief minister, the Marquis de Pombal, is virtual military dictator from **1775**.

**1751-1776** Denis Diderot compiles the *Encyclopedie*, which aims to record the total stock of knowledge of the time.

**1755** Corsicans rise against Genoese rule.

**1755** Publication of Samuel Johnson's *Dictionary*.

**1755** Earthquake destroys Lisbon, Portugal.

**1756** Joseph Black, Scottish chemist, produces carbon dioxide by heating chemicals.

**1756-1763** Seven Years' War caused by rivalry between Austria and Prussia in Europe, and Britain and France in America. Austria allies with France; and Britain with Prussia. Spain joins the Franco-Austrian alliance in **1759**.

*French navy commander*

1759

## NORTHERN AND EASTERN EUROPE

*Frederick's crown*

### FREDERICK THE GREAT

Frederick II of Prussia (**1740-1786**), known as Frederick the Great, was a brilliant soldier and statesman. By **1772**, he had merged Prussia's territories together, making Prussia the strongest German state after Austria. Frederick was also a keen musician, interested in the ideas of the Enlightenment. Although he was an 'absolute' ruler (keeping power firmly in his own hands), he tried to modernize the country, and to provide strong but efficient government in the interests of the people. He promoted education, agriculture and industry, brought in a fairer legal system, abolished torture and censorship, and declared religious freedom.

*Prussian soldier*

**1740** Frederick II of Prussia invades Silesia.

**1741** Ivan VI of Russia is deposed and replaced by Empress Elizabeth (**1741-1762**), Peter the Great's daughter. German influence and the power of the nobles increase.

**1741** French, Bavarian and Saxon troops occupy Prague. Charles Albert of Bavaria is recognized as King of Bohemia.

**1742** Anders Celsius, Swedish scientist, invents the centigrade thermometer.

**1744** Frederick II of Prussia invades Bohemia, but is repelled by Austrians and Saxons.

**1745** Ewald von Kleist, German priest, invents the Leiden jar, an instrument that stores electricity.

*The Leiden jar*

**1746** Russia and Austria ally against Prussia.

**1747** Sweden allies with Prussia. Russia allies with Britain.

**1749-1832** Life of Johann Wolfgang von Goethe, German poet, novelist and playwright.

**1753** Carl von Linné, also known as Linnaeus, a Swedish botanist, publishes his system for classifying plants, the starting point for the modern classification of species.

*A page from Linnaeus's Systema Naturae*

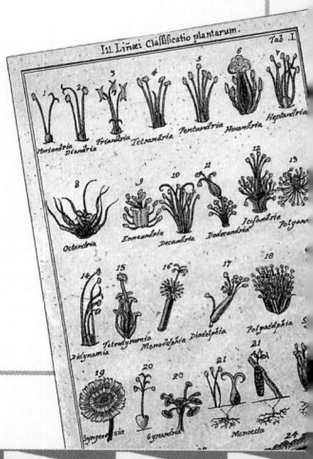

**1757** Russia joins the Franco-Austrian alliance and invades East Prussia. Prussian victory at Rossbach and Leuthen.

**1759-1805** Life of Johann Christoph Friedrich von Schiller, German poet, playwright and historian.

## AFRICA TO INDIA

**c.1740** Lunda kingdom of Kazembe is established in Central Africa.

**1740-1756** Bengal becomes independent of the Mogul empire.

*Bengal tiger*

**1746** French take Madras from the British.

**1746** East Africa: Mazrui dynasty in Mombasa becomes independent of Oman.

**1747-1748** West Africa: Yoruba conquer Dahomey, Benin.

**1748** British retake Madras: start of intense Anglo-French rivalry in India.

**1751** Robert Clive, young clerk in the East India Company, defeats the French at Arcot: the end of French influence in Madras.

*Shah Alam, Nawab of Bengal*

**1756** Black Hole of Calcutta: Nawab of Bengal puts 146 British people into a tiny prison and many die.

**1757** Clive captures Calcutta and defeats the Nawab of Bengal at Plassey: the start of British supremacy in India.

*Indian ivory chess pieces in form of British and Indian soldiers*

**1758** Marathas seize the Punjab and take Lahore.

## THE FAR EAST

**1743** Mataram, Java becomes a Dutch subject state.

**1751-1759** China overruns Tibet, Dzungaria and the Tarim Basin.

**1752** Mons people conquer Upper Burma. Burmese leader, Alaungpaya, rebels and proclaims himself king. He gains control of most of Upper Burma.

**1753** Alaungpaya takes the capital, Ava, and the Shan states.

**1755** Alaungpaya seizes Dagon (renamed Rangoon) from the Mons in Lower Burma.

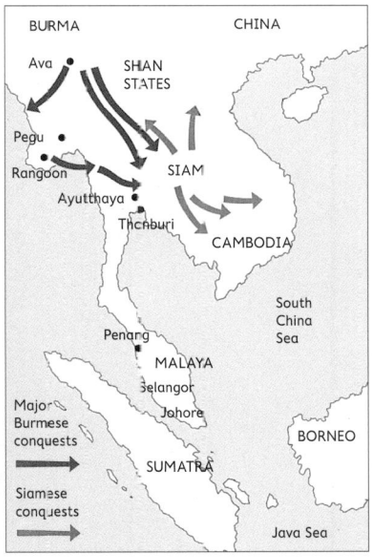


*Map of Southeast Asia*

**1755** Dutch East India Company holds supremacy in Java after war with Javanese Mataram kingdom.

*Dutch East India Company ships*

**1756** Alaungpaya takes Pegu and now controls all Burma. His dynasty rules until 1885.

**1757-1843** China reduces European influence by restricting foreign trade to Canton.

**1758** Bugis people of Johore recognize Dutch tin trade monopoly.

**1758-1759** China conquers East Turkestan.

## AMERICA AND THE PACIFIC

1740

**1742** Russians explore Alaska.

**1742** Venezuela becomes a separate province inside the Spanish South American empire.

**1744-1748** King George's War, between Britain and France in North America.

**1745** Vitus Bering, Danish navigator, discovers the Aleutian Islands.

*Arctic tern, found in Alaska*

**1745** Canada: British capture French fortress of Louisbourg.

**1748** British return Louisbourg to France, as a part of the peace settlement in Europe.

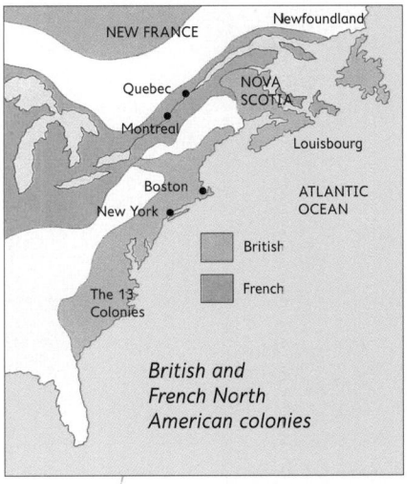


**1750** Boundary commission fails to settle British-French boundary disputes in North America.

**1752** Marquis Duquesne is appointed governor of Quebec.

**1752** Benjamin Franklin, a publisher and politician from Boston, Massachusetts, shows that lightning is caused by electricity.

*Benjamin Franklin*

**1754** French and Native Americans fight against the British in North America.

**1759** British troops, led by General Wolfe, capture Quebec from France.

*General Wolfe*

1759

## SOUTHERN AND WESTERN EUROPE

1760

**1761** Spain invades Portugal for refusing to close its ports to British ships.

**1762** Britain declares war on Spain.

**1763** Peace of Paris ends the Seven Years' War.

### THE INDUSTRIAL REVOLUTION

In the early 18th century, Britain was already richer than many other nations, with fertile well-farmed land, a flourishing cloth industry and expanding trade. Between **c.1750-1850**, this wealth increased, as new industries developed, transformed by the invention of machines powered by steam and water. This is known as the Industrial Revolution. Improved agriculture played a part, and advances in banking, foreign trade and transportation by road, rail and canal made the movement of goods cheaper and more efficient. In the 19th century other European countries, especially Germany, began industrializing too, followed by the United States and Japan.

*Spinning Jenny*

**1767** James Hargreaves, British inventor, invents the 'Spinning Jenny', which can spin up to 8 threads at a time.

**1768** France buys Corsica from Genoa.

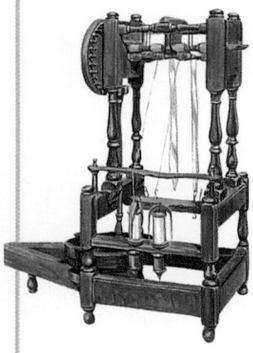

*Arkwright's water frame*

**1769** Richard Arkwright, British cotton manufacturer, invents the water frame, a water-powered spinning machine.

**1772** Slavery is declared illegal in Britain.

**1773** Pope Clement XIV suppresses the Jesuit order.

**1774** Joseph Priestley, a British scientist, isolates oxygen, which he calls 'dephlogisticated air'.

**1776** Adam Smith (**1723-1790**), Scottish economist, publishes *The Wealth of Nations*, advocating free trade and private enterprise.

**1777** James Watt, Scottish engineer, designs a steam engine, which leads to use of steam power in industry.

*James Watt's steam engine*

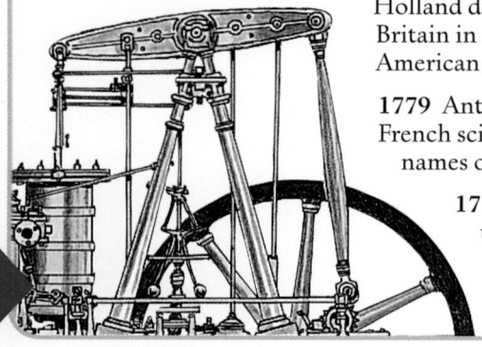

**1778** France and Holland declare war on Britain in support of American colonists.

**1779** Antoine Lavoisier, French scientist, names oxygen.

**1779** France and Spain unsuccessfully besiege Gibraltar.

1779

## NORTHERN AND EASTERN EUROPE

**1762-1796** Reign of Catherine II ('the Great') of Russia. A German princess, she marries the heir to the throne, Peter III, and is a party to his murder. Under her rule, Russia extends its boundaries, Russian culture develops and St. Petersburg becomes a magnificent city. She introduces reforms in government and allows religious freedom.

*Catherine the Great's crown and brooch*

**1768-1774** War between Russia and Turkey.

**1769** Austria seizes the Polish territories of Lvov and Zips.

*Salzburg cathedral*

**c.1770s** Great age of European orchestral music begins: Haydn (**1732-1809**), Mozart (**1756-1791**) and Beethoven (**1770-1827**).

*Mozart at the piano with his father*

**1771-1792** Reign of Gustavus III of Sweden.

**1772** First partition of Poland by Russia, Prussia and Austria. Russia makes modest gains. Prussia annexes most of the territory between Pomerania and Eastern Prussia. Austria annexes a large area north of Hungary.

*Marquee built for Gustavus III*

**1772** Gustavus III of Sweden forces through a new constitution giving himself greater power.

**1773-1775** Peasant uprisings in Russia, led by Cossack Pugachev.

**1774** Treaty of Kuchuk-Kainarji ends Russo-Turkish war. Russia gains Black Sea ports and the right to represent Christians in the Ottoman empire.

## AFRICA TO INDIA

**1761** Battle of Panipat: the Afghans defeat the Marathas.

**1761-1790** Rise of Sikhs in India.

### THE BRITISH IN INDIA

The British victory at Plassey in **1757** gave the East India Company effective control of Bengal, the richest area of India, and of Calcutta, its major port. In **1761**, they captured Pondicherry from the French, marking the final collapse of French power in India. The Company's prosperity grew steadily. Land and privileges were obtained from wealthy native rulers, in return for support and protection. A series of wars brought more territory, as well as recognition of British sovereignty. In **1764**, Clive was appointed governor and commander-in-chief in Bengal, and in **1773** Warren Hastings became first governor-general of British India. India became so important to Britain that, in **1784**, the government took direct control of the political administration: a significant step towards colonization.

*East India Company official with servants*

**1769-1772** James Bruce, Scottish explorer, visits Ethiopia.

**1775-1782** British and Marathas at war.

**c.1775** East Africa: Masai expand as far as Ngong Hills.

*Masai cattle herders*

## THE FAR EAST

**1767** Burmese invade Siam, destroy the capital, Ayutthaya, and take control of most of the country.

**1767-1769** China invades Burma and war breaks out between them. Burma becomes a Chinese dependency.

**1768** Taksin, a Siamese general, forms an army and drives out the Burmese. He defeats various local rulers and becomes the new King of Siam. His capital is at Thonburi.

### COOK'S TRAVELS

James Cook, a British navigator, reached the Pacific island of Tonga and New Zealand in **1769**, and the east coast of Australia (which he claimed for Britain) in **1770**. He named the spot where he landed Botany Bay, because of the abundant plant life. Further trips (**1772-1774** and **1776-1779**) took him to New Hebrides and Hawaii.

*Butterfly fish*

*Breadfruit*

*Captain Cook on his ship, the Endeavour*

## AMERICA AND THE PACIFIC

**1760** Britain takes Montreal and controls St. Lawrence river.

*A wrecked fur trade boat*

**1762** Britain captures Grenada and St. Vincent.

**1763** Peace of Paris establishes British supremacy over French in North America.

**1763** Rio de Janeiro becomes capital of Brazil.

**1763** Proclamation Line in North America defines limits of settler expansion. All land west of it is reserved for Native North Americans.

**1766** Britain occupies Falkland Islands.

**1767** New British taxes on goods to North America upset the colonists.

### THE AMERICAN WAR OF INDEPENDENCE

The American War of Independence (**1775-1783**) followed a decade of increasing dissatisfaction in the colonies with British rule. In **1770**, violent anti-tax protests took place (the 'Boston Massacre') and, in **1773**, Bostonians threw chests of tea into the sea (the 'Boston Tea Party'). In May **1775**, representatives from the colonies met at the Philadelphia Congress, and in June **1776**, an army was set up under George Washington. On July 4, **1776**, Congress signed the Declaration of Independence and war broke out.

*Paul Revere riding to warn fellow Americans that British troops are coming*

**1778** France and Spain ally with Americans against Britain.

**1779** James Cook is killed in Hawaii.

## SOUTHERN AND WESTERN EUROPE

1780

**1781** Joseph II of Austria (**1780-1790**) introduces religious toleration and major reforms, including abolition of serfs.

**1784** William Pitt the Younger becomes Prime Minister.

**1785** Edmund Cartwright, British clergyman, invents the power loom, which mechanizes weaving.

### THE FRENCH REVOLUTION

In May **1789**, facing mounting debts and growing unrest, Louis XVI called the national parliament for the first time since **1614**. Parliament consisted of three Estates: Nobility, Clergy and Commoners, but on June 17, the Commoners formed their own National Assembly. This marked the start of the French Revolution. Fears that the King might dissolve the Assembly led to riots, and on July 14, the mob stormed and destroyed the infamous Bastille Prison. Revolution spread through France and many nobles fled abroad for safety. In **1792**, the National Convention replaced the National Assembly, and monarchy was abolished. In **1793**, Louis XVI was executed and power passed to an extremist political group, the Jacobins, led by Maximilien Robespierre. The period **1793-1794** is known as the Reign of Terror: all those suspected of betraying the revolution were executed by guillotine. In July **1794**, Robespierre himself was executed and France came under the control of a group called the Directory (**1795-1799**).

*The storming of the Bastille on July 14th, 1789*

**1791** English politician William Wilberforce's bill for abolition of slavery is passed.

**1791-1792** Thomas Paine writes The Rights of Man, supporting the ideas behind the French Revolution.

**1793** France declares war on Britain, Netherlands and Spain.

**1795** European coalition forms against France.

**1796** Edward Jenner, British doctor, introduces vaccination against smallpox.

**1796-1797** French troops conquer much of Italy. Republics are established in Rome and Switzerland in **1798**.

**1798** Unsuccessful rebellion against the British in Ireland, led by Irish Protestant Wolfe Tone.

1799

**1799** Napoleon Bonaparte takes control in France.

## NORTHERN AND EASTERN EUROPE

**1781** Austro-Russian alliance against Turkey.

**1783** Russia annexes the Crimea.

**1784** Power struggle in Holland between the stadtholder, the Estates-General, and the Patriot party.

**1787-1791** Russia goes to war with Turkey and gains the Black Sea Steppes.

**1788** Austria declares war on Turkey and overruns Moldavia.

**1788** Gustavus III of Sweden declares war on Russia.

*Swedish soldier*

**1789** Revolt in Austrian Netherlands (Belgium) against centralizing policy of Joseph II. Proclamation of a Belgian Republic (**1790**), which is later reconquered by Austria.

*Leopold II of Austria*

**1790-1792** Reign of Habsburg Emperor Leopold II.

**1791** King of Poland adopts a new constitution to protect the country from Russian interference. Catherine II invades at the request of the nobles, destroys the constitution and divides large areas of Poland between Russia and Prussia.

**1792** Gustavus III of Sweden is assassinated at a masked ball.

**1792** France declares war on Austria and Prussia.

**1793** Second partition of Poland. Russia takes the eastern territory inhabited by Ukrainians and White Russians. Prussia gains Danzig, Thorn and Posen and expands its eastern frontier.

**1794** Polish uprising suppressed by Russia.

**1794** France occupies the Netherlands, and renames it the Batavian Republic (**1795-1806**).

**1795** Poland disappears after the third partition. Prussia takes Warsaw, Austria takes West Galicia, and Russia gains the remaining territory, including Lithuania.

*The 2nd partition of Poland in 1793*

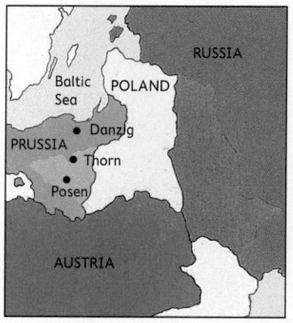


*The 3rd partition of Poland in 1795*

*Poland* *Russian gains* *Prussian gains* *Austrian gains*

## AFRICA TO INDIA

**1784** India Act: British government takes control of political affairs in British India.

**1786** Ottoman Turks send a fleet to restore control in Egypt, after period of unrest.

**1787** British establish a colony for freed slaves in Sierra Leone.

**c.1790** East Africa: Buganda kingdom expands its frontiers.

**1794** Aga Muhammed founds the Qaja dynasty in Persia, which lasts until **1925**.

**1795-1797** West Africa: Mungo Park, a British explorer, reaches Segu and Niger river.

*Mungo Park*

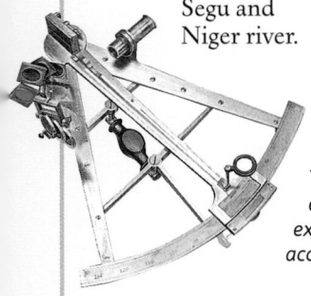

*The sextant, which enabled early explorers to navigate accurately*

**1795-1796** British take Cape of Good Hope, South Africa, and Ceylon (Sri Lanka) from the Dutch.

**1798-1799** Napoleon invades Egypt. Defeated by British at Battle of the Nile (**1798**), but defeats Turks at Aboukir Bay (1799).

*Napoleon Bonaparte*

**1799** Rosetta Stone is found in Egypt: the key to understanding Egyptian hieroglyphs.

**1799** British control South India. Tippoo, ruler of Mysore (**1750-1799**), is killed fighting the British.

*Tippoo's tiger, a musical toy showing a tiger attacking a European, from Seringapatam, capital of Mysore*

## THE FAR EAST

**1782** Siam: Taksin is deposed and executed after a rebellion. Prince Chakri seizes the throne and becomes Rama I, first king of the Chakri dynasty. He moves the capital to Bangkok. Siam grows in prosperity, the only Southeast Asian country to remain uncolonized by Europeans in the 19th century.

**1783-1823** Burmese capital moves to Amarapura.

**1785** François de la Pérouse, French explorer, leaves for the Pacific, in search of the Solomon Islands.

**1786** English East India Company sets up base in Penang, Malaysia: first British settlement in Southeast Asia.

**1787** Severe famine and rice riots in Edo (Tokyo), Japan.

*The city of Edo, Japan, in the 18th century*

**1788** François de la Pérouse lands on the coast of New South Wales, Australia, a day after the British had established a colony there.

**1788** Convicts are transported from Britain to Sydney, the first British settlement in Australia.

**1791-1792** China and Tibet at war.

**1795** Matthew Flinders and George Bass, British explorers, make first trip inland from east coast of Australia.

## AMERICA AND THE PACIFIC

**1780** British capture Charleston, South Carolina.

**1780-1782** Tupac Amaru II, the last of the Incas, leads the Peruvian Indians in an unsuccessful revolt against the Spaniards.

**1781** British General Cornwallis surrenders at Yorktown.

**1783** Treaty of Paris: Britain recognizes independence of the 13 Colonies, renamed United States of America. Britain gives Florida to Spain.

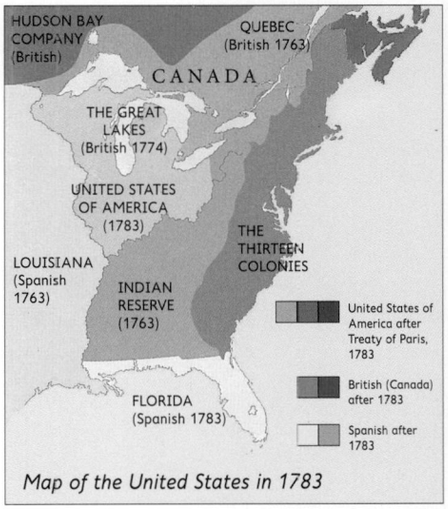


*Map of the United States in 1783*

**1787** New constitution is drawn up in United States by Thomas Jefferson.

**1789-1797** George Washington is first President of the United States.

*A bald eagle, used on the seal of the United States*

**1791** Canada Act: Canada is divided into English and French-speaking territories.

**1791** Slave revolt in Haiti against the French, led by Toussaint L'Ouverture. He is Lieutenant Governor in **1796**.

*Toussaint L'Ouverture*

**1797** Britain takes Trinidad from Spain.

**1798** Spaniards found Los Angeles, California.

Troupe de

# THE 19th CENTURY

## 1800 - 1899

## EUROPE

1800

**1800** Alessandro Volta, Italian physicist, invents the battery.

**1801** Act of Union unites Britain and Ireland.

**1804** Richard Trevithick, British engineer, builds first steam train to run on a track.

### THE RISE OF NAPOLEON

A young Corsican general named Napoleon Bonaparte rose to power in France after winning a dazzling reputation on campaigns in Italy and Egypt. In **1799**, he appointed himself First Consul (effectively military dictator) and disbanded the corrupt and ineffective Directory, and in **1804**, crowned himself Emperor. Napoleon was a successful statesman and administrator, introducing the *Code Napoléon* in **1804**, confirming property rights granted to peasants by the Revolution. In **1805**, Britain, Austria, Russia and Sweden allied against him, but he won important victories at Austerlitz (**1805**), Jena (**1806**) and Friedland (**1807**). In **1806**, he dissolved the Holy Roman Empire and reorganized the German states. He installed members of his family as rulers in Spain, Italy and Westphalia and in **1810** had his general, Jean Bernadotte, made heir to the Swedish throne. By **1812**, most of Western Europe was under his control. But his enemies continued to oppose his ambitions, and finally brought about his fall.

**1805** Battle of Trafalgar: the British, led by Admiral Nelson, defeat the French.

**1808-1814** Peninsular War: Britain successfully supports resistance movement against the French in Spain.

**1809** Russia gains Finland from Sweden.

**1809** Jean de Lamarck, a French zoologist, publishes his theories on the changes in living things, based on a study of fossils.

**1811** England: Luddites start smashing machines in protest at the Industrial Revolution.

**1812** Napoleon invades Russia, but is forced back.

*Napoleon's army was ill-prepared for the harsh Russian winter. Of 600,000 men, only about 30,000 returned.*

**1813** Austria, Prussia and Russia defeat Napoleon in Germany, causing the collapse of his rule in Germany, Italy and Holland.

**1814** The Allies reach Paris: Napoleon is forced to abdicate and is imprisoned on the island of Elba. Louis XVIII is restored.

**1815** The Hundred Days: Napoleon escapes from Elba and retakes power, but is defeated at Waterloo and imprisoned on the island of St. Helena in the middle of the Atlantic, where he dies.

**1815** Congress of Vienna meets to settle post-war boundaries.

1819

## AFRICA AND THE MIDDLE EAST

**1801** Russia takes Georgia.

**1802** Trutor and Somerville, British explorers, explore Bechuanaland (now Botswana).

**1805** Mungo Park, a Scottish doctor, sets out to explore the River Niger.

**1805-1848** Mehemet Ali massacres the ruling Mamelukes in Egypt and is installed as *pasha* (viceroy). His dynasty rules until **1952**.

*Mehemet Ali, at his palace in Alexandria. During his reign, Egypt was opened to European influences.*

**1806** Cape of Good Hope, South Africa, becomes a British colony (officially recognized in **1814**).

**1807** British politician William Wilberforce passes a law banning British ships from taking part in slavery.

**1807** Sierra Leone and Gambia become British Crown Colonies.

**1808** Import of African slaves into the U.S.A. is prohibited.

**1810** West Africa: Yoruba kingdom breaks up.

**1811** War between Russia and Persia.

*Fath Ali, ruler of Persia, attacking a Russian soldier*

**1818** The Mfecane, or time of troubles, in southern Africa. Shaka the Great (**c.1787-1828**) organizes an army of 40,000 men into uniformed regiments called *impi*. He founds the Zulu empire which extends over much of southern Africa and many local tribes are driven north.

*Zulu warriors*

## ASIA

**1800** British traders begin importing opium from India into China.

*Opium poppies*

**1801** English East India Company takes Tanjore and the Carnatic coast, India.

**1802** Siam (now Thailand) annexes Battambang, Cambodia.

**1802** Wars in the Deccan lead to the supremacy of the English East India Company in India.

**1802** Ceylon (now Sri Lanka) becomes a British Crown Colony.

**1803** Mogul emperor accepts British protection.

**1809-1824** Reign of King Rama II of Siam. Start of contact with Europe after a period of isolation.

**1810** Britain takes Mauritius from France.

**1811-1813** British occupy Dutch Java.

**1817-1823** Anglo-Maratha Wars end in British victory, removing final barrier to British supremacy in India.

**1817** Expansion of Burmese in Assam.

**1818** Java is restored to the Dutch.

### THE FOUNDING OF SINGAPORE

Singapore was founded in **1819** by Sir Stamford Raffles, as a base for the English East India Company. Strategically situated, at the opening of the Malacca Straits, it was chosen to rival the Dutch port of Malacca in Malaya. Raffles negotiated with the island's ruler and established a colony. Despite being disease-ridden and virtually uninhabited, Singapore grew to become the largest and most prosperous port in the region, and played an important part in the expansion of British influence in Asia.

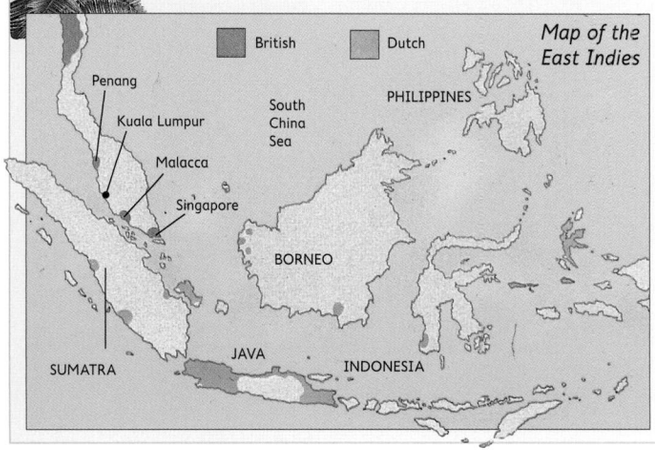


*Map of the East Indies*

## AMERICA AND AUSTRALASIA

1800

**1802-1803** The Australian coast is surveyed by English navigator, Matthew Flinders.

*A grey kangaroo, one of the unusual animals Europeans found in Australia*

**1803** Lousiana Purchase: U.S. buys French land in North America.

**1803** Britain acquires British Guiana, Tobago and St. Lucia.

**1804** Hobart, Tasmania, is founded.

**1808** Uprisings against the Spaniards begin in New Spain.

**1808-1825** Wars of independence from Spanish and Portuguese colonial rule in South and Central America. Argentina (Provinces of Rio de la Plata) declares independence in **1810**, Paraguay and Venezuela in **1811**, Colombia in **1813**, Uruguay in **1814** and Chile in **1816**.

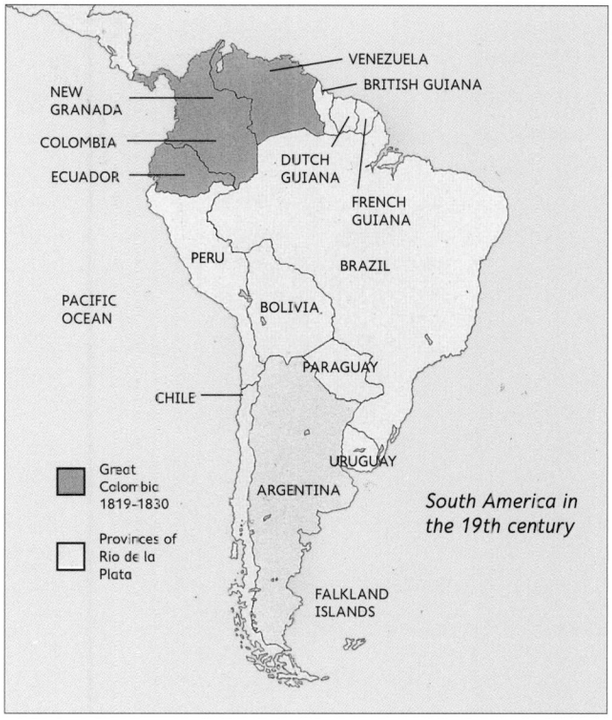


*South America in the 19th century*

**1812-1814** Trade war between the U.S.A. and Britain.

**1816** Argentina wins formal independence from Spain.

**1816-1824** Simón Bolívar, Venezuelan rebel leader, and José de San Martín, another rebel leader, help to win independence for many colonies.

**1818** A boundary is established between the U.S.A. and Canada.

**1818** Chile becomes independent.

**1819-1830** The state of Great Colombia is set up under Bolívar. It becomes independent from Spain in **1822**.

**1819** Spain loses Florida to the United States.

1819

## EUROPE

1820

**1820** Hans Oersted, a Danish scientist, shows that an electric current has a magnetic effect on a compass needle.

**1820** Revolutions in Spain and Portugal.

**1821** Napoleon dies on the island of St. Helena.

### THE GREEK WAR OF INDEPENDENCE

During the 19th century, many countries struggled for independence from foreign rule, asserting their national identity. The first successful nationalist struggle was the Greek War of Independence (**1821-1829**). Supported by Britain, Russia and Austria, the Greeks won independence from the Ottoman empire at the Treaty of Adrianople (**1829**) and in **1832** Prince Otto of Bavaria became their first king.

**1825** First passenger railway, from Stockton to Darlington, England.

**1826** J.-N Niépce (France) takes the world's first photograph.

**1827** Battle of Navarino: Greece's allies destroy the Turkish fleet.

**1829** George and Robert Stephenson, British engineers, build the *Rocket*, a steam engine, which reaches a top speed of 30 miles per hour.

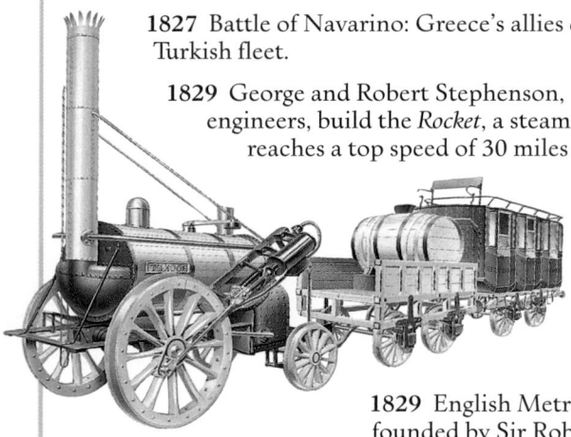

*Stephenson's Rocket pulling passenger cars*

**1829** English Metropolitan Police founded by Sir Robert Peel.

**1830** Belgium wins independence.

**1830** July Revolution in France installs Louis Philippe as king.

**1831** Michael Faraday, English scientist, produces electric current from a moving magnet, using a disc dynamo.

**1832** Reform Act in Britain gives the middle classes the vote.

**1834-1839** Carlist Wars in Spain: Don Carlos, the pretender, attempts to gain the throne.

**1834-1871** Charles Babbage designs an analytical engine, the first computer, helped by program designer Ada Lovelace.

**1836** Britain: Chartists demand the vote for all adult males.

**1837-1901** Reign of Queen Victoria of Great Britain.

**1837** First electric telegraph invented by W. Cooke and C. Wheatstone (British).

**1838** First practical photographic process produced by Louis Daguerre (French). His pictures are called daguerreotypes.

1839

## AFRICA AND THE MIDDLE EAST

**1820-1821** Egypt conquers the Sudan.

**1822** U.S.A. founds Liberia, West Africa, as a colony for freed African slaves.

**1823** William Wilberforce helps found the Anti-Slavery Society, which campaigns to abolish slavery. Slavery is abolished in the British empire in **1833**.

**1823-1831** War between the British and the Ashanti in Ghana.

**1824** René Caillié, French explorer, sets out for Timbuktu in West Africa.

*René Caillié (right) walking through the African jungle*

**1826-1828** War between Persia and Russia. Russia gains Armenian provinces.

**1830** French forces conquer Algiers.

**1831-1840** Syria and Lebanon are occupied by Egypt.

**1835** Tripoli, Libya, becomes an Ottoman province.

**1835-1837** Great Trek of Boers (Dutch settlers) from Cape of Good Hope, South Africa.

*Zulu warriors attacking Dutch settlers, known as Boers, during the Great Trek*

**1838** Boers defeat Zulus at Battle of Blood River, Natal.

**1838** War between the British and Afghans.

**1839** Dutch settlers found the Republic of Natal.

**1839** Britain takes Aden.

## ASIA

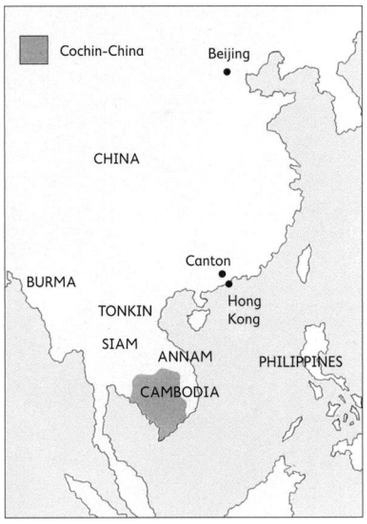


*Map of Southeast Asia*

**1821** Siam invades the Malay state of Kedah.

**1824-1826** First Anglo-Burmese War. British take Lower Burma and Assam.

**1825-1830** Java War: Indonesians revolt against Dutch rule.

**1830** English East India Company takes Mysore, India.

**1833** English East India Company trade monopoly with India and China is abolished.

*A clipper, a ship developed in the U.S.A. in the 1820s, for trade with the East*

**1839-1842** Opium War between Britain and China.

### THE OPIUM WARS

In **1838**, Emperor Tao-kuang of China sent an official, Lin Tse-hsu, to Canton to prohibit the importation and use of Indian opium. Lin burned 20,000 chests of opium and drove British traders out of Canton to Hong Kong. This attempt to ban the trade in opium led to the outbreak of war in **1839**. The British fleet blockaded the Chinese coast and defeated Chinese resistance. By the Treaty of Nanking of **1842**, the Chinese were forced to open five ports to British trade. Britain also acquired Hong Kong.

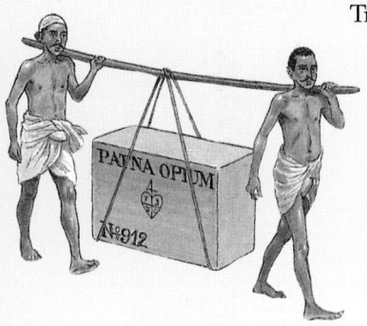


*Indians carrying an opium chest. British traders used opium to pay for Chinese goods.*

## AMERICA AND AUSTRALASIA

**1821** Mexico is proclaimed independent. Agustin Iturbide becomes Emperor Agustin I in **1822**.

**1822** Haiti is independent.

**1822** Brazil declares independence and is ruled by King Pedro I.

**1823** Monroe Doctrine in U.S.A.: President Monroe warns Europeans not to interfere in American affairs.

**1823** Formation of the United Provinces of Central America (see map below).

**1823-1824** Emperor Agustin I is overthrown and Mexico becomes a republic.

**1825** Simón Bolívar founds Bolivia.

**1826** The Black War in Tasmania between settlers and aborigines (the native people).

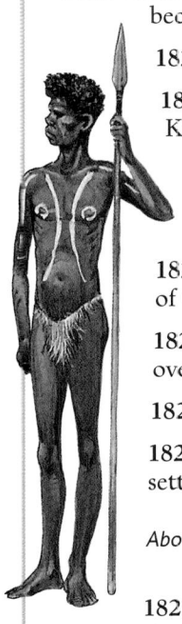

*Aborigine*

*Rainbow Lorikeet, found in Australia*

**1828** Uruguay, part of Argentina since **1816**, becomes a republic.

**1829** Swan River Settlement founded in Western Australia.

**c.1830s** U.S. settlers move West, driving many Native North Americans from their homes.

*Native North American teepee*

**1830** Colombia, Venezuela and Ecuador become independent republics.

**1833** Britain takes Falkland Islands.

**1834** Tolpuddle Martyrs, six English workers, are sent to Australia for trying to set up a Trade Union.

**1834** British settlement at Fort Philip Bay (Melbourne).

**1835-1836** Rebels in Texas (part of Mexico) fight for independence. Texan rebels are massacred by Mexican forces at the Alamo mission station. Texas breaks away and forms a republic.

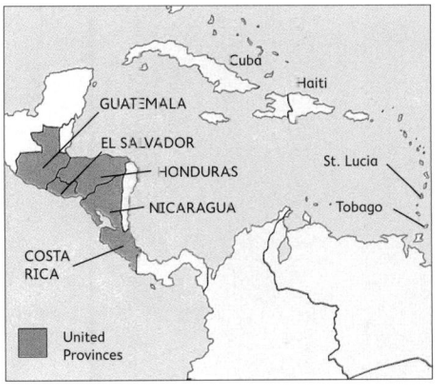


**1839-1840** El Salvador, Honduras, Nicaragua, Guatemala and Costa Rica become independent republics.

*Map of United Provinces of Central America*

## EUROPE

1840

**1840** First postage stamp, the Penny Black, issued in Britain.

**1845-1848** Irish famine leads to mass emigration to U.S.A.

**1847** Civil war in Switzerland.

### 1848: THE YEAR OF REVOLUTIONS

In **1848**, a wave of revolutions swept through Europe - with uprisings in Sicily, Paris, Vienna, Berlin, Milan, Sardinia, Warsaw and Prague. In France and Austria there had been growing opposition to conservative rulers, as well as economic difficulties - food shortages and rising prices. In Italy, Hungary, Bohemia and Poland, nationalist feeling was stirred by resentment of Habsburg rule. In Germany and Italy, there were also calls to found new nations by joining together the separate states. Both the French and Habsburg emperors were forced to abdicate, but in the end the rebellions were unsuccessful and short-lived, except in France. After temporary panic, the old regimes managed to reassert themselves.

*The retaking of the Pantheon, Paris, by government troops*

**1848-1851** Second Republic in France.

**1848** *Communist Manifesto* issued by Karl Marx and Friedrich Engels.

*Karl Marx*

**1849** Austria wins back her Italian possessions, after defeating Piedmont-Sardinia.

**1849** Guiseppe Garibaldi, Italian nationalist leader, marches to Rome, but his revolt is crushed.

**1851** Great Exhibition (international trade fair) in London.

### THE CRIMEAN WAR

In **1853**, Russia demanded the right to use the Dardanelles Straits for her ships, and to protect Turkish Christians. Turkey, France and Britain felt this gave Russia too much power and in **1854**, declared war. After much bloodshed on both sides, Russia was forced to make concessions at the Treaty of Paris in **1856**.

*The Charge of the Light Brigade at the Battle of Balaklava*

**1859** Charles Darwin, English naturalist, publishes his theory of evolution in *On the Origin of the Species*.

1859

**1859** Piedmont-Sardinia leads Italian uprising against Austria.

## AFRICA AND THE MIDDLE EAST

*David Livingstone*

**1841** David Livingstone, a Scottish missionary, makes his first journey of exploration in Africa.

**1841** Egypt loses Syria to Turkey.

**1842** Boers establish the Orange Free State, South Africa.

**1842-1843** Wars between Boers and British in Natal. Natal becomes a British colony.

**1844** War between France and Morocco.

**1846-1847** British defeat Bantus (Africans) in South Africa.

*Boers and cannon*

**1847** Liberia becomes independent.

**1852-1856** David Livingstone becomes first European to walk all the way across Africa. In **1855**, he discovers the Victoria Falls, southern Africa.

*Burton disguised as an Arab at a Bedouin camp*

**1853** Richard Burton, British explorer, reaches holy city of Mecca in Arabia, forbidden to non-Muslims.

**1854** Orange Free State is recognized as a Boer republic.

**1856** Pretoria becomes the capital of Transvaal, South Africa.

**1856** Richard Burton and John Speke leave England in search of the source of the Nile.

**1858** John Speke reaches the source of the Nile: Lake Victoria in East Africa.

*Speke on the shore of Lake Victoria*

**1858-1864** David Livingstone explores the Zambezi river.

**1859-1869** Suez Canal is built in Egypt.

## ASIA

**1842** British conquer Labuan, Borneo.

**1843** British conquer Sind, India.

**1845-1846** First Anglo-Sikh War: British gain control of the Punjab.

**1847** French expedition to Cochin-China.

**1848-1849** Second Anglo-Sikh War: British add the Punjab to their territory in India.

*Indian woman waving British flag*

**1850-1864** Taiping Rebellion in China against the decaying Manchu dynasty.

**1852** Second Anglo-Burmese War.

**1853** United States gunboats force Japan to open its ports to foreign trade. European contacts increase. A time of growing unrest and weakness for the Tokugawa dynasty.

*Europeans from a Japanese print*

**1856** English East India Company takes Oudh.

*Sword with East India Company crest*

**1856-1860** Second Opium War between Britain and China.

**1857-1860** Anglo-French forces occupy Beijing, China.

### THE INDIAN MUTINY

In **1857-1858** there was a series of uprisings against the British, which became known as the Indian Mutiny. It began in Meerut as a protest by Bengali soldiers in the British army, but soon spread throughout northern India, lasting over a year. After the relief of Lucknow (where British residents had been trapped for months), the British reasserted control. The government took over from the East India Company and administered India directly, through a viceroy, and the Mogul emperor was forced to give up his throne. India became the keystone of the British empire, and a focus for imperial rivalry, especially after the Russians began expanding in Central Asia.

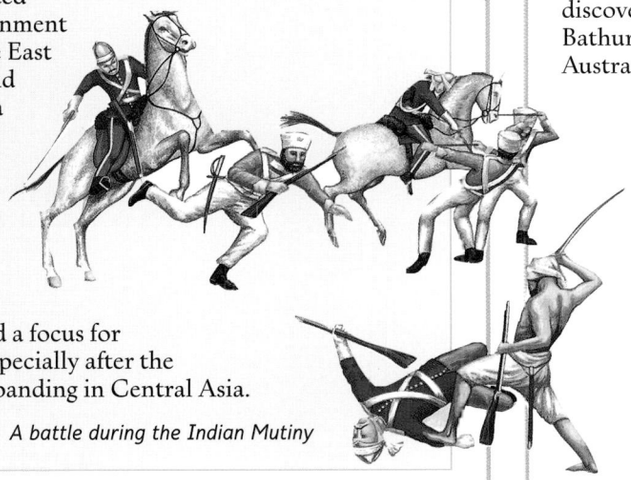

*A battle during the Indian Mutiny*

**1858** Treaty of Tientsin: 11 Chinese ports are opened to European trade.

**1859-1865** Mandalay becomes the capital of Burma.

## AMERICA AND AUSTRALASIA

1840

**1840** Captain Wilkes, American explorer, discovers the Antarctic coast.

**1840** Treaty of Waitangi: native Maori chiefs give up sovereignty over New Zealand to Britain.

*Maori warrior and sword*

**1840** Upper and Lower Canada united. Given self-government under British monarch in **1841**.

**1843** New telegraph code is designed by Samuel Morse (U.S.A.), replacing the one used by Cooke and Wheatstone.

**1844-1845** Charles Sturt, English explorer, leads an expedition into Central Australia.

**1844-1848** Unsuccessful uprisings in New Zealand by Maoris against the British.

**1845** Texas and Florida become states of the U.S.A.

**1846-1848** War between Mexico and U.S.A. over boundaries. Mexico loses California, New Mexico, Arizona, Utah and Colorado.

**1848-1849** Gold is discovered in California. This leads to a huge rush to the West by settlers in search of gold.

**1848** Otago, New Zealand, is founded.

**1851** Gold is discovered at Bathurst, Australia.

**1851** Isaac Singer (U.S.A.) produces the first practical sewing machine.

*American settlers heading west in the Gold Rush*

**1853-1854** Gold rush in Victoria, Australia.

**1857** Civil war in Mexico.

**1859** Queensland, Australia, becomes a separate colony.

**1859** Oil is discovered in Pennsylvania, which leads to the start of the modern oil industry.

1859

# EUROPE

1860

## THE UNIFICATION OF ITALY

Until the 19th century, Italy was just a collection of states, some independent, some under foreign rule. Unification came about mainly because of the ambitions of one of the states, Piedmont-Sardinia, and its chief minister, Camillo Cavour. In **1859**, Piedmont won Lombardy from Austria, and in **1860** most of northern Italy voted to join them. Giuseppe Garibaldi led a revolt against the Spanish Bourbon rulers in southern Italy, and joined it to the Italian kingdom. In **1861**, Victor Emmanuel II of Piedmont-Sardinia became first king of Italy. Venice joined in **1866** and Rome in **1870**.

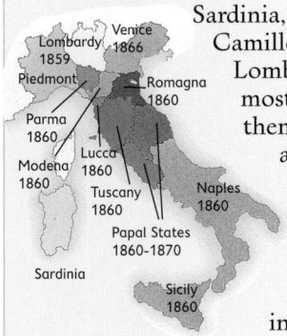


**1861** Alexander II of Russia frees the serfs (landless peasants).

**1863** World's first underground railway is built in London.

**1864** Red Cross Society founded in Geneva, to care for war casualties.

**1865** Louis Pasteur, French doctor, publishes his germ theory.

**1866** War between Austria and Italy. Italy gains Venice.

**1866** Gregor Mendel, Bohemian botanist, publishes his laws of inheritance.

*Mendel performed experiments on sweet pea plants.*

**1867** The Austrian empire is renamed the Austro-Hungarian empire.

**1867** Prussia, led by minister Otto von Bismarck, forms the Confederation of North German states.

**1867** Joseph Lister, British surgeon, describes use of antiseptics to reduce infections.

**1867** Second Reform Act extends the right to vote in Britain.

**1867** Karl Marx publishes *Das Kapital*, outlining his theories.

**1870** Irish Land Act gives Irish tenants compensation for eviction.

**1870-1871** Franco-Prussian War. Prussians overthrow Second Empire. Revolution sets up the Third Republic (**1870-1940**).

**1871** Paris Commune (a revolutionary group) is crushed.

**1871** Germany is united. Wilhelm I of Prussia becomes first Kaiser (emperor), with Bismarck as Chancellor.

**1872-1874** Civil war in Spain.

**1873** Home Rule League founded to promote Irish self-rule.

**1873** Alliance of Russia, Germany and Austria-Hungary.

**1874** Iceland becomes independent.

**1877-1878** Russo-Turkish War ends in Congress of Berlin. Romania, Montenegro and Serbia win independence.

**1878** Joseph Swan, British scientist, invents a light bulb.

1879

**1879** Dual Alliance between Germany and Austria-Hungary.

# AFRICA AND THE MIDDLE EAST

**1860** French begin expanding settlements in West Africa.

**1869** Diamond rush begins in South Africa.

**1869** Tunisia is controlled by Britain, France and Italy.

**1869** Suez Canal in Egypt is opened.

**1871** Ujiji, East Africa: Sir Henry Stanley, journalist, meets David Livingstone, an explorer who has been missing for years.

*Stanley meeting Livingstone*

**1872** British take over Dutch forts on Gold Coast (Ghana).

**1873-1874** British and Ashanti at war in Gold Coast.

**1874-1877** Sir Henry Stanley explores the Congo.

**1875** British Prime Minister Disraeli buys majority shares in the Suez Canal, ensuring control of the sea route to India.

**1876** Britain and France take control of Egypt's finances.

**1877** Britain annexes the Transvaal.

**1879** Britain and France control Egypt.

**1879** Zulus defeat British at Battle of Isandlwana, Natal, but are defeated at Ulundi.

*19th century Italian, French, British and German flags*

## THE SCRAMBLE FOR AFRICA

At the beginning of the 19th century, there was a handful of British and French settlements on the West coast of Africa, but most of the continent was still unknown to Europeans. The only established colonies were Angola and Mozambique (Portuguese), Cape Colony (which passed from Dutch to British control in **1814**) and Algeria (French). However, between **1877** and **1914** most of Africa was colonized by European powers. It happened so fast it became known as the 'Scramble for Africa'. There were many reasons for the scramble. Industrialization and expanding world trade produced a demand for new markets and materials. Exploration and the railways opened up new areas for development. Some colonies were acquired almost by accident, as a result of land-grabbing by men on the spot, such as Cecil Rhodes, founder of De Beers, the diamond mining company. But European rivalries also played a big part. Africa was the last continent to be opened up, and new nations, such as Germany, Italy and Belgium, saw it as an opportunity to acquire an empire.

*Guineas, named after Guinea, in West Africa, where the gold was mined*

*Cecil Rhodes*

## ASIA

**1860** British and French forces burn down the Summer Palace, Beijing. Second Opium War between Britain and China comes to an end. China cedes Kowloon to Britain.

**1861-1862** France goes to war with Cochin-China (South Vietnam) and establishes a protectorate over the province by **1867**.

**1862-1908** Dowager Empress Tz'u-hsi rules China, on behalf of her baby son.

*Summer Palace, Beijing, rebuilt by Empress Tz'u-hsi*

**1863** France establishes a protectorate in Cambodia.

**1865** Russia expands in Central Asia, taking the khanate of Tashkent.

**1868** Russia takes the khanate of Bukhara, Central Asia.

**1868** The major clans in Japan organize opposition to the Tokugawas. The last shogun, Kei-ki, abdicates after a coup d'état and the emperor's power is restored under a new government (the Meiji Restoration **1868-1912**). A period of growth and modernization.

*The young Emperor returning to Edo, to take power from the shogun*

**1873** Russia acquires Khiva and provinces of Central Asia.

*Map of the expansion of Russia into Central Asia in the 19th century*

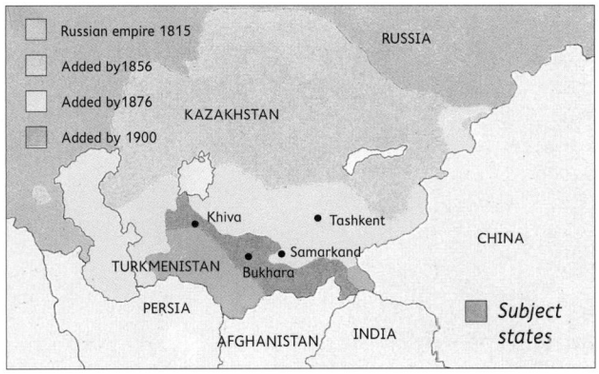


**1874** Annam (now part of Vietnam) is opened to French trade. Tonkin is made a French protectorate in **1883**.

**1876** Korea is declared independent by China.

**1877** Queen Victoria of Great Britain is proclaimed Empress of India.

**1878-1880** War between Britain and Afghanistan. British India makes frontier gains and British influence in Afghanistan grows.

## AMERICA AND AUSTRALASIA



*An Apache spear*

**1860s-1870s** Wars with settlers lead to huge reduction in population of Native North Americans.

**1860-1861** Robert Burke and William Wills, British explorers, cross Australia.

**1860-1864** War between Maoris (native peoples) and settlers in New Zealand.

### THE AMERICAN CIVIL WAR

In **1860**, Abraham Lincoln, a firm supporter of the abolition of slavery, was elected U.S. President. The following year, in **1861**, the southern states, whose economy was dependent on slavery, broke away and formed the Confederate States of America. A bloody civil war broke out with the northern Unionists, who fought to preserve national unity. After bitter fighting, with 635,000 people killed, the Unionists finally defeated the Confederates in **1865**.

*Abraham Lincoln*

**1863** Battle of Gettysburg: Unionist victory - Confederate General 'Stonewall' Jackson, is killed.

**1863** Gold rush in New Zealand.

**1864** France installs Archduke Maximilian of Austria as Emperor of Mexico. He is shot in **1867**.

**1865** Slavery abolished in the U.S.A. Lincoln is assassinated.

**1866** First transatlantic cable.

**1867** United States buys Alaska from Russia for $7 million.

**1867** Canada becomes a dominion (a self-governing colony).

**1868** 14th Amendment gives civil rights to African-Americans in the U.S.A.

**1868-1878** Cuba loses war of independence against Spain.

**1869** First U.S. trans-continental railroad built.

**1876** Battle of Little Big Horn (or 'Custer's Last Stand'): Native American Sioux and Cheyenne warriors defeat U.S. army, led by Colonel George Custer.

**1876** Telephone is patented in the U.S.A. by Alexander G. Bell.

*A Bell telephone in use*

**1877** Thomas Edison, a U.S. inventor, invents the record player.

**1877-1911** Rule of Porfirio Diaz, Mexican dictator. He establishes order, wealth and prosperity.

**1879** Thomas Edison invents a light bulb.

**1879-1884** Chile expands territory after war with Bolivia and Peru.

## EUROPE

1880

**1880-1885** Unrest in Ireland.

**1881** Russia: Alexander II is assassinated. Repression follows.

**1883** Russian Marxist Party is founded. Unrest follows.

**1884** Reform Act in Britain gives the vote to all men over 21.

**1885** Karl Benz, German engineer, builds the first motor car.

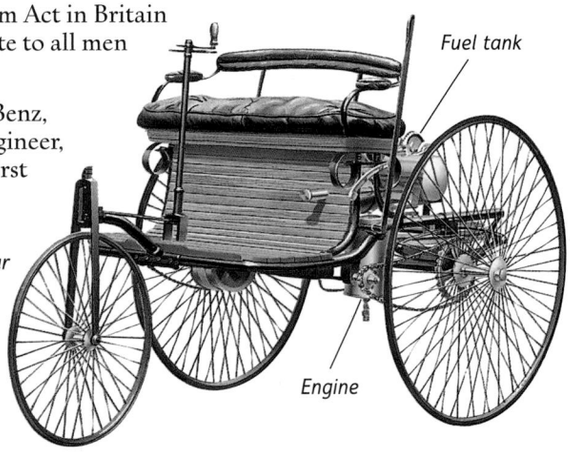


*First Benz car*

**1886** Gladstone's First Home Rule Bill for Ireland is defeated.

**1888-1918** Reign of Kaiser Wilhelm II of Germany.

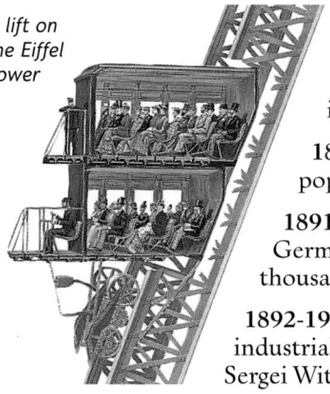

*A lift on the Eiffel Tower*

**1889** Eiffel Tower is built for the Paris Exposition.

**1890** Luxembourg becomes independent from Holland.

**1890s** Art Nouveau style is popular in Europe.

**1891-1896** Otto Lilienthal, German engineer, makes over a thousand flights in his gliders.

**1892-1903** Modernization and industrial growth in Russia under Sergei Witte (finance minister).

**1893** Britain: Keir Hardie founds Independent Labour Party.

**1893** France allies with Russia.

**1894** Nicholas II becomes Tsar of Russia.

**1894** Dreyfus Affair in France. Alfred Dreyfus, a Jewish army officer, is expelled for treason. Many believe he is innocent and it leads to a political battle. (He is cleared in **1906**.)

**1894-1897** Cretans rise against Turks and unite with Greece.

**1895** Guglielmo Marconi, Italian physicist, invents wireless.

**1895** Sigmund Freud, Austrian psychiatrist, publishes his first work on psychoanalysis.

**1895** Wilhelm Röntgen, German physicist, discovers x-rays.

**1896** First modern Olympic Games in Athens, Greece.

**1895** Motion pictures are premiered in Paris, France.

**1898** Pierre and Marie Curie, French scientists, observe radioactivity and isolate radium.

*Caricature of Pierre and Marie Curie*

1899

## AFRICA AND THE MIDDLE EAST

**1880-1881** First Anglo-Boer War: Boer victory at Majuba Hill. Britain forced to recognize independent Transvaal.

**1880-1900** French influence grows in the Sahara region.

*French Saharan soldier*

**1881-1882** Nationalist revolt in Egypt. British forces occupy Egypt and Sudan, to suppress anti-European riots.

**1881** Tunisia becomes a French colony.

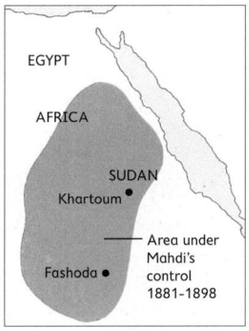


*Map of the Sudan*

**1884** Anti-British uprising in the Sudan, led by the Mahdi, a religious leader. General Gordon is sent to Khartoum.

*General Gordon*

**1884** Britain takes British Somaliland. Germany takes South West Africa, Cameroons and Togo.

**1885** The Mahdi takes Khartoum and Gordon is killed.

**1885** Britain takes Bechuanaland (Botswana). Germany takes Tanganyika. Italy takes Eritrea. Belgium takes Belgian Congo. Spain takes Rio de Oro and Spanish Guinea.

**1886** Royal Niger Company given control of British territories in Nigeria. Lagos and Kenya become British colonies.

**1886** Gold found in Transvaal. Johannesburg is founded.

**1888-1889** Cecil Rhodes's British South Africa Company expands British influence in Rhodesia (Zimbabwe).

**1889** French take Ivory Coast. Italy takes Italian Somaliland and claims a protectorate over Ethiopia.

**1890-1897** Armenian anti-Turkish revolutionary movement.

**1891** Emperor Menelik of Ethiopia rejects Italian protectorate. Italians invade in **1895**, but are forced to recognize Ethiopian independence.

**1894** French take Dahomey.

**1895** British take Uganda.

**1895-1896** Jameson Raid in South Africa: a failed attempt by Cecil Rhodes to take over the Transvaal.

**1896** French annex Madagascar.

**1898** Fashoda Crisis: French advancing north meet British advancing south at Fashoda, Sudan. French withdraw. Battle of Omdurman: British defeat Sudanese.

**1899** British government takes control of Nigerian territories. Sudan comes under Anglo-Egyptian rule.

**1899-1902** Second Anglo-Boer War. Britain annexes the Transvaal and Orange Free State.

*Queen Victoria's South Africa medal, awarded to British soldiers who fought in the Boer War*

## ASIA

**1883** Annam, in Indochina, becomes a French protectorate.

**1883-1884** The French expand in Southeast Asia.

**1884** Russia takes Turkmenistan.

**1884** Cambodia is annexed by France.

**1885** The founding of the Indian National Congress, which campaigns for independence.

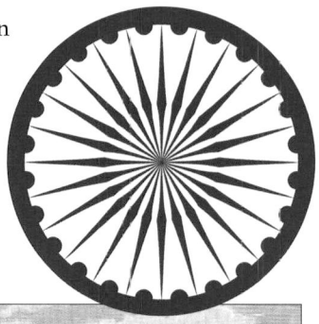

*A spinning wheel, the symbol of the Indian National Congress*

**1885-1886** The British attack and annex Ava in Burma.

*Indian army troops fighting in Upper Burma*

**1887** France establishes an Indo-Chinese Union.

**1894-1895** War between Japan and China. Japan gains Formosa. Korea becomes independent of China.

**1896** Britain sets up the Federated Malay States.

**1896** Rebellion against the Spanish in the Philippines.

**1897** Anglo-Siamese agreement on Malaya-Siam boundary.

*19th century Siamese king*

**1898** War between Spain and the U.S.A. over the Philippines. Spain cedes the Philippines to the U.S.A.

**1898-1909** Reactionary and repressive rule in China under Empress Tz'u-hsi. Attempts at liberal reforms are crushed.

## AMERICA AND AUSTRALASIA

1880

**1880** Start of the construction of the Panama Canal.

**1886** Statue of Liberty is completed in New York.

*The Statue of Liberty (below)*

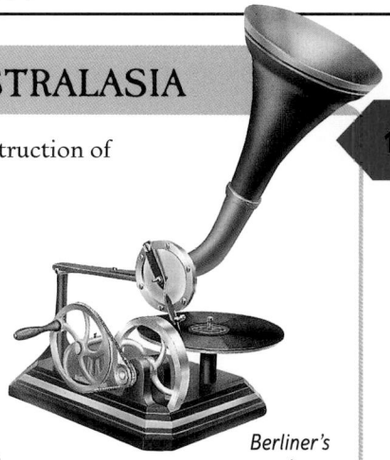

*Berliner's gramophone*

**1887** Emile Berliner (1851-1929), a German who emigrated to the U.S.A., patents the gramophone.

**1888** George Eastman (U.S.A.) mass markets his box camera, making photography more accessible.

**1889** Pedro II of Brazil is deposed and a republic set up.

**1890** Battle of Wounded Knee: last Native American uprising in the U.S.A. by the Sioux people. The Native Americans are defeated and their weapons taken away.

*Many tribes were rounded up and taken to live on special areas of land called reservations.*

*Many Sioux warriors wore special 'ghost shirts', believing they could protect them from the settlers' bullets.*

**1893** Hawaii becomes a U.S. protectorate.

**1893** Women in New Zealand become the first in the world to be given the vote.

**1898** Spanish-American War. Cuba becomes independent under temporary American control.

1899

# THE 20th CENTURY

## 1900 - 1999

## EUROPE

1900

**1901** Great Britain: death of Queen Victoria and accession of Edward VII.

*Queen Victoria*

**1902** Britain allies with Japan: the end of a long period of Japanese isolation.

**1903** King and Queen of Serbia are assassinated.

**1903** French minister Delcassé visits London. Growing Anglo-French friendship.

**1904** Entente Cordiale: friendship pact between Britain and France.

**1905** Revolts in St. Petersburg and other Russian cities. In St. Petersburg, soldiers open fire on protesters.

**1905** Norway becomes independent from Sweden.

**1905** Albert Einstein (Switzerland) publishes his Special Theory of Relativity.

*Albert Einstein*

**1908** Austria-Hungary takes Turkish provinces Herzegovina and Bosnia. Tension follows. Bulgaria wins independence.

**1908** Failed revolution in Portugal: the King and his heir are assassinated.

**1910** Revolution in Portugal: the King is deposed. A republic is declared in **1911**.

**1911** Ernest Rutherford (N.Z./U.K.) shows that atoms have a nucleus.

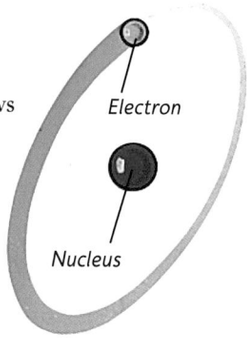


*Rutherford's model of an atom*

**1912** First Balkan War: Bulgaria, Greece, Serbia and Montenegro unite and defeat Turkey.

**1913** Second Balkan War: Turkey, Romania, Serbia and Greece defeat Bulgaria.

## AFRICA AND THE MIDDLE EAST

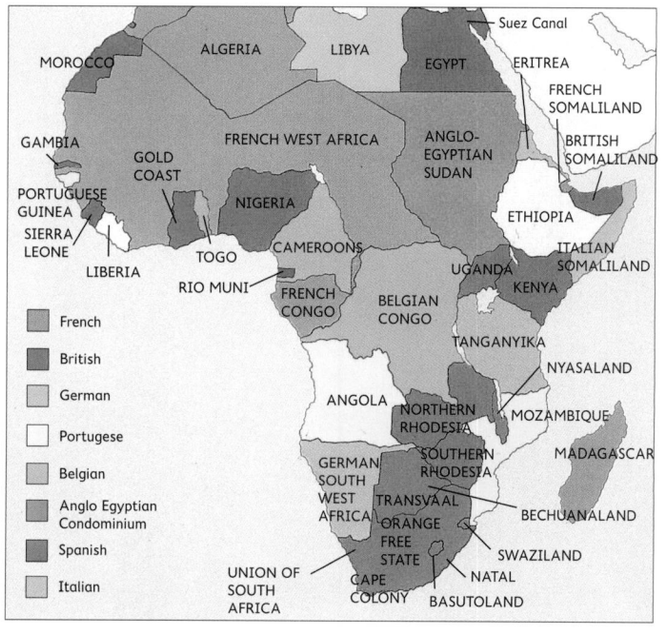


*Map showing European colonisation of African countries*

**1900** South Africa: British annex Transvaal and Orange Free State. Anglo-Boer War ends with Peace of Vereeniging (**1902**).

**1901** Britain joins Ashanti kingdom to the Gold Coast colony.

**1909** Ahmed Shah seizes power in Persia, at the age of 11, after his elder brother Muhammed Ali is deposed.

**1908** Belgium takes over Congo from Belgian King Leopold.

**1908-1909** Revolution in Turkey by the Young Turks, a group of army officers, including Mustafa Kemäl. Sultan is deposed.

**1910** Union of South Africa becomes a British dominion. French Congo is renamed French Equatorial Africa.

**1911** Agadir crisis: Germans send a gunboat to Agadir, Morocco, provoking tensions with France.

**1911-1912** Italians take Libya, after struggle with Turkey.

**1914-1915** Germany loses colonies to Britain and France.

**1914-1922** Egypt becomes a British protectorate.

## THE FIRST WORLD WAR

At the start of the 20th century, the balance of power in Europe was so delicately balanced that an attack on one country would automatically involve its allies and lead to war. In **June 1914**, Archduke Franz Ferdinand, heir to the Austrian throne, was assassinated by a Serbian nationalist in Sarajevo. Austria declared war on Serbia, and within weeks, war had broken out between Germany and Austria (the Central Powers) and Russia, France and Britain (the Allies).

The First World War (**1914-1918**), or 'Great War' as it was known at the time, was mainly a European war, fought across Europe and the Middle East: much of the fighting took place in northern France, where each side dug trenches to stop the other from advancing. But many other nations, especially the colonies - and later the U.S.A. - became directly involved. It dragged on for four years, killing 17 million people - more than in any other conflict in history.

*Poppies, a symbol of remembrance of the war*

1914

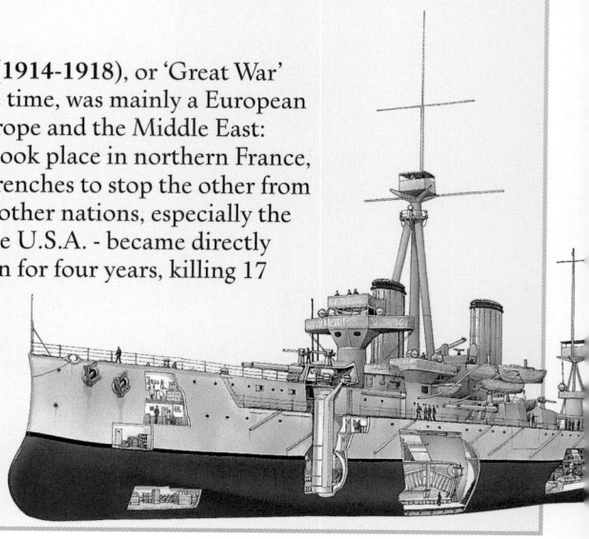

*Dreadnought, the most powerful ship of its day*

## ASIA

**1900** Boxer Rebellion in China against foreign influence is crushed by an international force.

*A dragon, ancient symbol of China*

**1904-1905** Russia and Japan at war over Manchuria and Korea.

**1905** Japan destroys Russian fleet at Tsushima. Treaty of Portsmouth gives Japan a protectorate over Korea and territory in China.

*Japanese painting showing the Russian defeat at Tsushima*

**1905** 10,000 people die in earthquake in Lahore, India.

**1909** Anglo-Siam Treaty: Siam recognizes British control over Malayan states.

**1909** China occupies Tibet. The Tibetan ruler, the Dalai Lama, flees to India.

**1910** Malayan states of Trengganu and Perlis accept British protection.

**1910** China: uprising in Yunnan province.

**1910** Nationalist movement in Burma led by Buddhist monks.

**1910-1945** Korea is a Japanese colony.

*Tibetan monk playing a trumpet at a festival*

*Japanese flag*

**1911** Chinese Revolution: a government is set up in Nanking under Sun Yat-sen.

**1912** Chinese Manchu dynasty is overthrown and a republic is established. This is followed by a period of great unrest and local rule by warlords.

## AMERICA AND AUSTRALASIA

1900

**1900** New Zealand takes the Cook Islands. Papua is transferred from Britain to Australia. Britain annexes Tonga.

**1901** The Commonwealth of Australia is established.

**1901** Guglielmo Marconi, Italian inventor, sends the first wireless transmission from U.S.A. to England.

**1902** Australia: women win the right to vote.

**1903** Revolution in Panama. Panama gains independence from Colombia as a U.S. protectorate.

**1903** Orville and Wilbur Wright (U.S.A.) make the first successful powered and controlled flight.

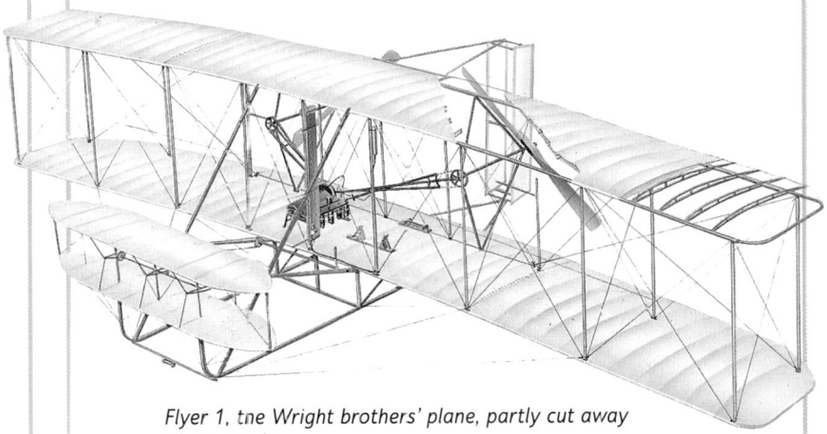

*Flyer 1, the Wright brothers' plane, partly cut away to see inside*

**1906** San Francisco: earthquake followed by a fire destroys much of the city.

**1907** New Zealand is given dominion (self-governing) status within the British empire.

**1908-1918** Unrest in Haiti.

**1909** Robert E. Peary and Matthew Henson of United States Navy claim to reach the North Pole.

*Seals in the North Pole*

**1910-1911** Revolution in Mexico overthrows Porfirio Diaz. Followed by disorder and the rise of dictators.

**1912** Sinking of ocean liner Titanic off the coast of Newfoundland.

**1912** Roald Amundsen, Norwegian explorer, is the first to reach the South Pole.

*Penguins at the South Pole*

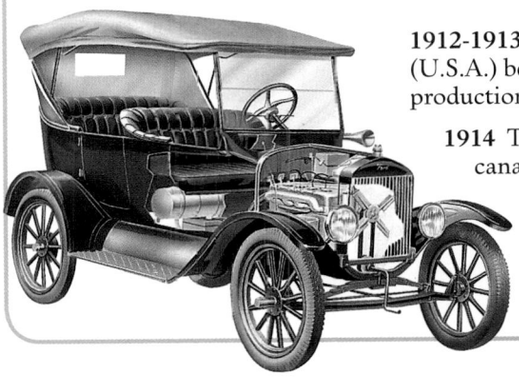

**1912-1913** Henry Ford (U.S.A.) begins the mass production of motor cars.

**1914** The Panama canal is opened.

*Ford Model T, the first mass-produced car*

1914

## EUROPE

1915

**1916** Easter Rising in Dublin: Irish nationalists against British.

### THE RUSSIAN REVOLUTION

In **1900**, Russia was one of the most underdeveloped places in Europe. Most people lived in poverty, under the oppressive, autocratic rule of the tsars. World War One led to starvation and huge loss of life, which fed growing discontent. In **April 1917**, the leader of the communist Bolshevik party, Vladimir Ilyich Ulyanov (known as Lenin), returned to Russia from exile. His influence spread fast and in **October** he and his supporters stormed the palace in St. Petersburg and seized power. The new government acted through a Congress of Soviets: they centralized control of the land, murdered the Tsar and his family, and held onto power through a campaign of fear, known as the 'Red Terror'. They won a civil war **(1918-1920)**, despite support for their opponents, the Whites, from foreign powers anxious to stop the spread of revolution. In **1922**, Russia became the Union of Soviet Socialist Republics (U.S.S.R.).

*Tsar Nicholas, Alexandra and children*

**1918** Peace of Brest-Litovsk between Russia and Germany.

**1918-1919** Revolution in Berlin: the Kaiser flees. The German Weimar Republic is set up in **1919**.

**1918** Britain: the vote is given to women over 30.

**1918-1919** Emperor of Austria-Hungary abdicates. New independent nations: Latvia, Estonia, Lithuania, Czechoslovakia and Yugoslavia.

**1919** Peace of Versailles between Germany and the Allies.

**1919** Benito Mussolini establishes Fascist movement in Italy.

**1919** Ernest Rutherford (N.Z./U.K.) splits the atom.

**1919** Solar eclipse (see below) confirms Einstein's theories.

**1919** Finland becomes a republic.

**1920** Six northern Irish counties set up parliament in Belfast. Irish Free State (the southern counties) becomes a British dominion from **1921**.

**1922** Benito Mussolini forms a Fascist government in Rome.

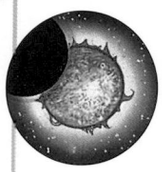

**1923** De Rivera is Spanish dictator.

**1926** Britain: 9-day General Strike.

**1928** Alexander Fleming discovers penicillin, the first antibiotic.

**1924-1953** Josef Stalin leads U.S.S.R.

**1924** Greece becomes a republic.

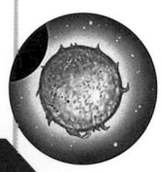

**1924** Ahmed Zogu seizes power in Albania.

**1926-1935** Józef Pilsudski leads Poland.

**1928** U.S.S.R.: Five Year Plan is launched: a period of rapid growth and industrialization.

1929

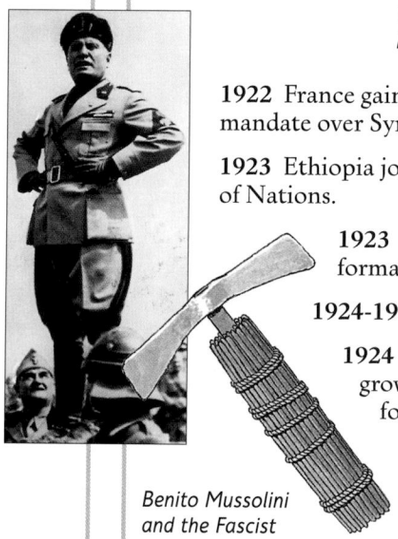

*Benito Mussolini and the Fascist symbol: a bundle of twigs tied around an axe*

## AFRICA AND THE MIDDLE EAST

**1916** Arab nationalists in the Hejaz, Saudi Arabia, rise against the Ottomans. Further uprisings follow.

**1916** British Colonel T.E. Lawrence explores the Hejaz area of Saudi Arabia.

*Colonel T.E. Lawrence*

**1917** Balfour Declaration: Britain supports Jewish homeland in Palestine, so long as Arab rights are respected.

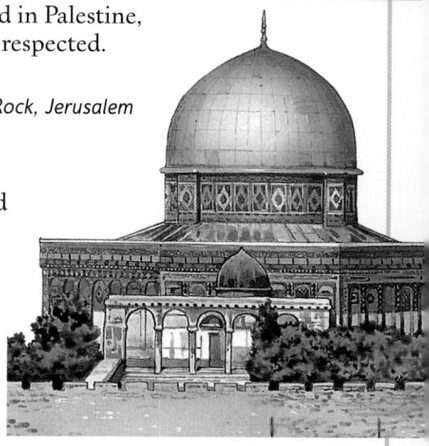

*Dome of the Rock, Jerusalem*

**1918** Syria proclaims independence. Not recognized by France or Britain. French forces take control in **1919**.

**1918** Ottoman empire collapses: Allies control Istanbul.

**1919** War begins between Britain and Afghanistan.

**1919** German African colonies are mandated to the Allies by the League of Nations.

**1919** Egypt: nationalist revolt against British protectorate. Britain recognizes Egyptian independence in **1922**.

**1920** Transjordan is separated from Syria.

**1920-1921** Uprising in Iraq. Britain installs an autonomous Arab government under King Faisal, brother of Abdullah, King of Jordan, and a member of the Hashemite dynasty.

**1921** Moroccan Berbers defeat Spaniards at Anual.

**1922** Mustafa Kemäl, or Atatürk, seizes power in Turkey. Greek army is expelled and Ottoman emperor deposed. Republic is proclaimed: reform and modernization follows.

*Turkish flag and Mustafa Kemäl Atatürk*

**1922** France gains League of Nations mandate over Syria.

**1923** Ethiopia joins the League of Nations.

**1923** Southern Rhodesia (Zimbabwe) is formally annexed as a British colony.

**1924-1925** Reza Khan becomes Shah of Persia.

**1924** Moroccan independence movement grows, but is crushed by Spanish and French forces in **1926**.

**1926** Ibn Saud becomes King of Hejaz and Nejd (later Saudi Arabia).

**1926** Lebanon becomes a republic.

**1927** Britain recognizes Ibn Saud as the ruler of Saudi Arabia.

## ASIA

**1919** India: British soldiers under the command of General Dyer fire on protesters at a peaceful political meeting in Amritsar. Leads to a rise in Indian nationalist feeling. General Dyer is fired.

**1920** Mohandas (Mahatma) Gandhi leads the Indian National Congress, a non-violent movement for independence. The first Indian Parliament meets in **1921**.

*Gandhi*

**1921** Mao Zedong (Mao Tse-tung) and Li Ta-chao form the Chinese Communist Party in Bejing.

*Mao Zedong*

**1923** An earthquake and fire destroy much of Tokyo, Japan.

*Tokyo after the earthquake*

**1925** China: Sun Yat-sen dies. He is succeeded by Jiang Jie Shi (Chiang Kai-shek), who campaigns against the warlords.

**1926** Hirohito becomes Emperor of Japan.

**1927** Jiang Jie Shi, leader of the Kuomintang (Chinese Nationalists), breaks with the Communist Party. Civil war follows. The Communists set up bases in remote areas.

**1928** Jiang Jie Shi becomes President of China.

**1929** Gandhi demands Indian independence and begins a campaign of civil disobedience.

## AMERICA AND AUSTRALASIA

1915

**1917** A number of U.S. passenger ships are sunk by German U-boats (submarines). U.S.A. declares war on Germany, joined by some South American states and Cuba.

**1918** World-wide influenza epidemic kills 20 million. In the U.S.A. alone, 500,000 die.

**1919** League of Nations is set up to preserve world peace.

**1920** The U.S. Senate votes not to join the League of Nations. Prohibition of alcohol and women's suffrage are introduced in the U.S.A.

**1923** Edwin Hubble (U.S.A.) proves the existence of other galaxies.

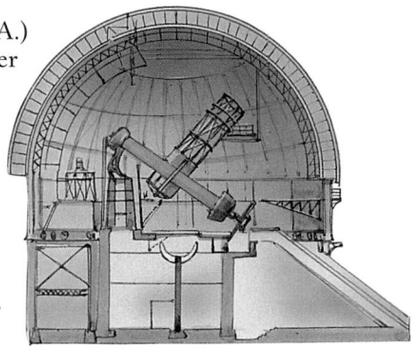

*The Hubble telescope*

**1927** Canberra becomes the federal capital of Australia.

**1927** *The Jazz Singer*, one of the first talking pictures, or movies, is made.

**1927** Charles Lindbergh makes the first solo flight across the Atlantic.

**1929** Hubble shows galaxies moving away from each other. Forms the basis of the Big Bang Theory.

**1929** The Wall Street Crash: U.S. stock market collapses. The beginning of the Depression.

### THE DEPRESSION

From **1929** until the mid **1930s**, nearly every country in the world experienced an economic crisis, known as the Depression. There was falling production, declining incomes and mass unemployment. The U.S.A., Germany, Eastern Europe and many places in Africa, Asia and Latin America were worst affected.

*Unemployed people lining up at a soup kitchen*

*The Chrysler building, New York, built between 1928 and 1930*

1929

## EUROPE

1930

**1930** U.S.S.R.: Stalin enforces collectivization of agriculture. Millions of kulaks, peasant farm owners who oppose this, are suppressed and murdered. Famine follows in **1932**.

**1931** Alphonso XIII leaves Spain and a republic is set up.

**1931** Statute of Westminster defines rights of British dominions: major step in founding of the Commonwealth.

**1932-1968** Antonio Salazar is Prime Minister and virtual dictator of Portugal.

**1933** Germany: Berlin parliament, the Reichstag, burns down. Adolf Hitler, leader of the fascist Nazi Party, becomes Chancellor. He takes the title *Führer* (leader) in **1934**.

**1934-1939** Stalin crushes opposition in U.S.S.R.

**1935** Germany increases its military strength.

**1935** Nuremberg Laws: German Jews persecuted.

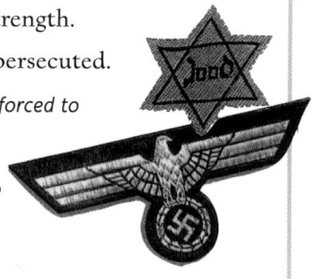

*The Star of David, which German Jews were forced to wear (top), and a Nazi officer's badge*

**1936** Britain: Edward VIII abdicates to marry Mrs. Simpson, a divorcée.

**1936** Germans occupy Rhineland.

**1936** German-Italian Axis Pact.

**1936-1939** The Spanish Civil War: General Franco, Nationalist leader, rebels against Republican government. Germany and Italy give him military aid. U.S.S.R. supports Republicans. Franco becomes dictator until his death in **1975**.

**1937** Southern Ireland becomes the sovereign state of Éire.

**1938** Hitler occupies Austria and joins the two countries under the Anschluss. At the Munich Conference, Germany is granted Sudetenland (German-speaking Czech territory), on the condition that no further expansion is made.

**1938** *Kristallnacht* ('the Night of Broken Glass'): Nazis attack thousands of Jewish shops and synagogues.

**1939** Hahn and Strassman (German) discover nuclear fission.

**1939** Mussolini seizes Albania.

## AFRICA AND THE MIDDLE EAST

**1930** Revolution in Ethiopia establishes Ras Tafari (**1892-1975**) as Emperor. He takes the name Haile Selassie.

*Emperor Haile Selassie*

**1932** Kingdom of Saudi Arabia is established by Ibn Saud.

**1932** Harry Philby, English explorer, crosses the Rub' al-Khali Desert in Arabia, known as 'the Empty Quarter', probably the first European to do so.

*A menorah candlestick, symbol of Judaism*

**1933** Arabs riot against Jewish immigration into Palestine. Britain limits the number allowed, to try to stop unrest.

**1935** Italy invades Ethiopia, disobeying the terms of the League of Nations.

**1935** Persia is renamed Iran.

**1935** Turkish women win the vote.

**1936** Anglo-Egyptian alliance ends the British protectorate over Egypt, but gives Britain control over the Suez Canal for 20 years. British troops garrison the Suez Canal zone.

**1936** Italian troops capture Addis Ababa, capital of Ethiopia, and annex the country. Haile Selassie appeals for League of Nations support. Britain and France agree to impose limited sanctions on Italy.

**1936** Arab revolt in Palestine against Jewish immigrants, in an attempt to stop the establishment of the state of Israel.

**1938** Mussolini declares Libya part of Italy.

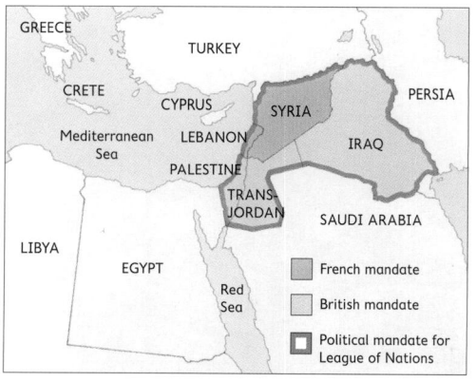


*A map of mandated territories in the Middle East*

## THE SECOND WORLD WAR

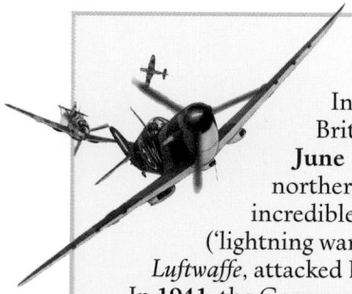

In **September 1939**, Hitler invaded Poland, and Britain and France ('the Allies') declared war. By **June 1940**, Germany had occupied much of northern Europe. They moved tanks and planes with incredible speed, using a technique known as *Blitzkrieg* ('lightning war'). Between **1940** and **1941**, its airforce, the *Luftwaffe*, attacked British airports, factories and cities (the *Blitz*). In **1941**, the Germans launched operation 'Barbarossa': a massive invasion of the Soviet Union, their former ally. A huge mistake, it drained German resources and forced them to retreat. In **1942**, the U.S.A. joined the Allies, after Germany's new ally, Japan, attacked Pearl Harbor in Hawaii. The Japanese won control of much of Southeast Asia and the Pacific. But, from **1942**, there were Allied victories in the Pacific and in North Africa, and in **June 1944**, the Allies landed in Normandy (D-Day). Meanwhile, the Soviets were pushing the Germans back from the East, and met the Allies in Berlin in **April 1945**. Hitler, facing inevitable defeat, committed suicide. In **May 1945**, Germany surrendered (VE day) followed in September by Japan (VJ day).

1939

## ASIA

**1931** Mohandas Gandhi marches 380km (238 miles) across India, in protest against British taxes.

**1931** Mao Zedong proclaims a Chinese Soviet Republic in the remote Jiangxi province.

**1931** Japanese occupy Manchuria. In **1932**, they set up Republic of Manchukuo, with Chinese ex-emperor Pu Yi as President.

*Gandhi*

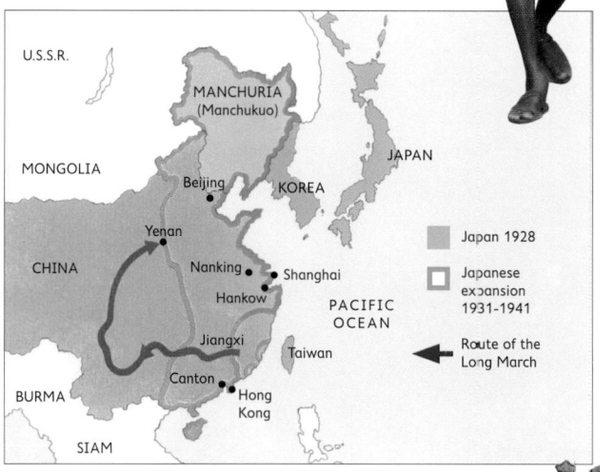


*Map showing the Japanese invasion of China*

**1934** Rapid military and naval rearmament begins in Japan.

**1934-1935** The Long March to northern China by Chinese Communists led by Mao Zedong. Driven from their stronghold in Jiangxi by Jiang Jie Shi, they are forced to make an 8,000km (5,000 mile) journey to Yenan, a mountainous region in northwest China. They set up government and plot to take over the whole country.

*The Communist Long March of 1934-1935, led by Mao Zedong*

**1937** Burma is separated from British India and ruled as an individual colony.

**1937-1945** The Japanese attack China. They take Shanghai and Nanking (**1937**), Canton and Hankow (**1938**).

## AMERICA AND AUSTRALASIA

1930

**1930** Amy Johnson, English aviator, flies from London to Darwin, Australia, becoming the first woman to fly solo across the world.

*Amy Johnson's plane*

**1930** Getulio Vargas seizes power in Brazil and becomes President.

*Peruvian textiles and bowl*

**1932** War between Peru and Colombia.

**1932** Sydney Bridge opens in Australia.

**1932** The Empire State Building, the world's tallest building, is opened in New York.

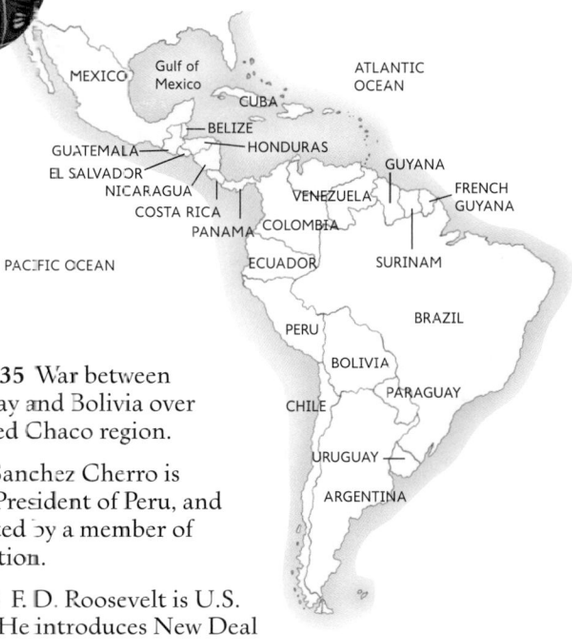


**1932-1935** War between Paraguay and Bolivia over disputed Chaco region.

**1933** Sanchez Cherro is elected President of Peru, and assassinated by a member of the opposition.

**1932-1945** F. D. Roosevelt is U.S. President. He introduces New Deal policies to deal with the Depression. The end of Prohibition.

**mid 1930s** Fierce winds in the U.S. plains destroy farms and wreck the landscape. The area, and the period, become known as 'the Dust Bowl'.

**1935** Mackenzie King becomes Prime Minister of Canada.

**1936** Jesse Owens, an African American, wins four gold medals at the Berlin Olympics.

*U.S. and German (Nazi period) flags, and a stopwatch used at the Olympics*

**1938** Unsuccessful Nazi plots in Chile and Brazil.

**1938-1945** Getulio Vargas is dictator of Brazil.

**1939** Igor Sikorsky, a Russian-born American, designs the first modern helicopter.

1939

## EUROPE

1940

**1940** Battle of Britain: British win air battle with Germany.

*British plane*

**1940** Germans occupy France. De Gaulle sets up Free French Forces (FFL) to continue fighting.

**1940-1945** Winston Churchill leads coalition government in Britain.

**1941** Operation Barbarossa: Germans invade U.S.S.R.

**1941** Frank Whittle, inventor of aircraft jet engine, flies the first British jet aircraft.

**1941-1945** Nazis build concentration camps in German-occupied countries and murder over 12 million: homosexuals, mentally ill, gypsies and over six million Jews. This is known as 'the Holocaust'.

**1942** Wernher von Braun, German scientist, launches the V-2, the first long-range jet rocket.

**1943** The first electronic computer, Colossus I, is built in U.K.

**1943** Italy surrenders. Germans occupy North Italy and Rome.

**1944** Allies advance on all fronts. France is liberated on June 6 (D-Day). De Gaulle sets up a government in Paris in August.

**1944-1949** Civil war in Greece.

**1945** French women are given the vote for the first time.

**1945** Hitler commits suicide. Germany surrenders on May 8 (VE Day) and splits into French, British, U.S. and Soviet zones.

*Churchill, Roosevelt and Stalin, the leaders of Britain, U.S.A. and U.S.S.R., meeting at Yalta, on the Black Sea, to make plans for a postwar settlement*

**1945-1946** Trials of Nazi leaders at Nuremburg, Germany.

**1946** Hungary, Albania and Bulgaria become republics.

**1946** King of Italy abdicates and a republic is proclaimed. Italian women are given the vote for the first time.

**1947** Belgium, Netherlands and Luxembourg form a Customs Union: the start of the movement for European unity.

**1947** Romania becomes a republic.

**1948** Communists seize power in Czechoslovakia, Hungary, Romania, Bulgaria and Poland.

**1947-1958** Fourth Republic in France.

**1948** Organization for European Economic Cooperation (OEEC) is established.

**1948-1949** Berlin Blockade: U.S.S.R. cuts off West Berlin in an attempt to force it to join the Eastern bloc. Blockade is broken by an Anglo-American airlift of supplies. East and West Germany are established as separate states.

**1949** U.K. Labour government begins nationalization policy.

1949

**1949** Éire leaves the British Commonwealth.

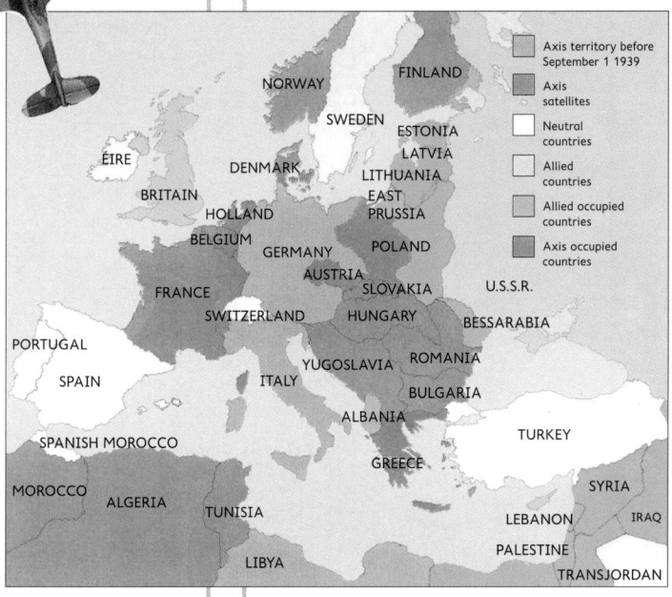


*Irish flag*

## AFRICA AND THE MIDDLE EAST

**1940** Italians invade Egypt, but are driven back by British, who occupy Libya.

**1940** Many French African colonies support General de Gaulle's Free French Forces.

**1941** General Erwin Rommel leads a German counterattack against the Allies in North Africa.

**1941** Italians expelled from Somalia, Eritrea and Ethiopia.

*Map showing the two sides across Europe, North Africa and the Middle East during the war*

**1942** Rommel is defeated by British under General Montgomery at El Alamein, Egypt.

*Rommel's troops after capture in 1941*

**1943** Germans surrender in Tunisia: the end of German involvement in Africa.

**1945** Formation of the Arab League in Cairo.

**1945** Uprising against the French in Algeria.

**1946** Transjordan wins independence under King Abdullah, and is renamed Jordan.

*Map of Israel and Palestine 1947-1948*

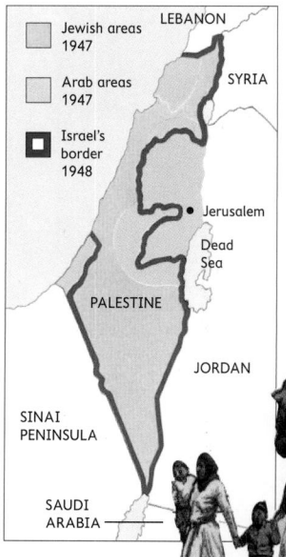


**1947** Partition of Palestine into Arab and Jewish states agreed by UN, but opposed by Arabs. Fighting breaks out after the British withdraw.

**1948** Nationalist Party is elected in South Africa on a policy of *apartheid* (a system of enforced racial segregation). Apartheid is introduced in **1949**.

**1948-1949** Arab League goes to war with Israel, but fails to stop the establishment of the state.

*Palestinian refugees leaving Israel*

## ASIA

**1940** Friendship treaty between Siam and Japan.

**1941** Neutrality pact between Soviet Union and Japan.

**1941-1942** Japanese occupy much of Southeast Asia and the islands of the Pacific.

**1942** Battle of Midway: U.S. halts Japanese expansion.

**1944** U.S. seizes Saigon, Vietnam, and launches bombing raids against Japan.

**1945** U.S. destroys Japanese fleet at Okinawa and drops atomic bombs on Japan. Hiroshima and Nagasaki are completely destroyed. Japanese surrender on August 14.

*This atomic bomb, named 'Fat Boy', was dropped on Nagasaki, Japan.*

*Inside the bomb was a substance called plutonium. Upon hitting the target, all the plutonium atoms in the bomb split, releasing huge amounts of energy.*

**1945** U.S.S.R. and U.S.A. jointly administer Korea.

**1945** Ho Chi Minh forms a government in Hanoi, Vietnam. French attempts to reassert control lead to a war of independence in Indochina (**1946-1954**).

**1945-1951** Allies occupy and administer Japan.

**1946-1949** Civil war between nationalists and communists in China leads to communist victory. Nationalists set up state of Nationalist China in Taiwan.

**1947** India is granted independence and divided into Hindu India and Muslim Pakistan. Massacres take place as people migrate to different parts of the subcontinent

*People migrating to different parts of India*

**1948** Mahatma Gandhi is assassinated.

**1948** Terrorism leads to a state of emergency in Malaya.

**1948** Two republics in Korea: a pro-communist regime in North Korea and a pro-western regime in South Korea.

**1948** Burma and Ceylon are granted independence from Britain.

**1949** Siam is renamed Thailand.

**1949** Japan: the U.S. launches a scheme to improve the Japanese economy.

**1949** Chairman Mao Zedong formally declares the communist People's Republic of China.

## AMERICA AND AUSTRALASIA

1940

**1941** Japanese attack U.S. naval base at Pearl Harbor, Hawaii. U.S.A. enters Second World War.

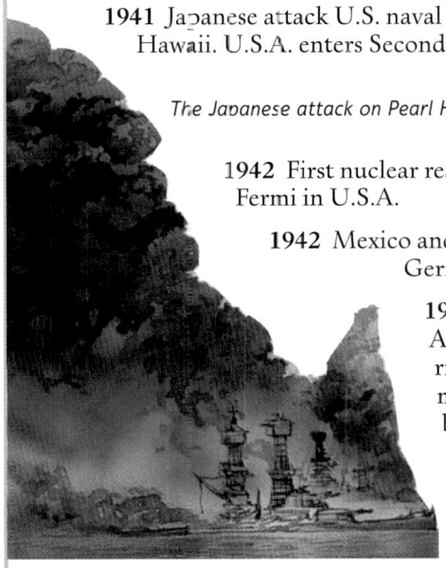

*The Japanese attack on Pearl Harbor*

**1942** First nuclear reactor is built by Enrico Fermi in U.S.A.

**1942** Mexico and Brazil declare war on Germany and Japan.

**1943** Revolution in Argentina: Juan Perón rises to power as virtual military dictator. He becomes President in **1946**.

**1945** U.S. explodes first atom bomb in New Mexico.

**1945** United Nations (UN) is set up in San Francisco, U.S.A. to encourage peace and protect human rights.

*UN symbol*

**1946** ENIAC, an early modern computer, is developed by John Mauchly and John Eckert.

**1946** U.S. conducts the first underwater atomic explosion at Bikini Atoll in the Pacific.

**1947** U.S. introduces the Marshall Plan, to give economic aid to non-communist countries.

*German poster advertising the Marshall Plan*

**1947** U.S. President Harry Truman offers to support groups fighting communism.

### THE COLD WAR

After World War Two, the two superpowers, the U.S.S.R. and the U.S.A., were driven apart by political differences and mutual suspicion. Both sides built up nuclear forces and engaged in a war of propaganda and threats. Although there was no direct fighting between them, the two sides supported armed struggles between communists and non-communists in other parts of the world. This state of hostility was known as the Cold War, and lasted from **1948** until the dissolution of the Soviet Union in **1991**.

**1948** Invention of the transistor miniaturizes electronic circuitry.

**1949** North Atlantic Treaty Organization (NATO) is formed: a military alliance to counter the communist threat.

1949

## EUROPE

1950

**1951** U.S.S.R. explodes its first atom bomb.

**1951** European Coal and Steel Treaty between Belgium, France, Holland, Italy, Luxembourg and West Germany.

**1952** Elizabeth II becomes Queen of Great Britain and Northern Ireland.

**1953** DNA structure is discovered by Francis Crick (U.K.) and James Watson (U.S.).

*The double helix shape of a DNA molecule*

**1953** U.S.S.R.: Death of Stalin. Nikita Khrushchev becomes first secretary, then premier (**1958-1964**).

**1953** Imre Nagy, liberal Communist Party leader, introduces reforms in Hungary.

**1953** Josip Broz, known as Tito, is elected President of Yugoslavia.

**1953** Soviet tanks crush anti-communist uprising in East Berlin.

**1954** Roger Bannister (U.K.) runs first four-minute mile.

**1954** EOKA movement in Cyprus struggles for union with Greece. Anti-British unrest until **1959**.

**1955** The Warsaw Pact is signed: a military treaty and association between the communist states of Eastern Europe.

*Map of divided Europe*

**1956** Anti-communist uprising in Hungary is crushed by the U.S.S.R. Imre Nagy is executed in **1958**.

*Soviet tanks putting down the anti-communist revolt in Hungary in 1956*

**1957** U.S.S.R. launches the first space satellite, *Sputnik 1*. Laika, a small dog, becomes first living creature in space.

**1957** Treaty of Rome establishes the European Economic Community (EEC). Members: France, Germany, Italy, Belgium, Netherlands and Luxembourg.

**1958** De Gaulle becomes Prime Minister, then President, of France (**1959-1969**). The Fifth Republic is established.

**1959** The first air cushioned vehicle (ACV), designed by Christopher Cockerell (U.K.), makes first sea crossing.

**1959** Archbishop Makarios becomes first president of new republic of Cyprus.

1959

## AFRICA AND THE MIDDLE EAST

**1951** Libya becomes first African colony to win independence.

**1951** King Abdullah of Jordan is assassinated. Crown Prince Hussein becomes King of Jordan.

**1952** Revolution in Egypt: King Farouk abdicates. A republic is proclaimed in **1953**.

**1952-1955** State of emergency in Kenya: uprisings by Mau Mau, a secret society opposed to British rule.

*Kenyan shields*

**1953** Federation of North and South Rhodesia and Nyasaland is established.

**1954** Gamal Abdul Nasser comes to power in Egypt. He is President from **1956-1970**.

**1954-1962** Bitter civil war between Algerian nationalists and French settlers leads to independence.

**1956** Second Arab-Israeli War.

**1956** Oil is discovered in Nigeria.

**1956** Sudan and Morocco become independent.

**1956** Suez Crisis: President Nasser of Egypt nationalizes the Suez Canal, opposed by Britain and France. Israel invades Egypt, and Britain and France occupy the Canal Zone. U.S. opposition and world opinion force them to withdraw.

**1957** Tunisia becomes a republic.

**1957** King Feisal II and Iraqi Prime Minister are assassinated in an army coup. Republic proclaimed.

**1957** Gold Coast (renamed Ghana) becomes independent under Kwame Nkrumah. Major step in the decolonization of Africa.

*Ghanaian flag*

**1958** Egypt and Syria form United Arab Republic (U.A.R.), later joined by Yemen. Syria leaves in **1960**.

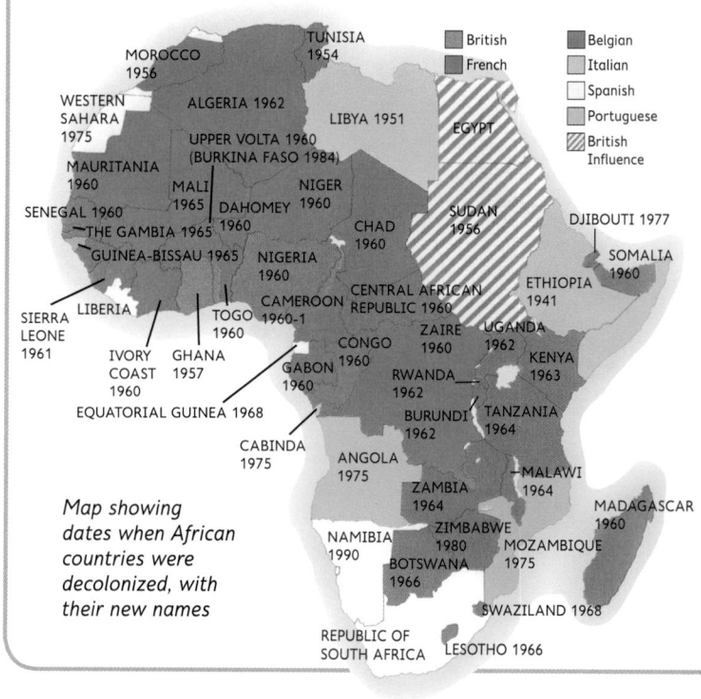


*Map showing dates when African countries were decolonized, with their new names*

## ASIA

*Map of Korea in 1953*

*U.S. tank from the Korean war*

**1950-1953** The Korean War: North Korea, backed by the U.S.S.R., invades South Korea. UN forces (mainly U.S.) support South Korea. China supports North Korea. Communists make gains at first, but in **1951** UN forces counterattack. Treaty of Panmunjon (**1953**) establishes the border between North and South Korea.

**1950** China invades Tibet.

**1951** Mussadeq, Prime Minister of Iran, nationalizes the Anglo-Iranian Oil Company. Tension with Britain follows.

**1951-1952** Postwar peace treaty gives full independence to Japan. Rapid economic growth begins. U.S. occupation ends.

**1953** Edmund Hillary (N.Z.) and Sherpa Tensing (Nepal) reach the summit of Everest, the world's highest mountain.

*The world's highest mountains*

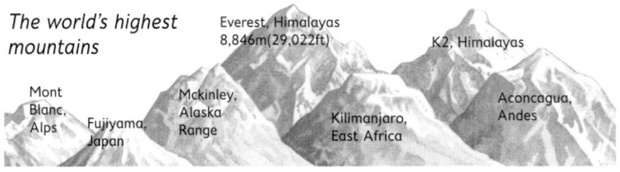


**1954** Southeast Asia Treaty Organization (SEATO) is set up by Australia, France, New Zealand, U.K., Pakistan, Philippines, Thailand and U.S.A. to check the spread of communism.

**1957** Malaya wins independence.

### THE VIETNAM WAR

*Map of Indochina 1953*

The struggle for independence in Indochina ended with the French defeat at Dien Bien Phu in **1954**. North Vietnam set up an independent communist state, based in Hanoi. The same year, at a conference in Geneva, Cambodia, Laos and South Vietnam were recognized as independent states. But North Vietnam refused to accept the division of Vietnam, and civil war broke out (**1954-1973**). The North supported the Viet Cong, southern rebels who wanted to join them, while the U.S. supported the South Vietnam government. From **1961**, the Americans became actively involved, bombing the north from **1965**. Despite a huge U.S. presence (half a million troops by **1968**), the Viet Cong were masters of jungle warfare. In **1973**, with demoralized troops and hostility to the war at home, the Americans withdrew. By **1975**, the Viet Cong had taken the southern capital, Saigon (now Ho Chi Minh city), and united the country.

**1958** China: Mao Zedong announces the Great Leap Forward, a plan for rapid industrial growth.

**1959** Unsuccessful uprising in Tibet against the Chinese. The Dalai Lama flees to India.

## AMERICA AND AUSTRALASIA

**1950** Death of Eva Perón, popular and influential wife of President Juan Perón of Argentina.

**1950** U.S. President Truman allows development of hydrogen bomb.

**1950-1954** Senator McCarthy leads drive against communism in U.S.A.

*American poster warning of the dangers of communism*

**1951** Australia, New Zealand and U.S.A. sign ANZUS pact.

**1952** Civil war in Cuba: General Batista seizes power, opposed by communists led by Fidel Castro.

**1954** First inoculations against polio in the U.S.

**1955** Revolution in Argentina overthrows Juan Perón.

**1955** Martin Luther King leads a boycott of buses in Alabama, U.S.A., in an attempt to end segregation.

**1958** Integrated circuit, or silicon chip, is demonstrated by Jack Kilby of Texas Instruments, U.S.A.

*The silicon chip (right) miniaturized electronic circuitry.*

**1958** Alaska becomes 49th state of U.S.A.

**1958-1967** Growing demands for civil rights for African Americans in U.S.A.

**1959** Failed invasion of Cuba by a small band of Cuban exiles trained by the American C.I.A.

**1959** Hawaii becomes 50th state of U.S.A.

*The number of stars on the American flag, known as the Stars and Stripes, equals the number of states in the union.*

**1959** Cuba: Fidel Castro overthrows President Batista, with the help of Che Guevara, an Argentinian Marxist experienced in guerilla warfare.

*Images of Che Guevara became a symbol of revolution all over the world.*

## EUROPE

1960

**1960** Cyprus becomes independent.

**1961** Yuri Gagarin (U.S.S.R.) makes first manned spaceflight. He completes an entire orbit of the Earth in Vostok 1.

**1961** Berlin Wall is built around West Berlin, to stop East Germans from fleeing to the West.

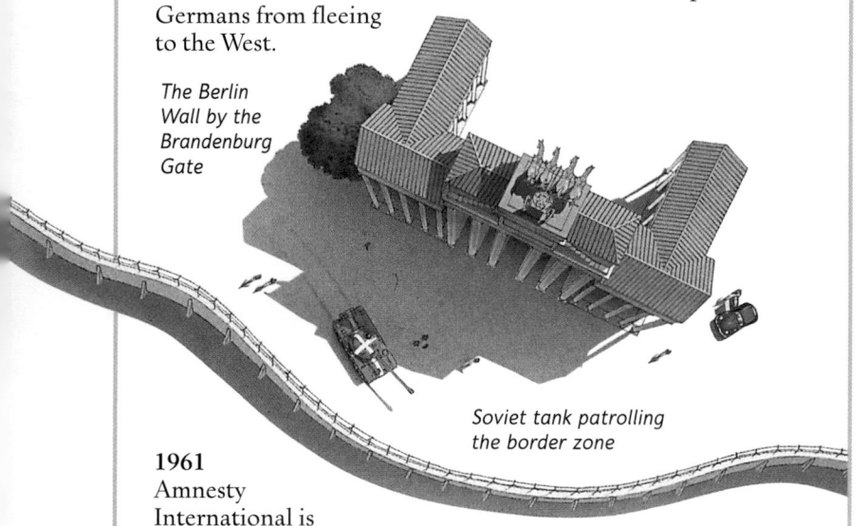

*The Berlin Wall by the Brandenburg Gate*

*Soviet tank patrolling the border zone*

**1961** Amnesty International is founded in London, to fight for human rights.

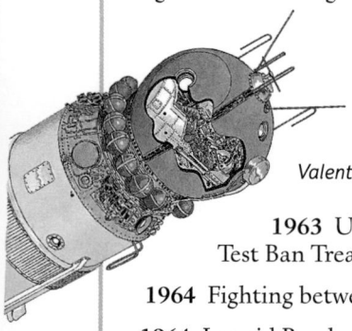

**1962** U.K. application to join EEC is rejected.

**1963** Valentina Tereshkova (U.S.S.R.) is first woman in space.

*Valentina in the command module of Vostok 6*

**1963** U.S.S.R., U.K. and U.S.A. sign Nuclear Test Ban Treaty.

**1964** Fighting between Greeks and Turks in Cyprus.

**1964** Leonid Brezhnev succeeds Khrushchev as Soviet leader.

**1965** Sir Winston Churchill, British wartime leader, dies.

**1965** Alexei Leonov (U.S.S.R.) is first to 'walk in space'.

**1967** Greek monarchy is abolished.

### MAY '68

In May **1968**, student demonstrations broke out in Paris against university conditions and other issues, including U.S. involvement in the Vietnam War, and quickly spread to other parts of France. Revolution was in the air, as suppression by the police led to violent clashes between riot police and up to 30,000 students. Workers joined forces with the students, ending in a general strike against President de Gaulle's policies. He resigned as President in **1969**.

October **1968** Soviet troops invade Czechoslovakia to crush the 'Prague Spring', a liberal movement in the Czech Communist Party, led by Prime Minister Alexander Dubcek.

**1968-1969** Civil rights riots in Northern Ireland. Period of violence and clashes between Unionists (who want to keep union with Britain) and Republicans (who want separation).

1969

## AFRICA AND THE MIDDLE EAST

*Flags of Uganda (1962), Botswana (1966), Ghana (1957), Swaziland (1968) and Togo (1960)*

**1960s** Most African countries become independent.

**1960** Organization of Petroleum Exporting Countries (OPEC) is set up in Baghdad, Iraq.

**1960** Sharpeville massacre in South Africa. 67 black Africans are killed when troops fire on a demonstration.

**1960-1965** Civil war in the Congo following independence from Belgium. A military coup brings President Mobutu to power. Katanga province declares independence.

**1961** South Africa leaves the Commonwealth.

**1962** Revolution in Yemen. The monarchy is abolished.

**1963** Organization for African Unity (OAU) is formed in Addis Ababa, Ethiopia, by 30 African countries.

**1963** Kenya becomes independent under Prime Minister Jomo Kenyatta. It becomes a republic in 1964.

**1964** Tanganyika and Zanzibar unite to become Tanzania.

**1964** Rebel activity against the Portuguese in Mozambique.

**1964** Last French forces leave Algeria.

**1965** Ian Smith, Rhodesian Front Party leader, declares Southern Rhodesia independent under white minority rule. This is known as the Unilateral Declaration of Independence, or UDI. Britain does not accept it and imposes sanctions. Long civil war follows, as black guerillas fight for power.

*Emblem used on Bokassa's robe*

**1966** Jean Bokassa seizes power in Central African Republic.

**1966** Milton Obote seizes power in Uganda.

**1966** Nkrumah is overthrown in Ghana by military coup.

**1966** South African Prime Minister Verwoerd is assassinated.

**1966** Revolution in Nigeria.

**1967** Six Days' War between Israel and Arab states. Israel occupies Sinai.

**1967** First successful heart transplant performed in South Africa by Dr. Christiaan Barnard.

**1967-1970** Nigerian Civil War: Eastern Nigeria breaks away and declares independence as Biafra.

**1969** Revolution in Libya overthrows King Idris I and puts Colonel Gadaffi in power.

**1969** Golda Meir becomes Prime Minister of Israel.

## ASIA

**1960** War between China and India over disputed border.

**1960** Worsening relations between China and U.S.S.R.

**1960** Mrs. Bandaranaike of Sri Lanka becomes first elected woman prime minister.

**1961** U.S. starts sending troops to South Vietnam, to fight attacks by communist North Vietnamese, the Viet Minh. They begin bombing North Vietnam in **1965**.

**1964** Death of Jawaharlal Nehru, popular Prime Minister of India since independence in **1947**.

**1964** State of emergency in Malaya after attacks by Indonesian guerillas.

**1965** U.S. sends first ground troops into Vietnam.

**1965** India and Pakistan fight over the Kashmir region on the border between them.

**1965** Singapore becomes independent from Malaya.

**1965** Ferdinand Marcos becomes President of Philippines.

**1966** Indira Gandhi becomes Prime Minister of India.

### THE CULTURAL REVOLUTION

*Chinese flag*

In **1966**, the Chinese leader, Mao Zedong, launched the Cultural Revolution: a period of terror during which supposed capitalist influences were crushed, in an attempt to keep to pure communist ideals. Young people were encouraged to join the Red Guards, who used spying, violence and intimidation to seek out anti-revolutionaries. This lasted until Mao's death in **1976**, and millions of people were killed or imprisoned.

*Support for Mao during the Cultural Revolution*

**1967** China explodes its first hydrogen bomb.

**1968** Tet offensive: North Vietnam launches a major campaign against South Vietnam. Peace negotiations begin.

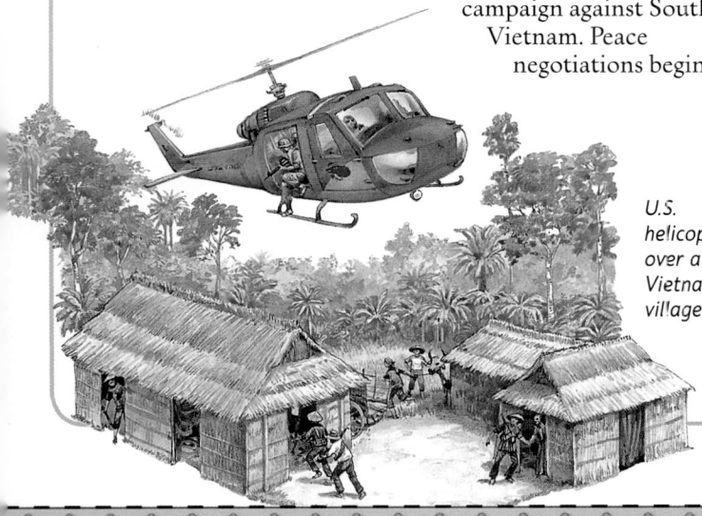

*U.S. helicopter over a Vietnamese village*

## AMERICA AND AUSTRALASIA

**1960** New city of Brasilia becomes the new capital of Brazil.

**1961** Bay of Pigs: an invasion of Cuba, backed by the U.S.A. to overthrow Fidel Castro, fails.

**1962** Jamaica, Trinidad and Tobago gain independence

**1962** The U.S. launches Telstar, the first satellite to relay live television and telephone calls.

*Telstar satellite*

### THE CUBAN MISSILE CRISIS

In **1962** came the most dangerous moment of the Cold War, as the world teetered for days on the brink of nuclear war. The U.S.A. discovered that the Soviet Union had established nuclear bases in Cuba. Seeing its security at risk, the U.S. began a naval blockade of the island, threatening war unless the bases were dismantled. Eventually, however, the U.S.S.R. was persuaded to back down.

**1963** U.S. President Kennedy is assassinated in Dallas, Texas.

**1963** Viking remains are found in North America dating back 500 years before Christopher Columbus.

**1964** President Johnson signs U.S. Civil Rights Bill, outlawing racial discrimination.

**1965** First U.S. spacecraft lands on the Moon.

**1965** Malcolm X, African American activist, is assassinated in New York.

**1966** British Guiana (Guyana) and Barbados become independent.

*An anti-war poster*

**1967** Che Guevara, leader of guerillas in Bolivia, is assassinated.

**1968** Martin Luther King, an African American civil rights leader, is assassinated.

**1968** Pierre Trudeau becomes Prime Minister of Canada.

**1968** U.S. Senator Robert F. Kennedy is assassinated.

**1969** Anti-Vietnam War demonstrations grow.

**1969** Half a million attend a rock festival at Woodstock, U.S.A.

**1969** July 21: U.S. astronaut Neil Armstrong is the first man on the Moon.

*'One small step' for Neil Armstrong*

## EUROPE

1970

**1970** First jumbo jet lands in London from New York.

**1970** British find oil in North Sea.

*An offshore oil rig*

**1970** Death of President de Gaulle of France.

**1970** Spain: serious unrest among Basque separatists (people from the Basque region who want separation from Spain).

**1971** Former Soviet leader Nikita Khrushchev dies.

**1971** Decimal currency is adopted in Britain.

**1971** Women are given the vote in Switzerland.

**1971** U.S.S.R. launches the world's first space station, *Salyut 1*.

*The Olympic logo*

**1972** Munich Olympic Games: Israeli athletes are murdered by *Black September*, an Arab terrorist organization.

**1972** Bloody Sunday in northern Ireland. Troops fire on rioters, killing 13. Britain imposes direct rule.

**1973** Éire, Denmark and U.K. join the EEC.

**1973** Greece becomes a republic. President Papadopoulos is overthrown in a military coup.

**1974** Turks invade Cyprus and split the island into northern Turkish sector and southern Greek sector.

**1974** Revolution in Portugal. The military dictatorship is overthrown and replaced by democracy.

**1975** Death of General Franco in Spain. The monarchy is restored under King Juan Carlos.

**1975** West Germany: trial of Baader-Meinhof terrorist gang.

**1976** Helsinki Convention on Human Rights is adopted.

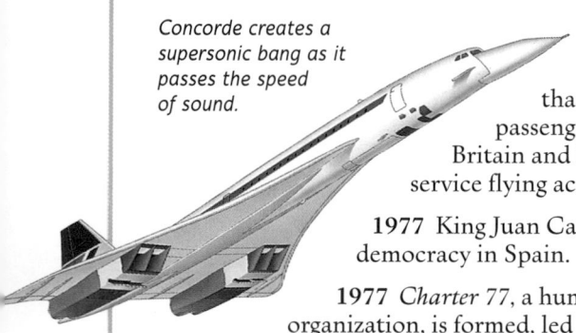

*Concorde creates a supersonic bang as it passes the speed of sound.*

**1976** Concorde, the world's first supersonic (faster than the speed of sound) passenger plane, designed by Britain and France, begins a service flying across the Atlantic.

**1977** King Juan Carlos restores democracy in Spain.

**1977** *Charter 77*, a human rights organization, is formed, led by Czech playwright Václav Havel.

**1978** First test-tube baby, Louise Brown, born in U.K.

**1978** World's worst oil spill: tanker *Amoco Cadiz* runs aground off French coast, losing 1.3 million barrels of oil.

**1979** Lord Mountbatten is killed by an IRA bomb.

**1979** Margaret Thatcher becomes the first woman prime minister in U.K.

1979

## AFRICA AND THE MIDDLE EAST

**1970** King Hussein of Jordan and Yasser Arafat of the PLO (Palestine Liberation Organization) sign a truce to end the war in Jordan.

**1970** Military coup in Uganda brings Idi Amin to power.

**1970** Israel and Egypt fight over Sinai.

*Israeli F4E fighter plane*

**1971** Aswan Dam is opened in Egypt.

**1972** Idi Amin expels over 40,000 Asians living in Uganda.

**1973** Yom Kippur War between Israel and Arab states. Egypt and Syria attack Israel and occupy Golan Heights. OPEC restricts oil supplies: this leads to huge increases in oil prices and a worldwide economic crisis.

*This oil 'supertanker' is so long that crew members need a moped to ride from one end to the other.*

**1974** Haile Selassie is deposed and a Marxist government is established in Ethiopia.

**1974** Civil war begins between rival religious (Christian and Muslim) and political groups in Lebanon.

**1975** Angola and Mozambique become independent. Civil war begins in Angola.

**1975** King Faisal of Saudi Arabia is assassinated.

**1976** Serious rioting in Soweto, near Johannesburg.

**1976** Raid on Entebbe: Israeli commandos free 100 hostages held by Palestinian terrorists at Entebbe, Uganda.

**1977** Jean Bokassa crowns himself emperor of the Central African Empire.

**1977** President Sadat of Egypt visits Israel for peace talks.

**1978** UN peace troops sent to Israel/Lebanon border.

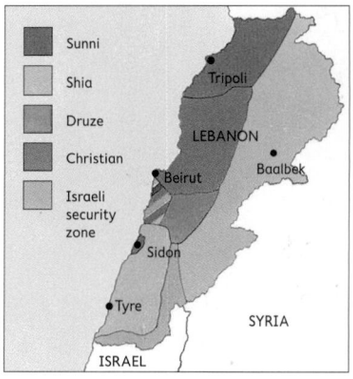


*Map of Lebanon, showing the majority religious group in each area*

**1979** Peace treaty between Israel and Egypt. Israel agrees to withdraw from Sinai.

**1979** Shah of Iran is overthrown, and an Islamic republic is set up, led by Ayatollah Khomeini.

*Zimbabwe flag*

**1979** Uganda: civil war and military invasion by Tanzania leads to the overthrow of Idi Amin.

**1979** Lancaster House Conference in London draws up a constitution for majority rule in Rhodesia, to be renamed Zimbabwe.

## ASIA

**1970** Military coup in Cambodia overthrows the government of Prince Sihanouk. Khmer Republic is set up by Lon Nol.

**1971** Pakistan attacks India, but is defeated.

**1971** Pakistan is forced to give up East Pakistan, which forms the independent state of Bangladesh.

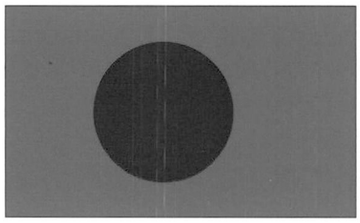

*The flag of Bangladesh*

**1972** Ceylon changes its name to Sri Lanka.

**1972** U.S. President Nixon makes an eight-day visit to China to meet Mao Zedong, after 20 years of strained relations between the two nations.

**1973** Ceasefire in Vietnam: the last American troops leave.

**1973** The King of Afghanistan is overthrown in a military coup. Muhammad Daoud reasserts control.

**1974** Largest ever tomb is discovered, belonging to Chinese emperor Shi Huangdi.

*The tomb of Emperor Shi Huangdi contained a terracotta army of over 7,500 soldiers, horses and chariots.*

**1975** North and South Vietnam are united under communist rule.

**1975** Communists seize power in Cambodia and Laos. Khmer Rouge, Cambodian communists, are led by dictator Pol Pot. Millions die under his rule.

**1976** China: Mao Zedong dies. Fall from power of the 'Gang of Four', Mao's closest associates, including his widow.

**1977** Thousands of Vietnamese people leave in boats, fleeing the communist regime in South Vietnam.

**1977** Military coup in Pakistan by General Zia al-Haq. Former President Bhutto is overthrown and later hanged.

**1978** Vietnamese invade Cambodia to help rebels overthrow Khmer Rouge government. A pro-Vietnamese regime is set up.

**1979** Civil war against the pro-Soviet regime in Afghanistan. Soviet troops invade in support of the government. Guerilla war follows.

**1979** The Killing Fields: huge graves are found in Cambodia, evidence of mass murder under Pol Pot's regime.

## AMERICA AND AUSTRALASIA

**1970** U.S. national guardsmen shoot four students dead at a demonstration at Kent State University, Ohio.

**1971** Death of François 'Papa Doc' Duvalier, President of Haiti since **1957**. He is succeeded by his son Jean-Claude 'Baby Doc'.

**1972** U.S.A. and U.S.S.R. sign SALT (Strategic Arms Limitation Treaty) to reduce the number of missiles.

**1973** Australia: opening of the Sydney Opera House.

**1973** U.S.-backed military coup in Chile, led by General Pinochet. Marxist President Allende is killed.

*Chilean flag*

**1973** Juan Perón becomes President of Argentina again.

**1973** Civil war in Nicaragua, between the *Sandinistas* (nationalist and communist guerillas) and the government (ruled by the Somoza family since **1933**).

**1974** Isabel Perón becomes President of Argentina, after the death of her husband, Juan Perón. She is deposed in **1976**.

**1973-1974** Watergate scandal in U.S.A.: bugging devices found in Democrat election campaign headquarters. President Nixon faces impeachment by Congress and resigns.

**1975** Altair, the first personal computer, is sold in the U.S.A.

**1975** First international meeting in space: Soviet and U.S. spacecraft dock together and astronauts shake hands through the hatches.

**1975** Constitutional crisis in Australia after Labour Prime Minister Gough Whitlam is dismissed.

**1977** The Space Shuttle, the first reusable spacecraft, is tested.

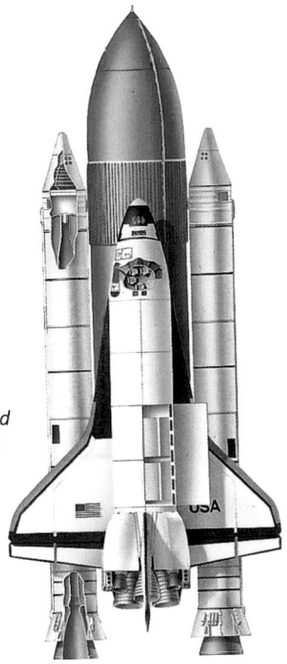

*The first Space Shuttle was named 'Enterprise' after the spaceship in the popular TV series Star Trek.*

**1978** Camp David Agreement between Israel and Egypt.

**1978** U.S. begins diplomatic relations with China.

**1978** Over 900 members of a religious cult die in a mass suicide in Guyana.

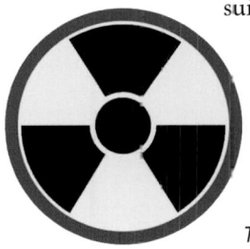

*The radioactive symbol*

**1979** Nicaragua: Somoza is overthrown. Sandinista government comes to power.

**1979** Three mile island: worst nuclear leak in U.S. history.

## EUROPE

1980

**1980** Death of President Tito, ruler in Yugoslavia since **1945**.

*Solidarity logo*

**1980** Unrest in Poland, as independent trade union *Solidarnosc* (Solidarity), led by Lech Walesa, wins support. Government declares martial law, bans Solidarity, and imprisons many of its leaders.

**1980** Terrorist bomb kills 84 at Bologna railway station, Italy.

**1981** François Mitterand is first socialist President of France.

**1981** United Kingdom: Charles, Prince of Wales marries Lady Diana Spencer.

**1981** Greece joins the EEC.

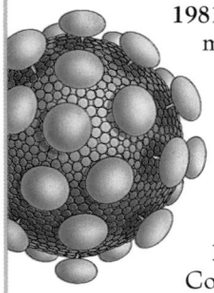

*Model of the AIDS virus*

**1982** AIDS virus is identified in France.

**1984** U.K.: IRA bomb hits Conservative Conference.

**1984-1985** Irish singer Bob Geldof organizes Band Aid and Live Aid, raising millions for Ethiopia.

**1985** Mikhail Gorbachev becomes leader in the U.S.S.R.

**1985** Talks between Reagan and Gorbachev in Geneva.

**1986** Reykjavik talks between Reagan and Gorbachev fail.

**1986** Major nuclear power disaster at Chernobyl, U.S.S.R.

**1986** Spain and Portugal join EEC.

**1987** Hurricane hits southern Britain and northern France.

**1987** Gorbachev encourages *glasnost* ('openness') and *perestroika* ('restructuring') in the U.S.S.R.

**1988** Plane crashes in Lockerbie, Scotland, killing all 259 passengers and crew, after terrorist bomb explodes on board.

**1988** Communist government is forced to resign in Czechoslovakia after peaceful pro-democracy demonstrations. Václav Havel is elected President.

**1988** Strikes by Polish union Solidarity bring the economy to a standstill and the government is forced to hold talks.

**1989** British writer Salman Rushdie is condemned to death by Ayatollah Khomeini for his book *The Satanic Verses*.

**1989** Tim Berners-Lee, British scientist, invents World Wide Web.

**1989** Hungary opens border with Austria, allowing the free flow of people from East to West for the first time.

**1989** Pro-democracy demonstrations all over Germany: the government gives in and the Berlin Wall is knocked down.

*Berliners celebrating the opening up of the wall*

**1989** Civil war in Romania. President Ceausescu is executed.

**1989** Tadeusz Mazowiecki is elected Prime Minister of a Solidarity-led government in Poland.

1989

## AFRICA AND THE MIDDLE EAST

**1980** Rhodesia becomes independent as Zimbabwe, with Robert Mugabe as Prime Minister.

**1980** War breaks out between Iran and Iraq.

**1981** President Sadat of Egypt is assassinated. Hosni Mubarak is elected president.

**1982** Israel invades Lebanon, in an attempt to drive out the PLO (Palestine Liberation Organization) and establish a strong Christian government in Beirut. Syria opposes Israel. Civil war follows. Hundreds of Palestinians are massacred in Shabra and Shatila refugee camps.

*PLO poster*

**1984-1985** 10-year drought and civil war lead to famine in Ethiopia, Sudan and Chad. Thousands die.

**1985** War between Iran and Iraq intensifies.

*Flags of Iran (top) and Iraq (bottom)*

**1985** Israeli troops withdraw from Lebanon.

**1985** Riots in Eastern Cape, South Africa.

**1986** State of Emergency declared in South Africa. Serious rioting and hundreds of deaths follow police violence.

**1986** Desmond Tutu becomes first black archbishop of Cape Town, South Africa.

**1986** U.S. bombs Libya, after Libyans carry out acts of terrorism in Europe.

**1986** Commonwealth and U.S. agree to economic sanctions against South Africa.

**1986** New constitution is adopted in Ethiopia. Colonel Mengistu Mariam becomes first president.

**1987** Mohammed Barre is re-elected President of Somalia.

**1988** Refugees flee to Ethiopia from Sudan.

**1988** South Africa signs peace agreement with Angola and Cuba.

**1988** Refugees flee to Rwanda after massacres in Burundi.

**1988** Yasser Arafat, PLO leader, renounces terrorism and recognizes right of Israel to exist.

**1989** F. W. de Klerk becomes President of South Africa.

**1989** Death of Iranian leader, Ayatollah Khomeini.

*Mourners at Khomeini's funeral*

## ASIA

**1982** First compact disc (CD) introduced by Sony (Japan) and Phillips (Holland).

*Compact disc*

**1983** Unrest and violence between Tamil separatists and Sinhalese majority in Sri Lanka.

**1983** Korean Air Lines flight 007 is shot down by Soviet fighter plane, killing 269 people on board.

**1983** Philippines opposition leader Benigno Aquino is assassinated.

**1984** Britain and China agree on terms for the handing over of Hong Kong to China.

**1984** Golden temple at Amritsar, India, is occupied by Sikh extremists demanding an independent state. Indian police storm the temple, fighting breaks out and hundreds die. Months later, Prime Minister Indira Gandhi is assassinated by a Sikh bodyguard. She is succeeded by her son, Rajiv.

**1984** Chemical leak at factory in Bhopal, India, kills more than 3,500 people.

**1986** President Marcos is ousted after 20 years in power in the Philippines. He is succeeded by Corazon Aquino.

**1987** India sends troops to Sri Lanka to control Tamil rebels.

**1987** China: Chairman Deng Xiaoping resigns from all posts, except control of the army.

**1988** President Zia al-Haq, military ruler of Pakistan, is killed when his plane explodes mid-air. Benazir Bhutto becomes first woman Prime Minister of Pakistan.

**1988** World's longest tunnel opens between islands of Honshu and Hokkaido in Japan.

**1988** Over 1,000 people die in floods in Bangladesh.

**1988** Major earthquake in Armenia, killing 100,000 people.

**1988** President of Burma resigns after riots and anti-government demonstrations.

**1989** Soviet army completes withdrawal from Afghanistan.

**1989** Death of Emperor Hirohito of Japan, the longest reigning monarch in the world.

**1989** Soviet troops withdraw from Afghanistan.

**1989** Chinese troops massacre peaceful pro-democracy protesters at Tiananmen Square, Beijing (see below).

## AMERICA AND AUSTRALASIA

**1980** Archbishop Romero is murdered in church in El Salvador.

**1980** John Lennon, former member of pop group *The Beatles*, is killed by a gunman in New York.

**1981** The first IBM Personal Computer (PC) is made.

**1981** Ronald Reagan becomes U.S. President.

**1981** The Space Shuttle makes its first spaceflight.

**1982** British Honduras becomes independent Belize.

**1982** Falklands War: Argentina invades the Falkland Islands. British naval task force retakes the islands.

**1982** Scientists spot a hole in the ozone layer over Antarctica.

**1983** Left-wing coup in Grenada is put down with U.S. intervention.

**1983** Military regime falls and democracy is restored in Argentina.

**1985** Democracy is restored in Brazil and Uruguay.

**1985** U.S. supplies aid to the Contra rebels in Nicaragua.

**1985** Colombian volcano erupts.

**1985** French sink Greenpeace boat *Rainbow Warrior* in New Zealand. Greenpeace had been trying to stop French nuclear testing in the Pacific.

*The Rainbow Warrior, and a blue whale, one of the endangered species Greenpeace is trying to protect.*

**1986** *Voyager* 2 sends pictures of Uranus.

**1986** *Challenger* Space Shuttle explodes on liftoff, killing all seven astronauts.

**1986** U.S. Iran-Contra scandal.

**1987** Washington treaty eliminates medium-range nuclear missiles.

**1987** Stock Market crash begins in New York.

**1988** Australia celebrates 200th anniversary of first settlers from Britain

**1989** Stealth bomber B-2 developed by Northrop and U.S. Air Force.

**1989** U.S. invades Panama. Dictator Noriega is removed from power.

**1989** Oil tanker *Exxon Valdez* runs aground off Alaska, spilling thousands of barrels of crude oil.

*A sea bird suffering the ill effects of the oil spill*

## EUROPE

1990

**1990** Germany is reunified.

**1990** Tadeusz Mazowiecki takes up position as Prime Minister of a Solidarity-led government in Poland. Former Solidarity leader Lech Walesa is President.

**1990** Boris Yeltsin is elected President of Republic of Russia.

**1990** Latvia, Lithuania and Estonia claim independence.

**1990** Free elections are held in Hungary, won by the non-communist Democratic Forum.

**1990** Coalition government is elected in Romania.

**1990** Margaret Thatcher resigns as British Prime Minister.

**1990** Mary Robinson becomes the first woman President of Éire.

**1991** Soviet leader, Mikhail Gorbachev, is ousted in a coup led by military and KGB leaders. Gorbachev is restored, but later resigns. U.S.S.R. is dissolved, and renamed the Commonwealth of Independent States (C.I.S.).

*Flags of the old Soviet Union (U.S.S.R.) and the new Commonwealth of Independent States (Russia)*

*Soviet peace poster*

**1991** Latvia, Lithuania and Estonia become independent.

**1991** Civil war breaks out in Yugoslavia. Croatia, Macedonia and Slovenia declare independence.

**1992** Bosnia-Herzegovina becomes independent.

**1993** Czechoslovakia splits into Czech and Slovak republics.

**1993** Single European Market is established.

**1993** Downing Street Declaration: British and Irish prime ministers work for peace in northern Ireland.

**1994** Channel Tunnel opens between Britain and France (see left).

**1994-1996** IRA (Irish Republican Army) ceasefire.

**1994** Ferry *Estonia* sinks in the Baltic Sea. Over 900 drowned.

**1994** Russian tanks invade breakaway region of Chechnya, which is demanding independence from Russia.

**1995** End of fighting in Bosnia between Bosnian Serbs and government forces.

**1995** Scientists in Geneva create antimatter for the first time.

**1995** Austria, Finland and Sweden join the EU.

**1995** Jacques Chirac is elected President of France.

**1995** London: collapse of Barings Bank, after trader Nick Leeson makes huge losses in Singapore.

1995

## AFRICA AND THE MIDDLE EAST

**1990** Rwanda invaded by Tutsi-led rebels. The invasion is contained, and multiparty democracy is established.

**1990** Namibia becomes independent from South Africa.

**1990** Worldwide ban on ivory trade is introduced to protect elephants from dying out.

**1990** Iraqi leader Saddam Hussein invades Kuwait. Leads to worldwide protest and a rise in oil prices.

**1990** ANC (African National Congress) ban is lifted in South Africa. *Apartheid* begins to break up. Nelson Mandela is released after 27 years in prison.

**1990-1991** Gulf War: UN operation 'Desert Storm' forces Iraq to withdraw from Kuwait. Iraqi forces leak two million barrels of oil into the Persian Gulf, causing the worst oil pollution in history.

**1991** Mogadishu, Somali capital, is captured by rebel forces and President Barre is overthrown.

**1991** Famine in Sudan.

**1992-1995** UN peacekeepers fail to keep peace in Somalia.

**1992** Civil war in Algeria. Fundamentalist Islamic Salvation Front wins control of local government.

**1993** Peace agreement between Yasser Arafat, PLO leader, and Israeli Prime Minister Yitzhak Rabin. Some self-rule for Palestinians on Gaza Strip and West Bank of River Jordan.

**1993** Ethiopia recognizes Eritrea's independence.

**1994** Nelson Mandela becomes the first black President of South Africa, after the first multiracial elections.

*The new South African flag*

*Nelson Mandela*

**1994** Civil war in Rwanda between Hutu people and the Tutsi government. Thousands die.

**1995** Nigerian military government executes dissident writer Ken Saro-Wiwa and eight environmental campaigners.

**1995** Israeli Prime Minister Yitzhak Rabin is assassinated by a Jewish extremist.

## ASIA

**1990** Benazir Bhutto, Prime Minister of Pakistan, is dismissed by the President on charges of corruption. She is re-elected for a second term in **1993**.

**1991** Rajiv Gandhi, former Prime Minister of India, is murdered by a suicide bomber during an election rally near Madras.

**1991** A military junta, led by General Sunthorn Kongsompong, takes power in Thailand.

**1991** Cyclone in Bangladesh kills 125,000 people, leaving 10 million homeless.

*Flooded Bangladeshi village*

**1991** Burmese opposition leader, Aung Sang Suu Kyi, under house arrest in Burma, is awarded the Nobel Peace Prize.

*Aung Sang Suu Kyi*

**1994** Death of Kim Il Sung of North Korea, longest-ruling dictator of the 20th century.

**1995** Meeting of APEC (Asia-Pacific Economic Co-operation): mutual opening of markets planned for **2020**.

**1995** Earthquake destroys much of Kobe, Japan.

**1995** Religious sect releases poison gas on trains in Tokyo, Japan, killing 10 people.

**1995-1996** France carries out nuclear testing at Mururoa atoll, South Pacific.

## AMERICA AND AUSTRALASIA

**1990** Hubble Space Telescope is launched from Cape Canaveral, U.S.A., to probe the furthest reaches of the universe.

**1990** Sandinista government is defeated in Nicaraguan elections by a U.S.-backed coalition.

**1991** Paul Keating becomes Australian Prime Minister.

**1992** Virtual Reality is developed by Gilman Louie in U.S.A.

**1992** Boutros Boutros-Ghali becomes UN Secretary-General.

**1992** The first UN summit on the environment, to try to tackle air pollution and global warming, is held in Brazil.

*Rainforest wildlife*

**1992** Mass riots in Los Angeles, U.S.A., after four white policemen are acquitted of beating a black motorist.

**1993** Bill Clinton becomes U.S. president.

**1993** Huge bomb damages World Trade Center in New York.

**1993** 51-day siege in Waco, Texas. 80 cult members commit suicide.

**1993** Yitzak Rabin, Israeli Prime Minister, and Yasser Arafat, leader of the PLO, sign peace accord in Washington D.C.

**1993** Native Titles Bill is passed in Australia. A tribunal is set up to try to restore land rights to native Aboriginals.

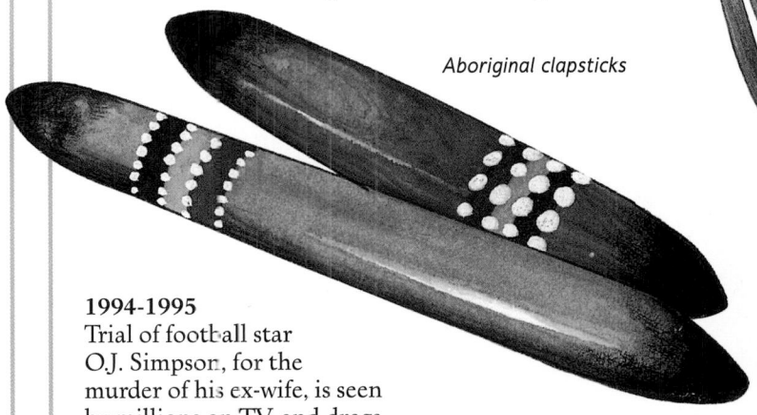

*Aboriginal clapsticks*

**1994-1995** Trial of football star O.J. Simpson, for the murder of his ex-wife, is seen by millions on TV, and drags on for months.

**1994** U.S. forces occupy Haiti and restore elected President Aristide to power after military coup.

**1995** Bomb wrecks federal building in Oklahoma City, killing 168 people.

**1995** Quebec votes to remain part of Canada.

*Quebec flag*

## EUROPE

1996

**1996** Outbreak of BSE, or 'mad cow disease', in Britain leads to widespread concern. Many countries ban British beef.

**1996** Ceasefire between Chechen rebels and Russian troops in Chechnya. Peace treaty signed.

**1997** Dolly, first sheep cloned using the cells of adult sheep, is born in Scotland.

*Sheep cloned in a laboratory*

**1997** Economic collapse leads to popular uprising in Albania. Government falls.

**1997** U.K.: Tony Blair becomes Labour Prime Minister in a landslide victory, after 18 years of Conservative rule.

*Tony and Cherie Blair (and family) outside number 10 Downing Street after the 1997 election victory*

**1997** Diana, Princess of Wales, is killed in a car crash in Paris.

**1998** Former Chilean dictator, General Pinochet, is arrested in London for human rights abuses.

**1998** Good Friday Agreement, between Protestant loyalists and Catholic republicans, brings fragile peace to Northern Ireland.

**1998** Russia faces economic collapse.

**1998** European Union agrees on a single currency, to be called the *Euro*.

**1998** Civil war in Kosovo province of Yugoslavia between Serbs and ethnic Albanians.

**1999** Northern Ireland becomes self-governing.

**1999** Czech Republic, Poland and Hungary join NATO.

**1999** NATO bombs Serbia to try to end the war in Kosovo.

**1999** Around 17,000 people die in an earthquake in Turkey, and 600,000 are left homeless.

## AFRICA AND THE MIDDLE EAST

**1996** Hardliner Benjamin Netanyahu becomes Israeli Prime Minister. Middle East peace process is in doubt.

**1996** U.S. bombs southern Iraq after Iraqi forces invade safe havens designated for Kurdish minority in Iraq.

**1996** Ethiopian forces attack Muslim fundamentalist militia in northern Somalia.

**1996** 225,000 Hutus flee to Rwanda from eastern Zaire.

**1997** President Mobutu of Zaire deposed. Replaced by rebel leader Laurent Kabila. Zaire renamed Democratic Republic of Congo.

**1997** Israel hands back part of Hebron (and other land) to Palestinians but establishes Jewish settlement in Arab East Jerusalem. Middle East peace process at a deadlock.

**1997** Atrocities in Algeria, allegedly carried out by anti-government forces.

**1997** Massacre of over 60 tourists near Luxor, Egypt, allegedly by Islamic extremists.

*Queen Hatshepsut's tomb, near the site of the massacre*

**1998** Terrorists bomb U.S. embassies in Kenya and Tanzania. U.S. launches missile strikes against Sudan and Afghanistan.

**1998** Wye Mills Agreement between Israeli Prime Minister Netanyahu and PLO leader Yasser Arafat.

**1998** U.S.A. and U.K. launch air strikes against Iraq, after Iraq fails to allow UN weapons inspections.

**1999** King Hussein of Jordan and King Hassan II of Morocco die.

**1999** Peace accord between Ehud Barak, new Prime Minister in Israel, and Yasser Arafat.

**1999** Nelson Mandela retires and is succeeded by Thabo Mbeki.

2000

## ASIA

**1996** Bombing campaign in Sri Lanka by the Tamil Tigers. State of emergency extended.

**1996** Taliban Islamic fundamentalists seize Kabul, Afghanistan.

**1997** Death of former Chairman Deng Xiaoping in China.

**1997** Violent demonstrations in Seoul, South Korea.

**1997** Fires caused by forest clearance in Indonesia grow out of control, spreading pollution through Southeast Asia.

**1997** Asian economic crisis begins as Japan raises consumption tax and Thailand floats its currency.

**1997** Hong Kong: 99-year lease to Britain expires on June 30. Britain returns Hong Kong to China on July 1.

*Hong Kong street scene*

**1998** India and Pakistan both conduct atomic tests.

**1998** Thousands die in an earthquake in Afghanistan.

**1998** Economic problems in Indonesia: dictator Suharto resigns.

**1999** Indonesia: hardliner Abdurrahman Wahid is elected president in the first free election since **1955**. East Timor votes for independence from Indonesia, leading to massacres and violence. UN peace-keeping force intervenes.

**1999** Russia sends ground troops into Dagestan and Chechenia, where fighting intensifies. President Yeltsin resigns, but hand-picks his successor, Vladimir Putin.

**1999** Pakistani government overthrown by military coup. Benazir Bhutto is imprisoned, allegedly for taking bribes.

**1999** Nuclear accident in Japan: dozens exposed to radiation.

## AMERICA AND AUSTRALASIA



**1996** American scientists warn that global warming has reached record high, introducing possibility of new diseases.

**1997** Tupac Amaru guerillas besiege Japanese embassy residence in Peru, holding hundreds hostage for four months.

**1997** Climatic change due to El Niño phenomenon causes extensive damage in South America and southern U.S.A.

*Hurricane force winds devastated parts of South and Central America.*

**1997** Two unmanned NASA spacecraft land on Mars.

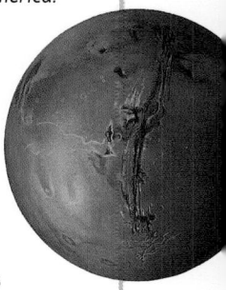

*Mars, fourth planet from the Sun*

**1997** Landmark ruling as tobacco industry is forced to pay billions of dollars to lung disease sufferers.

**1998** U.S. President Clinton is impeached by the House of Representatives for lying to Congress over his affair with Monica Lewinsky. He is acquitted in **1999**.

**1998** Hurricane Mitch hits the Caribbean and Central America, killing 9,000 people.

**1999** Australians vote to keep the British Queen as Head of State.

**31st December 1999** Millions all over the world take part in millennium celebrations, such as the firework display (shown below) held in New York, United States of America.

# Glossary

**amnesty** General pardon given by a government for crimes committed. Sometimes granted in an attempt to reach a settlement during a civil war.

**annex** To join a territory to a larger one by conquering or occupying it.

**apartheid** South African policy of the separation of races.

**aristocracy** Government by nobles, or a privileged class.

**autocracy** Government by a person such as a king, who has unrestricted authority and does not allow any opposition. Government of this kind is described as autocratic.

**autonomy** Self-government, often limited, granted to a nation or people by a more powerful nation.

**Bantu** African languages and peoples found between the equator and the Cape of Good Hope.

**baptize** To immerse a person in water, as part of the initiation ceremony into the Christian Church.

**caliph** Title given to the successors of Mohammed, rulers of Islamic states. The office or state is called a caliphate.

**canonize** To declare a person a saint.

**capitalism** A system in which the means of production (industries, businesses, etc.) are owned by a relatively small group, who provide the investment and take a major share of the profits.

**cede** To give up or surrender a territory, often as part of the terms of a peace treaty following a war.

**charter** Document issued by a government, granting certain rights, such as the right to found a colony.

**Christendom** The people and nations who belong to the Christian Church.

**Christianity** The religion founded in Palestine by Jesus of Nazareth, known as Jesus Christ.

**city-state** A state that is made up of a city and its surrounding territory, such as the city-states of Ancient Greece or Italy during the Renaissance.

**civil rights** Equality in social, economic and political matters.

**coalition** Temporary alliance between different groups or parties, such as in a government.

**collectivization** Organization of the ownership of the means of production (factories, farms etc.) into groups, or collectives.

**colony** A settlement in a country distant from the homeland. A Crown colony is one whose administration is controlled by the King or Queen.

**Commonwealth** Organization of former member countries of the British empire, with the purpose of mutual co-operation and aid.

**communism** An ideology mainly based on the ideas of Karl Marx, which advocates a society without social classes or private ownership, in which the means of production (factories and businesses) are owned by the state. In the 20th century, the U.S.S.R. and eastern European countries were communist states, as well as China and Cuba, which are still communist today.

**Congress** The government of the U.S.A., made up of the Senate and the House of Representatives.

**coup d'état** Sudden overthrow of an existing government by a small group, often army officers.

**demilitarization** The removal of any soldiers, weapons, etc. from an area.

**democracy** An ideology which originated in Ancient Greece, meaning 'rule by the people'.

**dependency** Territory subject to a nation, to which it is not usually linked geographically.

**despot** An 'absolute' or autocratic ruler, or tyrant, who rules unjustly.

**dictator** A non-royal autocratic ruler, who imposes his rule by force. The government is called a dictatorship.

**dominion** The name formerly used for a self-governing colony within the British empire, such as Canada.

**ecclesiastical** Relating to the Church.

**egalitarian** System that promotes equality between people.

**enlightened despot** A despot who tries to govern in the interests of the people, according to the ideals of the Enlightenment, an 18th century philosophical movement, which stressed the importance of reason.

**excommunicate** To expel a person from the Catholic Church. This is done by the Pope.

**fascism** A political ideology first developed by Mussolini. A form of government which allows no rival political parties and which controls the lives of its citizens. The Nazi Party in Germany was a fascist party.

**federal** Relating to a type of government in which power is shared between central government and several regional governments.

**guerilla** A fighter operating in secret, usually against the government. From the Spanish *guerra*, meaning war.

**hegemony** Domination of one power or state within a league or federation.

**homage** Public display of respect to someone, such as a feudal lord.

**infallibility** Being incapable of error. A principle applied to certain pronouncements by the Pope.

**Islam** The religion of Muslims, based around the holy book the *Koran*, which teaches that there is only one God and Mohammed is his prophet.

**Judaism** The religion of the Jewish people, based on the *Old Testament* of the *Bible* and the *Talmud*, with a central belief in one God.

**junta** Government by a group of army officers, often after a coup d'état.

**left-wing** Term used to describe any ideology that tends toward socialism or communism.

**liberalism** Political ideology advocating individual freedom and the idea that governments should interfere as little as possible in people's lives.

**mandate** Authority given to a country by the League of Nations, which met between **1920** and **1946**, to administer another country under its trusteeship.

**martial law** Rule of law established by military courts, and maintained by the army, in the absence of civil authority.

**Marxist** Person or government following the teachings of Karl Marx. The belief that actions and institutions are determined by economics, that the struggle between social classes is the instrument of change and that capitalism will eventually be overcome by communism.

**medieval** Relating to the Middle Ages, a period in European history dating loosely from **c.500-1500**.

**minority rule** Government by a group of people who are different, politically or racially, from a larger group over whom they rule.

**monopoly** Sole right to trade in a specific product or a specific area.

**nationalism** Common cultural characteristics, such as race or language, that link groups of people together. It sometimes leads to a movement for national independence, or separation from another ruling state.

**nepotism** Granting of an official position, or other privilege, to a member of the family, or friend.

**nomads** People who move continually from place to place.

**oligarchy** Government by a small group of people, such as in Ancient Greece.

**one-party-state** Nation that is dominated by the one and only party that is allowed to exist.

**papal bull** Formal document issued by the Pope.

**parliamentary democracy** Modern form of democracy, in which representatives elected by the people make decisions on their behalf.

**patent** Document issued by a government, granting specific rights.

**plebiscite** Direct vote by the people on an issue of particular importance, such as unification with another state.

**pretender** Someone who makes a claim to a throne or a title.

**privateer** Privately-employed soldier, sailor or vessel commissioned for service by a government.

**protector** Someone who exercises royal authority during the reign of a child, or an ill or unfit monarch.

**protectorate** Territory largely controlled by, but not annexed to, a more powerful nation.

**radical** Tending toward extreme or fundamental social, political or economic changes.

**regent** Ruler of a country during the reign of a child or the absence or incapacity of the monarch.

**republic** State ruled by representatives of the people, without a king or queen. The first republic was in Ancient Rome.

**residency** Official house of a British governor in an Indian princedom.

**sack** Plunder or destruction of a place by an army or mob.

**secular** Relating to worldly, as opposed to religious matters.

**serf** A person with no freedom, who is bound to the land. Found in medieval Europe and pre-revolutionary Russia.

**separatist** Person or organization that advocates separation from a larger unit.

**socialism** Ideology that stresses equality of income and wealth, and public (state) ownership of industries (the means of production).

**sovereignty** Supreme authority or power of a sovereign or state.

**state of emergency** Crisis during which a government temporarily suspends all the usual rights and liberties of a people.

**suffragette** A woman who fought a militant campaign for votes for women, especially in Britain at the start of the 20th century.

**sultan** Supreme ruler of a Muslim state, such as the Ottoman empire.

**suzerainty** Position of a state exercising a degree of domination over a dependent state.

**temporal** *See* **secular**.

**terrorist** Someone who uses terror (bombing, assassinations, etc.) as a means of political persuasion.

**Third World** Term once used to describe the relatively unindustrialized countries outside what used to be the Eastern (communist) and Western (non-communist) blocs.

**tribute** Payment made by one nation or people to another, more dominant one, acknowledging submission.

**triumvirate** Coalition of three rulers, such as Caesar, Crassus and Pompey in Ancient Rome.

**tyranny** Oppressive and unjust government by a despotic ruler.

**ultimatum** A final offer by a government or party, in which it insists on certain conditions.

**vassal** A person or nation in a subordinate relationship to another person or nation.

# Prime Ministers and Presidents

## PRIME MINISTERS OF GREAT BRITAIN

Party: Conservative (C), Labour (Lab), Liberal (Lib), Conservative-Unionist (CU), Coalition (Coal), National (N), Tory (T), Whig (W)

| | |
|---|---|
| **1721-1742** | (W) Sir Robert Walpole |
| **1742-1743** | (W) Sir Spencer Compton |
| **1743-1754** | (W) Henry Pelham |
| **1754-1756** | (W) Duke of Newcastle |
| **1756-1757** | (W) Duke of Devonshire |
| **1757-1762** | (W) Duke of Newcastle |
| **1762-1763** | (T) John Stuart, Earl of Bute |
| **1763-1765** | (W) George Grenville |
| **1765-1766** | (W) Marquis of Rockingham |
| **1766-1768** | (W) William Pitt the Elder |
| **1768-1770** | (W) Duke of Grafton |
| **1770-1782** | (T) Lord North |
| **1782-1783** | (W) Earl of Shelburne |
| **1783** | (Coal) Duke of Portland |
| **1783-1801** | (T) William Pitt (Younger) |
| **1801-1804** | (T) Henry Addington |
| **1804-1806** | (T) William Pitt (Younger) |
| **1806-1807** | (W) Lord Grenville |
| **1807-1809** | (T) Duke of Portland |
| **1809-1812** | (T) Spencer Perceval |
| **1812-1827** | (T) Earl of Liverpool |
| **1827** | (T) George Canning |
| **1827-1828** | (T) Viscount Goderich |
| **1828-1830** | (T) Duke of Wellington |
| **1830-1834** | (Lib) Earl Grey |
| **1834** | (Lib) Lord Melbourne |
| **1834-1835** | (C) Sir Robert Peel |
| **1835-1841** | (Lib) Lord Melbourne |
| **1841-1846** | (C) Sir Robert Peel |
| **1846-1852** | (Lib) Lord John Russell |
| **1852** | (C) Earl of Derby |
| **1852-1855** | (Lib-Coal) Earl of Aberdeen |
| **1855-1858** | (Lib) Lord Palmerston |
| **1858-1859** | (C) Earl of Derby |
| **1859-1865** | (Lib) Lord Palmerston |
| **1865-1866** | (Lib) Lord John Russell |
| **1866-1868** | (C) Earl of Derby |
| **1868** | (C) Benjamin Disraeli |
| **1868-1874** | (Lib) William Gladstone |
| **1874-1880** | (C) Benjamin Disraeli |
| **1880-1885** | (Lib) William Gladstone |
| **1885-1886** | (C) Marquess of Salisbury |
| **1886** | (Lib) William Gladstone |
| **1886-1892** | (CU) Marquess of Salisbury |
| **1892-1894** | (Lib) William Gladstone |
| **1894-1895** | (Lib) Earl of Rosebery |
| **1895-1902** | (CU) Marquess of Salisbury |
| **1902-1905** | (CU) Arthur James Balfour |
| **1905-1908** | (Lib) Sir H. Campbell-Bannerman |
| **1908-1915** | (Lib) Herbert Henry Asquith |
| **1915-1916** | (Coal) Herbert Henry Asquith |
| **1916-1922** | (Coal) David Lloyd George |
| **1922-1923** | (C) Andrew Bonar Law |
| **1923-1924** | (C) Stanley Baldwin |
| **1924** | (Lab) J. Ramsay MacDonald |
| **1924-1929** | (C) Stanley Baldwin |
| **1929-1931** | (Lab) J. Ramsay MacDonald |
| **1931-1935** | (Nat) J. Ramsay MacDonald |
| **1935-1937** | (Nat) Stanley Baldwin |
| **1937-1940** | (Nat) Neville Chamberlain |
| **1940-1945** | (Coal) Sir Winston Churchill |
| **1945-1951** | (Lab) Clement Attlee |
| **1951-1955** | (C) Sir Winston Churchill |
| **1955-1957** | (C) Sir Anthony Eden |
| **1957-1963** | (C) Sir Harold Macmillan |
| **1963-1964** | (C) Sir Alec Douglas-Home |
| **1964-1970** | (Lab) Sir Harold Wilson |
| **1970-1974** | (C) Sir Edward Heath |
| **1974-1976** | (Lab) Sir Harold Wilson |
| **1976-1979** | (Lab) James Callaghan |
| **1979-1990** | (C) Margaret Thatcher |
| **1990-1997** | (C) John Major |
| **1997-2007** | (Lab) Tony Blair |
| **2007-2010** | (Lab) Gordon Brown |
| **2010-2015** | (Coal) David Cameron |
| **2015-2016** | (C) David Cameron |
| **2016-2019** | (C) Theresa May |
| **2019-2022** | (C) Boris Johnson |
| **2022-2022** | (C) Elizabeth Truss |
| **2022-** | (C) Rishi Sunak |

## PRESIDENTS OF U.S.A.

Inauguration date followed by Party: Federation (F), Republican (R), Democrat (D), Whig (W)

| | | |
|---|---|---|
| **1789** | (F) George Washington | 1732-1799 |
| **1797** | (F) John Adams | 1735-1826 |
| **1801** | (R) Thomas Jefferson | 1743-1826 |
| **1809** | (R) James Madison | 1751-1836 |
| **1817** | (R) James Monroe | 1758-1831 |
| **1825** | (R) John Quincy Adams | 1767-1848 |
| **1829** | (D) Andrew Jackson | 1767-1845 |
| **1837** | (D) Martin Van Buren | 1782-1862 |
| **1841** | (W) William Harrison | 1773-1841 |
| **1841** | (W) John Tyler | 1790-1862 |
| **1845** | (D) James Knox Polk | 1795-1849 |
| **1849** | (W) Zachary Taylor | 1784-1850 |
| **1850** | (W) Millard Fillmore | 1800-1874 |
| **1853** | (D) Franklin Pierce | 1804-1869 |
| **1857** | (D) James Buchanan | 1791-1868 |
| **1861** | (R) Abraham Lincoln | 1809-1865 |
| **1865** | (R) Andrew Johnson | 1808-1875 |
| **1869** | (R) Ulysses S. Grant | 1822-1885 |
| **1877** | (R) Rutherford Hayes | 1822-1893 |
| **1881** | (R) James Garfield | 1831-1881 |
| **1881** | (R) Chester Arthur | 1830-1886 |
| **1885** | (D) Grover Cleveland | 1837-1908 |
| **1889** | (R) Benjamin Harrison | 1833-1901 |
| **1893** | (D) Grover Cleveland | 1837-1908 |
| **1897** | (R) William McKinley | 1843-1901 |
| **1901** | (R) Theodore Roosevelt | 1858-1919 |
| **1909** | (R) William Taft | 1857-1930 |
| **1913** | (D) Woodrow Wilson | 1856-1924 |
| **1921** | (R) Warren Harding | 1865-1923 |
| **1923** | (R) Calvin Coolidge | 1872-1933 |
| **1929** | (R) Herbert Hoover | 1874-1964 |
| **1933** | (D) Franklin Roosevelt | 1882-1945 |
| **1945** | (D) Harry S. Truman | 1884-1972 |
| **1953** | (R) Dwight Eisenhower | 1890-1969 |
| **1961** | (D) John F. Kennedy | 1917-1963 |
| **1963** | (D) Lyndon B. Johnson | 1908-1973 |
| **1969** | (R) Richard Nixon | 1913-1994 |
| **1974** | (R) Gerald Ford | 1913-2006 |
| **1977** | (D) Jimmy Carter | 1924- |
| **1981** | (R) Ronald Reagan | 1911-2004 |
| **1989** | (R) George Bush | 1924-2018 |
| **1993** | (D) Bill Clinton | 1946- |
| **2001** | (R) George W. Bush | 1946- |
| **2009** | (D) Barack Obama | 1961- |
| **2017** | (R) Donald Trump | 1946- |
| **2021** | (D) Joseph R. Biden | 1942- |

## PRIME MINISTERS OF CANADA

In **1867**, Lower Canada (Quebec), Upper Canada (Ontario), Nova Scotia, and New Brunswick united to form the Dominion of Canada.
Party: Conservative (C), Progressive Conservative (Prog.C), Liberal (Lib), Unionist (UN)

**1867-1873** (C) Sir John A. Macdonald
**1873-1878** (Lib) Alexander Mackenzie
**1878-1891** (C) Sir John A. Macdonald
**1891-1892** (C) Sir John J. Abbott
**1892-1894** (C) Sir John S. D. Thompson
**1894-1896** (C) Sir MacKenzie Bowell
**1896** (C) Sir Charles Tupper
**1896-1911** (Lib) Sir Wilfred Laurier
**1911-1920** (C/UN) Sir Robert L. Borden
**1920-1921** (UN) Arthur Meighen
**1921-1926** (Lib) W. L. Mackenzie King
**1926** (C) Arthur Meighen
**1926-1930** (Lib) W. L. Mackenzie King
**1930-1935** (C) Richard Bedford Bennett
**1935-1948** (Lib) W. L. Mackenzie King
**1948-1957** (Lib) Louis St. Laurent
**1957-1963** (Prog.C) John G. Diefenbaker
**1963-1968** (Lib) Lester B. Pearson
**1968-1979** (Lib) Pierre Elliott Trudeau
**1979-1980** (Prog.C) Joe Clark
**1980-1984** (Lib) Pierre Elliott Trudeau
**1984** (Lib) John Turner
**1984-1993** (C) Brian Mulroney
**1993** (Prog.C) Kim Campbell
**1993-2003** (Lib) Jean Chrétien
**2003-2006** (Lib) Paul Martin
**2006-2015** (C) Stephen Harper
**2015-** (Lib) Justin Trudeau

## PRESIDENTS OF EIRE

Party: Fianna Foil (FF), Fine Gael (FG), Labour (Lab), United Ireland (UI)

**1938-1945** (No party) Douglas Hyde
**1945-1959** (FF) Sean O'Kelly
**1959-1973** (FF) Eamon de Valera
**1973-1974** (FF) Erskine Childers
**1974-1976** (FF) Cearbhall O'Dalaigh
**1976-1989** (FF) Patrick John Hillery
**1989-1997** (Lab) Mary Robinson
**1997-2011** (FF) Mary McAleese
**2011-** (Lab) Michael D. Higgins

## PRIME MINISTERS OF ÉIRE

**1922-1932** (UI) William Cosgrave
**1932-1948** (FF) Eamon de Valera
**1948-1951** (FG) John Aloysius Costello
**1951-1954** (FF) Eamon de Valera
**1954-1957** (FG) John Aloysius Costello
**1957-1959** (FF) Eamon de Valera
**1959-1966** (FF) Sean Lemass
**1966-1973** (FF) Jack Lynch
**1973-1977** (FG) Liam Cosgrave
**1977-1979** (FF) Jack Lynch
**1979-1981** (FF) Charles Haughey
**1981-1982** (FG) Garrett Fitzgerald
**1982** (FF) Charles Haughey
**1982-1987** (FG) Garrett Fitzgerald
**1987-1992** (FF) Charles Haughey
**1992-1994** (FF) Albert Reynolds
**1994-1997** (FG) John Bruton
**1997-2008** (FF) Bertie Ahern
**2008-2011** (FF) Brian Cowen
**2011-2017** (FG) Enda Kenny
**2017-2020** (FG) Leo Varadkar
**2020-2022** (FF) Micheál Martin
**2022-** (FG) Leo Varadkar

## PRIME MINISTERS OF NEW ZEALAND

From **1856-1907**, self-government was granted in New Zealand. In **1907** the country became a dominion.
Party: Liberal (Lib), Labour (Lab), Reform (Ref), United (U), National (Nat)

**1906-1912** (Lib) Sir G. Joseph Ward
**1912** (Lib) Thomas MacKenzie
**1912-1925** (Ref) William F. Massey
**1925** (Ref) Sir Francis Bell
**1925-1928** (Ref) Joseph G. Coates
**1928-1930** (U) Sir Joseph G. Ward
**1930-1935** (U) George W. Forbes
**1935-1940** (Lab) Michael J. Savage
**1940-1949** (Lab) Peter Fraser
**1949-1957** (Nat) Sir Sidney G. Holland
**1957** (Nat) Sir Keith J. Holyoake
**1957-1960** (Lab) Sir Walter Nash
**1960-1972** (Nat) Sir Keith J. Holyoake
**1972** (Nat) John Ross Marshall
**1972-1974** (Lab) Norman E. Kirk
**1974** (Lab) Hugh Watt (acting)
**1974-1975** (Lab) Sir Wallace Rowling
**1975-1984** (Nat) Robert D. Muldoon
**1984-1989** (Lab) David R. Lange
**1989-1990** (Lab) Geoffrey Palmer
**1990** (Lab) Mike Moore
**1990-1997** (Nat) Jim Bolger
**1997-1999** (Nat) Jenny Shipley
**1999-2008** (Lab) Helen Clark
**2008-2016** (Nat) John Key
**2017-2023** (Lab) Jacinda Ardern
**2023-** (Lab) Chris Hipkins

## PRIME MINISTERS OF AUSTRALIA

In **1901**, the separate British colonies in Australia joined the Commonwealth and became states with a central government.
Party: Free Trade/Protectionist (FT/P), Protectionist (Pro), Labour (Lab), Liberal (Lib), United Australian (UAus), United Country (UC), Nationalist (Nat), Nationalist Country (N/C), Country (Co)

**1997-1999** (Nat) Jenny Shipley
**1999-2008** (Lab) Helen Clark
**1901-1903** (Pro) Edmund Barton
**1903-1904** (Pro) Alfred Deakin
**1904** (Lab) John Christian Watson
**1904-1905** (FT/P) Sir George H. Reid
**1905-1908** (Pro) Alfred Deakin
**1908-1909** (Lab) Andrew Fisher
**1909-1910** (Pro) Alfred Deakin
**1910-1913** (Lab) Andrew Fisher
**1913-1914** (Lib) Joseph Cook
**1914-1915** (Lab) Andrew Fisher
**1915-1923** (Lab/Nat) William M. Hughes
**1923-1929** (Nat/Co) Stanley M. Bruce
**1929-1932** (Lab) James Henry Scullin
**1932-1939** (UAus/Co) Joseph A. Lyons
**1939** (April) (UC) Sir Earle Page
**1939-1941** (UAus) Sir Robert G. Menzies
**1941** (Co) Sir Arthur Wm. Fadden
**1941-1945** (Lab) John Joseph Curtin
**1945** (Lab) Francis Michael Forde
**1945-1949** (Lab) Joseph B. Chifley
**1949-1966** (Lib) Robert G. Menzies
**1966-1967** (Lib) Harold E. Holt
**1967-1968** (Co) John McEwen
**1968-1971** (Lib) Sir John Grey Gorton
**1971-1972** (Lib) Sir William McMahon
**1972-1975** (Lib) Gough Whitlam
**1975-1983** (Lab) John Malcom Fraser
**1983-1991** (Lab) Bob Hawke
**1991-1996** (Lab) Paul Keating
**1996-2007** (Lib) John Howard
**2007-2010** (Lab) Kevin Rudd
**2010-2013** (Lab) Julia Gillard
**2013** (Lab) Kevin Rudd
**2013-2015** (Lib) Tony Abbott
**2015-2018** (Lib) Malcolm Turnbull
**2018-2022** (Lib) Scott Morrison
**2022-** (Lab) Anthony Albanese

# Kings and Queens

Here are the reign dates of some of the most important monarchies and dynasties of Europe.

## KINGS AND QUEENS OF ENGLAND

| | |
|---|---|
| Saxons | **c.500-1066** |
| Normans | **1066-1154** |
| Plantagenets | **1154-1399** |
| Lancastrians | **1399-1461** |
| Yorkists | **1461-1485** |
| Tudors | **1485-1603** |
| Stuarts | **1603-1714** |
| Hanoverians | **1714-1910** |
| Windsors | **1910-** |

| | |
|---|---|
| **c.500-802** | Rulers of seven kingdoms of England |
| **802-839** | Egbert |
| **839-858** | Ethelwulf |
| **858-860** | Ethelbald |
| **860-866** | Ethelbert |
| **866-871** | St. Ethelred I |
| **871-899** | Alfred the Great |
| **899-925** | Edward the Elder |
| **925-939** | Athelstan |
| **939-946** | Edmund I |
| **946-955** | Eadred |
| **955-959** | Edwy |
| **959-975** | Edgar |
| **975-978** | Edward the Martyr |
| **978-1016** | Ethelred II 'The Unready' |
| **1016** | Edmund II 'Ironside' |
| **1016-1035** | Canute (or Cnut) |
| **1037-1040** | Harold I |
| **1040-1042** | Harthacnut |
| **1042-1066** | Edward the Confessor |
| **1066** | Harold II |
| **1066-1087** | William I 'The Conqueror' |
| **1087-1100** | William II |
| **1100-1135** | Henry I |
| **1135-1154** | Stephen |
| **1135** | Matilda declared Queen |
| **1154-1189** | Henry II |
| **1189-1199** | Richard I |
| **1199-1216** | John |
| **1216-1272** | Henry III |
| **1272-1307** | Edward I |
| **1307-1327** | Edward II |
| **1327-1377** | Edward III |
| **1377-1399** | Richard II |
| **1399-1413** | Henry IV |
| **1413-1422** | Henry V |
| **1422-1461** | Henry VI |
| **1461-1470** | Edward IV |
| **1470-1471** | Henry VI regains crown |
| **1471-1483** | Edward IV regains crown |
| **1483** | Edward V |
| **1483-1485** | Richard III |
| **1485-1509** | Henry VII |
| **1509-1547** | Henry VIII |
| **1547-1553** | Edward VI |
| **1553** | Lady Jane Grey |
| **1553-1558** | Mary I |
| **1558-1603** | Elizabeth I |

## KINGS AND QUEENS OF ENGLAND AND SCOTLAND

| | |
|---|---|
| **1603-1625** | James I (James VI of Scotland) |
| **1625-1649** | Charles I |
| **1649-1660** | Britain is ruled as a Commonwealth (**1653-1658** Oliver Cromwell is Lord Protector) |
| **1660-1685** | Charles II |
| **1685-1688** | James II |
| **1689-1694** | William III and Mary II |
| **1694-1702** | William III reigns alone |
| **1702-1714** | Anne |

## KINGS AND QUEENS OF UNITED KINGDOM

| | |
|---|---|
| **1714-1727** | George I |
| **1727-1760** | George II |
| **1760-1820** | George III |
| **1820-1830** | George IV |
| **1830-1837** | William IV |
| **1837-1901** | Victoria |
| **1901-1910** | Edward VII |
| **1910-1936** | George V |
| **1936** | Edward VIII |
| **1936-1952** | George VI |
| **1952-2022** | Elizabeth II |
| 2022- | Charles III |

## KINGS AND QUEENS OF SCOTLAND

| | |
|---|---|
| **843-860** | Kenneth MacAlpin |
| **1005-1034** | Malcolm II |
| **1057-1093** | Malcolm III |
| **1124-1153** | David I |
| **1153-1165** | Malcolm IV |
| **1214-1249** | Alexander II |
| **1249-1286** | Alexander III |
| **1286-1290** | Margaret of Norway |
| **1292-1296** | John Balliol (removed by Edward I of England) |
| **1306-1329** | Robert I 'the Bruce' |
| **1329-1371** | David II |
| **1371-1390** | Robert II |
| **1390-1406** | Robert III |
| **1406-1437** | James I |
| **1437-1460** | James II |
| **1460-1488** | James III |
| **1488-1513** | James IV |
| **1513-1542** | James V |
| **1542-1567** | Mary Stuart |
| **1567-1603** | James VI (who becomes James I of England, Scotland and Ireland) |

## FRANKISH KINGDOMS

(includes part of France, Germany, Italy)

| | |
|---|---|
| Merovingian dynasty | **447-751** |
| Carolingian dynasty | **751-987** |

| | |
|---|---|
| **447-458** | Merovich |
| **458-481** | Childeric I |
| **481-511** | Clovis I |

(Clovis's kingdom is divided into three. Here are some of the main kings.)

| | |
|---|---|
| **511-558** | Childebert I |
| **558-562** | Clothaire I |
| **562-566** | Caribert |
| **566-584** | Chilperic |
| **584-628** | Clothaire II |
| **628-637** | Dagobert I |
| **637-655** | Clovis II |
| **655-668** | Clothaire III |
| **668-674** | Childeric II |
| **674-691** | Thierry III |
| **691-695** | Clovis III |
| **695-711** | Childebert II |
| **711-716** | Dagobert III |
| **716-721** | Chilperic II |
| **721-737** | Thierry IV |
| **737-743** | Interregnum: Charles Martel is governor between **714-741.** |
| **743-751** | Childeric III |
| **751-768** | Pepin 'The Short' |
| **768-814** | Charlemagne (Emperor of the Romans **800-814**) |
| **814-840** | Louis I |
| **840-877** | Charles I 'The Bald' |
| **877-879** | Louis II 'The Stammerer' |
| **879-882** | Louis III |

| | |
|---|---|
| 882-884 | Carloman |
| 884-888 | Charles II, 'The Fat' |
| 888-898 | Odo (Count of Paris) |
| 898-929 | Charles III, 'The Simple' |
| 929-936 | Interregnum |
| 936-954 | Louis IV, 'The Foreigner' |
| 954-986 | Lothaire |
| 986-987 | Louis V |

## KINGS OF FRANCE

| | |
|---|---|
| Capetians | **987-1328** |
| Valois | **1328-1589** |
| Bourbons | **1589-1883 (48)** |

| | |
|---|---|
| 987-996 | Hugh Capet |
| 996-1031 | Robert II 'The Pious' |
| 1031-1060 | Henri II |
| 1060-1108 | Philippe I |
| 1108-1137 | Louis VI 'The Grand' |
| 1137-1180 | Louis VII 'The Young' |
| 1180-1223 | Philippe II Augustus |
| 1223-1226 | Louis VIII 'The Lion' |
| 1226-1270 | Louis IX 'Saint Louis' |
| 1270-1285 | Philippe III 'The Strong' |
| 1285-1314 | Philippe IV 'The Fair' |
| 1314-1316 | Louis X |
| 1316 | Jean I |
| 1316-1322 | Philippe V 'The Tall' |
| 1322-1328 | Charles IV 'The Fair' |
| 1328-1350 | Philippe VI |
| 1350-1364 | Jean II 'The Good' |
| 1364-1380 | Charles V 'The Wise' |
| 1380-1422 | Charles V |
| 1422-1461 | Charles VII 'The Victorious' |
| 1461-1483 | Louis XI 'The Spider' |
| 1483-1498 | Charles VIII |
| 1498-1515 | Louis XII |
| 1515-1547 | François I |
| 1547-1559 | Henri II |
| 1159-1560 | François II |
| 1560-1574 | Charles IX |
| 1574-1589 | Henri III |
| 1589-1610 | Henri IV |
| 1610-1643 | Louis XIII |
| 1643-1715 | Louis XIV 'The Sun King' |
| 1715-1774 | Louis XV |
| 1774-1789 | Louis XVI |

1789-1804 Revolutionary period: France is ruled by National Assembly, National Convention, Directory, Consulate and then 1st Republic.

| | |
|---|---|
| 1804-1814 | Napoleon I (Emperor) |
| 1815-1824 | Louis XVIII |
| 1824-1830 | Charles X |
| 1830-1848 | Louis Philippe |
| 1848-1852 | 2nd Republic |
| 1852-1870 | Napoleon III (Emperor) |
| 1870-1940 | 3rd Republic |
| 1940-1944 | German occupation/ Vichy government |
| 1944-1946 | Provisional government |
| 1946-1958 | 4th Republic |
| 1958- | 5th Republic |

## EMPERORS OF THE GERMANS AND OF THE HOLY ROMAN EMPIRE

The coronation of Otto I as 'Holy Roman Emperor of the German nation' marked a new stage in medieval thinking. The emperors saw themselves as inheriting the old Roman empire as well as the Christian empire of Europe. The area they ruled over, and their degree of control, varied from period to period, but it consisted roughly of Germany, with parts of Austria and Italy.

| | |
|---|---|
| 962-973 | Otto I 'The Great' |
| 973-983 | Otto II |
| 983-1002 | Otto III |
| 1002-1024 | Henry II 'The Saint' |
| 1024-1039 | Conrad II |
| 1039-1056 | Henry III 'The Black' |
| 1056-1106 | Henry IV |
| 1106-1125 | Henry V |
| 1125-1137 | Lothar II of Luxembourg |
| 1138-1152 | Conrad III |
| 1152-1190 | Frederick I Barbarossa |
| 1190-1197 | Henry VI |
| 1198-1215 | Otto IV |
| 1198-1208 | Philip of Swabia |
| 1220-1250 | Frederick II |
| 1250-1254 | Conrad IV |
| 1254-1273 | Great Interregnum |
| 1273-1291 | Rudolf I of Habsburg |
| 1292-1298 | Adolf I of Nassau |
| 1298-1308 | Albert I of Habsburg |
| 1308-1313 | Henry VII of Luxembourg |
| 1314-1346 | Louis IV of Bavaria |
| 1314-1330 | Frederick the Fair (co-regent) |
| 1346-1378 | Charles IV of Luxembourg |
| 1378-1400 | Wenceslas the Lazy |
| 1400-1410 | Rupert of the Palatinate |
| 1410-1437 | Sigismund of Luxembourg |
| 1438-1439 | Albert II of Habsburg |
| 1440-1493 | Frederick III |
| 1493-1519 | Maximilian I |
| 1519-1556 | Charles V |
| 1558-1564 | Ferdinand I |
| 1564-1576 | Maximilian II |
| 1576-1612 | Rudolf II |
| 1612-1619 | Matthias |
| 1619-1637 | Ferdinand II |
| 1637-1657 | Ferdinand III |
| 1657-1705 | Leopold I |
| 1705-1711 | Joseph I |
| 1711-1740 | Charles VI |
| 1740-1745 | Charles VII of Bavaria |
| 1745-1765 | Maria Theresa & Francis I |
| 1765-1790 | Joseph II |
| 1790-1792 | Leopold II |
| 1792-1806 | Francis II |

(Napoleon abolishes the Holy Roman Empire in **1806**, and Francis II becomes Emperor of Austria.)

## EMPERORS OF AUSTRIA

| | |
|---|---|
| 1806-1835 | Francis II |
| 1835-1848 | Ferdinand I |
| 1848-1916 | Francis Joseph I |

(The Austrian empire is renamed Austria-Hungary in **1867**.)

| | |
|---|---|
| 1916-1918 | Charles I |
| 1918-1938 | 1st Republic |
| 1938-1945 | Anschluss |
| 1945- | 2nd Republic |

## RULERS OF GERMANY

| | |
|---|---|
| Holy Roman Empire | **962-1806** |
| Confederation of 39 German states | **1815-1866** |
| Confederation of Northern Germany | **1867-1870** |
| Emperors of Germany | **1871-1918** |

| | |
|---|---|
| 1871-1888 | Wilhelm I |
| 1888 | Friedrich III |
| 1888-1918 | Wilhelm II |
| 1919-1933 | Republic of Weimar |
| 1933-1945 | 3rd Reich |
| 1945-1990 | Division of Germany into East and West |
| 1990 | Germany united |

# Kings and Queens

## KINGS AND QUEENS OF PORTUGAL

| | |
|---|---|
| 1085-1139 | Henrique (Founder of Portugal) |
| 1139-1185 | Alfonso I (first king) |
| 1185-1211 | Sancho I |
| 1211-1223 | Alfonso II |
| 1223-1246 | Sancho II |
| 1248-1279 | Alfonso III 'The Brave' |
| 1279-1325 | Dinis 'The Farmer' |
| 1325-1357 | Alfonso IV |
| 1357-1367 | Pedro I |
| 1367-1383 | Fernando I |
| 1383-1433 | João I |
| 1433-1438 | Duarte |
| 1438-1481 | Alfonso V |
| 1481-1495 | João II |
| 1495-1521 | Manuel |
| 1521-1557 | João III |
| 1557-1578 | Sebastian |
| 1578-1580 | Cardinal Henry |
| 1580-1598 | Philip I (Philip II of Spain) |
| 1598-1621 | Philip II (Philip III of Spain) |
| 1621-1640 | Philip III (Philip IV of Spain) |
| 1640-1656 | João IV |
| 1656-1667 | Alfonso VI |
| 1667-1706 | Pedro II |
| 1706-1750 | João V |
| 1750-1777 | Joseph Emanuel (Power held by statesman Sebastiao José de Carvalho e Mello) |
| 1777-1816 | Maria I |
| 1816-1826 | João VI (Ruled in Maria I's name in 1792 after she became insane, becoming regent in 1799) |
| 1826-1834 | disputed succession |
| 1834-1853 | Maria III & (from 1837) Ferdinand |
| 1853-1861 | Pedro V |
| 1861-1889 | Luís I |
| 1989-1908 | Carlos |
| 1908-1910 | Manuel II |
| 1910 | Portuguese Republic |

## KINGS OF ITALY

| | |
|---|---|
| 1861-1878 | Victor Emmanuel II |
| 1878-1900 | Umberto I |
| 1900-1946 | Victor Emmanuel III |
| 1925-1943 | Mussolini's dictatorship |
| 1946 | Umberto II |
| 1946 | Italian Republic |

## KINGS AND QUEENS OF SPAIN

| | |
|---|---|
| 1492-1516 | Isabella of Castile and Ferdinand V of Aragon |
| 1516-1556 | Charles I |
| 1556-1598 | Phillip II |
| 1598-1621 | Philip III |
| 1621-1665 | Philip IV |
| 1665-1700 | Charles II |
| 1700-1724 | Philip V |
| 1724 | Louis I |
| 1724-1746 | Philip V |
| 1746-1759 | Ferdinand VI |
| 1759-1788 | Charles III |
| 1788-1808 | Charles IV |
| 1808 | Ferdinand VII |
| 1808-1813 | Joseph Bonaparte |
| 1813-1833 | Ferdinand VII |
| 1833-1868 | Isabella II |
| 1668-1873 | disputed succession |
| 1873-1875 | 1st Republic |
| 1875-1885 | Alphonso XII |
| 1885-1931 | Alphonso XIII (overthrown) |
| 1931-1939 | 2nd Republic & Civil War |
| 1939-1975 | Franco's dictatorship |
| 1975 | Monarchy restored |
| 1975-2014 | Juan Carlos (abdicated) |
| 2014- | Felipe VI |

## TSARS AND TSARINAS OF RUSSIA

| | |
|---|---|
| 1462-1505 | Ivan III 'The Great' |
| 1505-1533 | Vassily III |
| 1533-1584 | Ivan IV 'The Terrible' |
| 1584-1598 | Feodor I |
| 1598-1606 | Boris Godunov (Protector) |
| 1603 | Feodor II |
| 1603-1606 | Grigoriy Otrepieff, usurper, claims to be Dimitri I, son of Ivan IV |
| 1606-1610 | Vassily IV (usurper) |
| 1610-1613 | Vladyslav (not crowned) |

### THE ROMANOV DYNASTY

| | |
|---|---|
| 1613-1645 | Michael Romanov (elected king) |
| 1645-1676 | Alexis |
| 1676-1682 | Feodor III |
| 1682-1696 | Ivan V and Peter I 'The Great' (co-tsars) |
| 1682-1725 | Peter I 'The Great' (known as 'emperor' from 1721) |
| 1725-1727 | Catherine I |
| 1727-1730 | Peter II |
| 1730-1740 | Anna |
| 1740-1741 | Anna Leopoldovna (regent for her son Ivan VI) |
| 1741-1762 | Elizabeth |
| 1762 | Peter III (replaced by his wife Catherine) |
| 1762-1796 | Catherine II 'The Great' |
| 1796-1801 | Paul I |
| 1801-1825 | Alexander I |
| 1825-1855 | Nicholas I |
| 1855-1881 | Alexander II |
| 1881-1894 | Alexander III |
| 1894-1917 | Nicholas II |
| 1917 | Russian Revolution |
| 1922-1991 | U.S.S.R. (Soviet Union) |
| 1991- | Russian Federation Dissolution of U.S.S.R. into 15 nations |

# Internet Links

For links to websites where you can explore interactive timelines of world history, examine artifacts from around the world and watch video clips about important people from different eras, go to the Usborne Quicklinks website at www.usborne.com/quicklinks and type the keywords 'timelines of world history'.

**Internet safety**

When using the internet, please make sure you follow our three basic rules:

- Always ask an adult's permission before using the internet.
- Never give out personal information, such as your name, address, the name of your school or telephone number.
- If a website asks you to type in your name or email address, check with an adult first.

To find out more about internet safety, go to the "Help and advice" page at the Usborne Quicklinks website. We recommend that children are supervised while using the internet.

The recommended websites are regularly reviewed and updated but, please note, Usborne Publishing is not responsible for the content of any website other than its own, or for any exposure to harmful, offensive or inaccurate material which may appear on the Web. Usborne Publishing will have no liability for any damage or loss caused by viruses that may be downloaded as a result of browsing the sites it recommends.

**Research on the internet**

The internet is often the first place we go to find information on just about anything. However, finding information you can trust is sometimes tricky. The websites recommended at the Usborne Quicklinks website have been reviewed, but it is still a good idea to check the information for yourself.

Here are some tips to help you:

- Check the name and url of the website you are visiting. If it is a well-known organization, museum or reference site, the information will probably (but not necessarily) be reliable.
- Look for signs that the website has been updated recently. If you spot old news or dates, missing pictures, broken links or spelling mistakes, this may indicate that the website is no longer looked after and could contain information that is out of date.
- If you arrive at a website you haven't visited before, look for an 'About Us' section which may provide details about the people or organization responsible for the site. This may help you judge whether the information can be trusted.
- Experts often disagree about dates in very early history, so you may find that some of the dates shown in this book are slightly different from other timelines.
- Always visit several websites when carrying out research. This way you can compare information from different sources and check if any facts differ.
- Most organizations are happy for students and educational establishments to download images for use in schoolwork and projects, but do check the website terms and conditions before downloading.
- Be sure to credit all online sources you use.

# Index

Page numbers in **bold** type refer to a short feature on the subject.


## A

Abbas the Great, Shah of Persia, 51, 57
Abbasid dynasty, 23, 27
Abd al Rahman, Caliph of Córdoba, 24
Abdullah, King of Jordan, 92, 96, 98
Aborigines, 81, 107
Abdurrahman, Wahid, 109
Aboukir Bay, Battle of, 75
absolutism, 60
Abu Bakr, Caliph, 21
Acamapitzin, Aztec ruler, 37
Acre, crusader state, 28, 29, 33
Actium, Battle of, 14
ACV (air cushioned vehicle), 98
Addis Ababa, Ethiopia, 94, 100
Aden, Arabia, 47, 80
Adena people, 11, 13
Adrianople, Battles of, 16, 22
Adrianople, Treaty of, 80
Aga Muhammed, 75
Afghanistan, 13, 25, 45, 47, 51, 85, 92, 103, 105, 108, 109
Afghans, 47, 67, 69, 73, 80
Afonso of the Kongo, 45
Africa, Scramble for, **84**
African-Americans, 85, 99, 101
Agadir, Morocco, 90
Agadir Crisis, 90
Agincourt, Battle of, 38
Agra, India, 47, 61
Agung of Mataram, 55
Agustin Iturbide, Agustin I, Emperor of Mexico, 81
Ahmed Shah, ruler of Persia, 90
Ahuizotl, Aztec emperor, 45
AIDS, 104
Ain Jalut, Battle of, 33
Aix-la-Chapelle, Peace of, 70
Akbar the Great, Mogul emperor, 47, 49, 51, 55
Akbar, Prince of India, 63
Akhenaten, King of Egypt, 9
Akkad, 6, 8
al-Ksar al-Kabir, Battle of, 51
al Mansur, Ahmed, 51
Alabama, U.S.A., 99
Alam, Shah, Nawab of Bengal, 71
Alamo, the, U.S.A., 81
Alans, 14
Alaska, 71, 85, 99, 105
Alaungpaya, King of Burma, 71
Albania, 92, 94, 96, 98, 108
Albert I, Habsburg, Holy Roman Emperor, 32
Albert II, Habsburg of Austria, 38
Albert of Hohenzollern, 46
Albert, Duke of Austria, 32
Albi, France, 30
Albigensian Crusade, 30
Albigensians, 30
Alemanni, 14
Aleppo, Syria, 28, 29
Aleutian Islands, 71
Alexander the Great, **12**, 13
Alexander of Novgorod, ('Nevsky'), 30, 32
Alexander VI, Pope, 41
Alexander II, Tsar of Russia, 84, 86
Alexandria, Egypt, 13, 14, 17, 78
Alexius Comnenus, Byzantine emperor, 26
Alfonso of Aragon, 38
Alfonso I, King of Portugal, 28
Alfred the Great, 22
Algeria, 84, 90, 96, 98, 100
civil war, 98, 106, 108
Algiers, Algeria, 80
Algonquin people, 59
al-Haq, General Zia, 103, 105
Ali, Fath, ruler of Persia, 78
Ali, Mehemet, Viceroy of Egypt, 78
Ali, Muhammed, ruler of Persia, 90
al-Ksar al-Kabir, Battle of, 51
Allende, President, 103
Almohad dynasty, 29
Almoravid dynasty, 27
Alodia, 21
Alphonso XIII, King of Spain, 94
Altair, personal computer, 103
Altan-Khan, 49
Altranstadt, Treaty of, 66
Amaru, Tupac, 75
Amarapura, Burma, 75
Amazon river, 47, 49
Amboyna, massacre at, 57
Ambuila, Battle of, 61
American Civil War, **85**
American War of Independence, **73**
Amin, Idi, 102
Amnesty International, 100
Amorites, 8
Amritsar, India, 61, 63, 93, 105
Amundsen, Roald, 91
Anabaptists, 46
Anasazi people, 23, 25
ANC (African National Congress), 106
Andreas II, King of Hungary, 30
Angeli dynasty, 28
Angkor kingdom, 23, 27, 29
Angkor Wat, 29
Angles, 14, 16
Anglican Church, 48
Anglo-Boer wars, 86, 90
Anglo-Burmese Wars, 81, 83
Anglo-Dutch trade wars, 58, 60
Anglo-Egyptian Condominium, 90
Anglo-Iranian Oil Company, 99
Anglo-Maratha Wars, 79
Anglo-Saxons, 16, 20, 24
Anglo-Siam Treaty, 90
Anglo-Sikh Wars, 83
Angola, 49, 84, 90, 102, 104
Anjou, France, 30
Annam, Indochina, 47, 51, 81, 85, 87
Anne, Queen of England, 62, 66
Anschluss, 94
Antarctic coast, of America, 83
Antarctica, 105
antibiotics, 92
Antigonid dynasty, 12
antimatter, first created, 106
Antioch, Syria, 21, 28, 33
antiseptics, introduction of, 84
anti-slavery movements, 63, 74, 78, 80
Anti-Slavery Society, 80
anti-war movements, 101
Antony, Mark, 14
Antwerp, Belgium, 50
Anual, Battle of, 92
ANZUS pact, 99
apartheid, 96, 106
APEC (Asia-Pacific Economic Co-operation), 107
Apulia, Italy, 26, 28
Aquinas, Thomas, 30
Aquino, Benigno, 105
Aquino, Corazon, 105
Arab League, 96
Arabia, 10, 21, 82, 94
Arabic numerals, 30
Arab-Israeli War, 98
Arabs, 10, 20, 21, 22, 23, 24, 25, 26, 37, 38, 41, 54, 59, 69, 92, 94, 96, 100, 102, 104
Arafat, Yasser, 102, 104, 106, 107, 108
Aragon, Spain, 26, 30
Arbroath, Declaration of, 34
Archaic period, Greece, 10
Arcot, India, 71
Arctic, 57
Ardashir I, King of Persia, 16
Argentina, 47, 79, 81, 95, 97, 99, 103, 105
Aristide, President, 107
Arizona, U.S.A., 23, 83
Arkwright, Richard, 72
Armenia, 14, 31, 37, 80, 105
Armenians, 24, 37, 86
Armstrong, Neil, 101
Arpad dynasty, 22, 34
Arras, Peace of, 50
Art Nouveau style, 86
Arthur, King, 20
Aryans, 8, 9
Ashanti kingdom, 63, 67
people, 63, 67, 80, 84
Ashur, Assyria, 6, 8
Ashurbanipal, King of Assyria, 10
Ashurnasirpal II, 10
Asia Minor, 10, 12, 14, 26, 27, 28
Asoka, King of Maurya dynasty, 7, 13
Assam, 79, 81
Assassins, 27
Assyria, **8**, **10**, 11
Astrakhan, Russia, 49
Asturias, Spain, 22
Asunción, Paraguay, 47
Atatürk, 92, *see also* Mustafa Kemäl
Aswan Dam, Egypt, 102
Athabascan people, 33, 35
Athelstan, King of England, 24
Athens, Greece, 10, 12, 86
Atlantic Ocean, 59
atom, splitting the, 92
atomic bomb, 98
exploded, 97
exploded underwater, 97
tests, 109
*see also* nuclear weapons
Augsburg, League of, 62
Augsburg, Peace of, 48
Augustus II, Elector of Saxony and King of Poland, 66, 68
Augustus III, King of Poland, 68
Augustus, Roman emperor, 14
Aung Sang Suu Kyi, 107
Aurangzeb, Mogul emperor, 59, 61, 63, 67
Austerlitz, Battle of, 78
Australia, 55, 59, 63, 73, 75, 79, 81, 83, 85, 91, 93, 95, 99, 103, 105, 107, 109
Austria, 10, 34, 38, 40, 44, 46, 49, 62, 66, 68, 70, 72, 74, 78, 80, 82, 84, 94, 104, 106
Austro-Hungarian empire, 84
Austria-Hungary, 84, 90, 92
Austrian Netherlands (Belgium), 70, 74
Austrian Succession, War of the, 70
Ava, Burma, 49, 71, 87
Avars, 20
Avignon, France, 34, 36
Axis Pact, 94, 96
Axum, Ethiopia, 17, 21
Ayatollah Khomeini, 102, 104
Ayutthaya, Siam, 71, 73
Ayyubid dynasty, 29, 31, 33
Azores, 39
Azov, Russia, 62, 68
Aztec culture, 29, 31, 33, **35**, 37, 39, 45

## B

Baader-Meinhof, 102
Baalbek, Lebanon, 102
Babar, Prince of Ferghana, Afghanistan, 41, 45, 47
Babbage, Charles, 80
Babylon, 6, **8**, 10, 12
Bach, Johann Sebastian, 66
Bacon, Roger, 30
Bactria, 7, 15, 17
Baffin Island, 27
Baghdad, Iraq, 23, 27, 33, 39, 55, 100
Bahamas, 41
Bahlol Lodi, Pathan king of Delhi, 41
Baibars, Sultan of Egypt, 33
Balaklava, Battle of, 82
Balfour Declaration, 92
Balkans, the, 6, 20, 26, 28, 36, 40, 45, 90
Balkan Wars, 90
ballet, first known, 50
Baltic Sea, 30, 34, 48, 50, 56, 58, 62, 66, 106
Bambara kingdoms, 61, 67
Band Aid, 104
Bandaranaike, Mrs., 101
Bangkok, Thailand, 75
Bangladesh, 103, 105, 107
banknote, first, 60
Bannister, Roger, 98
Bannockburn, Battle of, 34
Bantu people, 82
Bar Cochba, 16
Barak, Ehud, 108
Barbados, 55
barbarian tribes, 14, 16
Barbarossa, Operation, 94, 96
Barbary Coast, 32
Bari, Italy, 26
Barings Bank, 106
Barnard, Dr. Christiaan, 100
Baroque art and music, 46, 66
Barre, Mohammed, 104, 106
Basil II, Byzantine emperor, 24
basket makers culture, 17
Basle, Peace of, 40
Basque separatists, 102
Bass, George, 75
Bastille prison, Paris, 74
Basutoland, 90, *see also* Lesotho
Batavia (Jakarta), East Indies, 59
Batavian Republic, 74
Bathurst, Australia, 83
Batista, General Fulgencio, 99
Battambang, Cambodia, 79
battery, invention of, 78
Batuta, Ibn, 35, 36
Bavaria, 54, 58, 62, 70
Bavarians, 66
Bay of Pigs invasion, 101
Bayeux tapestry, 27, 62
Beaker Ware culture, 6
Bechuanaland, 78, *see also* Botswana
Beethoven, Ludwig van, 72
Beijing, China, 35, 39, 59, 61, 81, 83, 85, 93, 105
Beirut, Lebanon, 8, 102, 104
Belfast, Ireland, 92
Belgian Congo, 86, 90
Belgian Republic, 74
Belgium, 80, 84, 86, 90, 96, 98, 100, *see also* Austrian,

Southern *or* Spanish Netherlands
Belgrade, Serbia, 44, 62, 66
Belize, 95, 105
Bell, Alexander G., 85
Benedictines, 24
Bengal, 23, 47, 49, 51, 67, 71, 73
Benin, 27, 35, 37, 67, 71
Benz, Karl, 86
Berber people, 92
Berber states, 33
Bering Strait, 59, 69
Bering, Vitus, 69, 71
Berlin airlift, 96
Berlin Blockade, 96
Berlin, Congress of, 84
Berlin, Germany, 58, 82, 92, 94, 95, 100, 104
East, 96, 100
West, 96
Berlin Olympics, 95
Berlin Wall, 87, 100, 104
Berliner, Emile, 87
Bermuda, 55, 63
Bern, Switzerland, 32
Bernadotte, Jean, 78
Berners-Lee, Tim, 104
Bernini, Gian Lorenzo, 46
Bethlehem, Judea, 14
Bey, Ahmed, 67
Bey, Ali, 59
Bhonsla, Sivaji, 61, 63
Bhopal, India, 105
Bhutto, Ali, 103
Bhutto, Benazir, 105, 107, 109
Biafra, 100
Big Bang Theory, 93
Bikini Atoll, Pacific, 97
Bismarck, Otto von, 84
Bithynia, 12, 14
Black Death, **34**
Black Hole of Calcutta, 71
Black, Joseph, 70
Black Sea, 62, 68, 72, 96
Black Sea Steppes, 74
Black September, 102
Black War, 81
Blair, Tony, 108
Blenheim, Battle of, 66
*Blitzkrieg*, 94
blood, circulation of, 54
Blood River, Battle of, 80
Bloody Sunday, 102
boat people, Vietnamese, 103
Boers, 86, 90
Bohemia, 24, 26, 32, 34, 36 38, 54, 56, 70, 82
Bokassa, Jean, 100, 102
Boleslav I, of Bohemia, 24
Bolívar, Simón, 79, 81
Bolivia, 17, 79, 81, 85, 95, 100
Bologna, Italy, 30, 104
Bolsheviks, 92
Bombay, India, 61, 63, 67
Bonaparte, Napoleon, 74, **78**
Boniface VIII, Pope, 36
Borneo, 39, 67, 71, 79, 83
Bornhöved, Battle of, 30
Bornu, West Africa, 69
Bosnia, 90, 106
Bosnia-Herzegovina, 106
Boston, U.S.A., 71, 73
massacre, 73
tea party, 73
Bosworth, Battle of, 40
Botany Bay, Australia, 73
Botswana, 98, 100, *see also* Bechuanaland
Boudicca, Queen of the Iceni, 16
Bourbon dynasty, 50, 66, 68, 84
Boutros Boutros Ghali, 107
Bouvines, Battle of, 30
Boxer Rebellion, 91
boycott of buses, U.S.A., 99
Boyle, Robert, 60
Boyne, Battle of the, 62
Braganza, house of, 58
Brandenburg, Germany, 38, 58, 60
Brasilia, Brazil, 101
Brazil, 47, 49, 69, 73, 79, 81, 87, 95, 97, 101, 105, 107
Breda, Peace of, 60
Breitenfeld, Battle of, 56
Brest-Litovsk, Treaty of, 92
Brétigny, Treaty of, 34
Brezhnev, Leonid, 100
Brian Boru, High King of Ireland, 26
Britain, 6, 16, 22
Britain, Great, 66, 67, 70, 71, 72, 73, 74, 75, 78, 79, 80, 82, 83, 84, 86, 90, 91, 92, 94, 96, 102, 105, 106, 108, 109
Britain, Battle of, 96
British, 69, 71, 73, 75, 78, 79, 80, 81, 82, 83, 84, 85, 86, 87, 90, 91, 92, 96
British Africa Company, 69
British Guiana, 70, 101, *see also* Guyana
British Honduras, 105
British India, **73**, 75, 85, 95
British Somaliland, 86, 90
British South Africa Company, 86
Britons, 24
Brittany, 6
Bronze Age, 6, 7, 8, 9, 10, 15
Brown, Louise, 102
Broz, Josip (Tito), ruler of Yugoslavia, 98
Bruce, James, 73
Bruce, Robert, King of Scotland, 34
Brulé, Etienne, 55
Brunanburh, Scotland, Battle of, 24
Brunelleschi, Filippo, 38
BSE, 'mad cow disease', 108
Buddha, 11, *see also* Siddhartha, Gautama
Buddhism, 11, 13, 17, 21, 51, 91
Buenos Aires, Argentina, 47
Buganda, 67, 75
Bugis people, 67, 71
Bukhara, 25, 85
Bulgaria, 22, 90, 96, 98
Bulgarians, 24, 28
Bulgars, 20, 22
Burgundians, 14, 16, 46
Burgundy, 24, 40
Burke, Robert, 85
Burkina Faso, 98
Burma, 27, 47, 49, 55, 67, 71, 73, 75, 81, 83, 87, 91, 95, 97, 105, 107
Burmese, 73, 79
Burton, Richard, 82
Burundi, 98, 104
Byzantine empire, **20**, 21, **22**, 24, 26, 28, 30, 32, 36, 40
Byzantium, 16, 20, *see also* Constantinople

# C

Cabinda, 98
Cabot, John, 41, 47
Cadiz, Spain, 50
Caesar, Julius, 14
Cahokia, U.S.A., 23, 29
Caillié, René, 80
Cairo, Egypt, 25, 35, 96
Calabria, Italy, 26, 28
Calais, France, 34, 48
Calcutta, India, 71, 73
California, U.S.A., 51, 55, 75, 83
Calvin, John, **46**
Calvinism, **46**, 48
Cambodia, 23, 27, 37, 55, 61, 71, 79, 81, 85, 87, 97, 103
Cambrai, Peace of, 46
camera, box, 87
Cameroon, 98
Cameroons, 86, 90
Camlan, Battle of, 20
Camp David, U.S.A., 103
Campbell clan, 62
Canaan, 8
Canada, 47, 55, 59, 61, 71, 75, 79, 83, 85, 95, 101, 107
Canada Act, 75
Canary Islands, 37, 39
Canberra, Australia, 93
Canmore, Malcolm, 26
*Canterbury Tales The*, 36
Canton, China, 45, 57, 63 67, 69, 71, 81, 95
Cape Colony, South Africa, 84
Cape Horn, Chile, 55
Cape of Bojador, Chile, 39
Cape of Good Hope, 39, 41, 59, 75, 78, 80
Cape Town, South Africa, 59, 104
Capetian dynasty, 24
Caribbean Sea, 48, 59
Carlist Wars, 80
Carloman, 22
Carnatic Coast, 79
Carolinas,
North and South, U.S.A., 61, 63, 69, 75
Carolingian dynasty, 22, 24
Carthage, North Africa, 11, 12, 14, 15, 21
Cartier, Jacques, 47
Cartwright, Edmund, 74
Casi di San Georgio, 38
Casimir III the Great, King of Poland, 34
Caspian Sea, 25, 68
Castile, Spain, 26, 30, 36, 42
Castro, Fidel, 99, 101
Çatal Hüyük, Turkey, 6
Cateau-Cambresis, Treaty of, 43
Cathars, 30
Catherine de Medici, 48
Catherine I, Tsarina of Russia, 68
Catherine II ('the Great'), of Russia, 72, 74
Catholic Church, 24, 26, 36, 44, 46, 48, 50, 54, 56, 57, 58
cave painting, 6
Cavour, Camillo, 84
Cayenne, Guiana, 57
Ceausescu, President, 104
Celsius, Anders, 70
Celts, 10, 12, 20
centigrade thermometer, 70
Central African Empire, 102
Central African Republic, 98, 100
Central Powers, 90
Cervantes, Miguel, 54
Ceuta, North Africa, 39
Ceylon, 59, 63, 75, 79, *see also* Sri Lanka
Chaco region, 95
Chad, 98, 104
Chaeronea, Battle of, 12
Chakri dynasty, 75
Chakri, Prince of Siam, 75
Châlons, Battle of, 16
*Challenger*, space shuttle, 105
Champa kingdom, 17
Champlain, Samuel de, 55
Chancellor, Richard, 48
Chanchan, Peru, 29
Chandragupta Maurya, Indian emperor, 7, 13
Chandragupta II, 17
Channel Islands, 34
Channel Tunnel, 106
Charge of the Light Brigade, Crimean War, 82
Charlemagne, **22**
Charles Albert, of Bavaria, 70
Charles of Anjou, 32
Charles VI, Emperor of Austria, 68, 70
Charles the Bold, Duke of Burgundy, 40
Charles I, King of England and Scotland, 56, 58
Charles II, King of England and Scotland, 60
Charles VIII, King of France, 40
Charles IX, King of France, 48
Charles I, King of Spain, **44**, *see also* Charles V, HRE
Charles II, King of Spain, 62, 66
Charles IV Luxembourg, King of Bohemia, Holy Roman Emperor, 34, 36
Charles IX, King of Sweden, 54
Charles V, Holy Roman Emperor, **44**, 45, 46, 47, 48
Charles XI, King of Sweden, 60
Charles XII, King of Sweden, 66
Charles Edward Stuart, 70
Charles Martel, 22
Charles, Prince of Wales, 104
Charles the Simple, King of the Franks, 24
Charleston, U.S.A., 75
*Charter 77*, 102
Chartists, 80
Chaucer, Geoffrey, 36
Chavín culture, 9, 11, 15
Chechenia, 106, 108, 109
Cheng Ho, Admiral, 39
Chernobyl, Ukraine, 104
Cherro, Sanchez, 95
Cheyenne people, 85
Chichen Itzá, Mexico, 25, 29, 31, 33
Ch'ien Lung, Emperor of China, 69
Chile, 47, 79, 85, 95, 103
Chimu people, 29, 31, 33, 41
Ch'in, *see* Qin dynasty, 31
Ch'ing dynasty, 57, **59**, *see also* Manchus
Chin dynasty, 29
China, 7, 9, 11, 13, **15**, 17, 21, 23, 25, 29, 31, 33, 35 37, 39, 45, 49, 51, 55, 57, **59**, 61, 63, 67, **69**, 71, 73, 75, 79, 81, 83, 85, 87, 91, 93, 95, 97, 99, 101, 103, 105, 109
China, Great Wall of, 15, 17
Chinese Communist Party, 93
Chinese Nationalists, 93
Chinese Revolution, 91
Chinese Soviet Republic, 95
Chirac, Jacques, 106
chocolate, 44
Chola kingdom, 23, 25
Choson dynasty, 37
Chou dynasty, *see* Zhou dynasty
Christ, Jesus, 14, 16
Christianity, 16, 17, 20, 21, 22, 24, 30, 44, 45, 47, 67
Christians, 26, 27, 28, 29, 33, 36, 45, 47, 57, 72, 82, 102, 104
Christina, Queen of Sweden, 56, 58
Chrosroes I, Sassanid emperor, 21
Chrysler Building, New York, 93
Chu Yuan-chang, 37
Churchill, John, Duke of Marlborough, 66
Churchill, Sir Winston, 96, 100
C.I.A.(Central Intelligence Agency), 99
C.I.S. (Commonwealth of Independent States), 106
Civil Rights Bill, 101
civil rights movement, 99, 100, 101
Classical Greece, **12**
classification of species, 70
Cleisthenes, 10
Clement VII, Pope, 46
Clement XIV, Pope, 72
Cleopatra, Queen of Egypt, 14, 15

Clinton, Bill, President, 107, 109
clipper ships, 81
Clive, Robert, of India, 71
Clontarf, Battle of, 26
Clovis, King of the Franks, 16
Cluny, France, 24
Cnut, King of Denmark, 26
Cochin-China, 81, 83, 85
Cochise people, 7
Cockerell, Christopher, 98
*Code Napoléon*, 78
coffee, first import of, 44
coins, first, 10
Colbert, Jean Baptiste, 60
Cold War, **97**, 101
Colombia, 47, 79, 81, 91, 95, 105
colonies, African, 84
Colorado, U.S.A., 83
Colosseum, Rome, 16
*Colossus I*, 96
Columbus, Christopher, 41, 101
Commonwealth,
Australian, 91
British, 94, 96, 100, 104
English, 58
communism, 92, 96, 97, 99, 100, 102, 104
*Communist Manifesto*, 82
Comneni dynasty, 26
compact disc (CD), 105
computer, first electronic, 96
Concordat of Worms, 26, 28
Concorde, plane, 102
Confederate States of America, 85
Confederation of North German States, 84
Confucius, *see* Kung Fu-tze, 11
Congo, 84, 90, 98, 100
Congo, Democratic Republic of, 108
Congress of Berlin, 84
Congress of Soviets, 92
Connecticut, U.S.A., 67
conquistadors, 45, 47, 49
Conrad of Franconia, 24
Constance of Sicily, 28
Constance, Council of, 38
Constantine, Roman emperor, 16
Constantinople, Roman and Byzantine capital, 14, 16, 20, 22, 28, 30, 32, 38, 40, 45
Contra rebels, 105
convicts, first transported to Australia, 75
Cook Islands, 91
Cook, James, **73**
Cooke, W., 80
Copernicus, Nicolaus, 46
Corded Ware culture, 6
Córdoba, Spain, 22, 24, 26
Cornwallis, General, 75
Corsica, France, 70, 72
Cortés, Hernando, 45
Cosimo de Medici, 38
Cossacks, 59, 60, 72
Costa Rica, 81, 95
Council of Nicaea, 16, 22
Counter Reformation, **46**
Courtrai, Battle of, 34
Crécy, France, Battle of, 34
Crespi, Peace of, 46
Cretans, 86
Crete, 8, 24, 60, 94
Crick, Francis, 98
Crimea, Russia, 34, 48, 74, 82
Crimean War, **82**
Cristofori, Bartolomeo, 66
Croatia, 34, 62
Croesus, King of Lydia, 10
Cromwell, Oliver, 58
Crusades, **27**, 28, 29, 30, 31, 33, 46
Cuba, 81, 85, 87, 93, 95, 99, 101, 104
Cuban Missile Crisis, **101**
Culloden, Battle of, 70
Cultural Revolution, **101**
Cumbria, England, 28
cuneiform writing, 6
Curaçao, 57
Curie, Marie, 86
Curie, Pierre, 86
Custer, Colonel G., 85
Customs Union, European, 96
Cuzco, Peru, 29, 33, 35, 39, 41
Cyprus, 8, 16, 94, 98, 100, 102
Cyrenaica, North Africa, 16
Cyrillic alphabet, 22
Cyrus II, King of Persia, 10, 12
czars, *see* tsars
Czech Republic, 106, 108
Czechoslovakia, 92, 96, 98

# D

Da Gama, Vasco, 41
da Vinci, Leonardo, 38, 40
Dagestan, Central Asia, 109
Dagon (Rangoon), 71
Daguerre, Louis, 80
Dahomey, 71, 86, 98
Dalai Lama, 91, 99
Dallas, Texas, 101
Damascus, Syria, 21, 25, 27, 28, 35, 39
Dampier, William, 63, 67
Danegeld, 24
Danelaw, 22, 24, 26
Danes, 22, 24, 58, 60, *see also* Denmark
Daniel, Prince of Moscow, 32
Dante, Alighieri, 32, 38
Danube, river, 6
Danzig, Poland/Prussia, 34, 74
Daoud, Muhammad, 103
Dardanelles Straits, 82
Darius I, King of Persia, 12
Dark Ages, Greece, 8
Darwin, Australia, 95
Darwin, Charles, 82
*Das Kapital*, 84
David, Askia, King of Songhai, 47
Davis, John, 51
D-Day, 94, 96
de Balboa, Núñez, 45
De Beers, 84
de Buffon, Georges, 70
De Chéseaux comet, 70
de Gaulle, General, 96, 98, 100, 102
de Guise, Duke Henri, 50
de Klerk, F.W., 104
de la Pérouse, François, 75
de la Salle, Robert, 61, 63
de Lamarck, Jean, 78
de León, Ponce, 45
de Orellana, Francisco, 47
de Pombal, Marquis, 70
de Quesada, Gonzalo Jiminez, 47
De Rivera, 92
de Valdivia, Pedro, 47
Deccan, India, 35, 47, 49, 57, 59, 63, 69, 79
decimal currency, 102
Declaration of Independence, American, 73
Declaration of Rights, 62
decolonization, of Africa, 98
Deerfield, Massachusetts, massacre, 67
Delaware, U.S.A., 67
Delcassé, French minister, 90
Delhi, India, 35, 37, 41, 47, 63, 69
Delhi, Islamic Sultanate of, 31
Delphi, Greece, 12
Democratic Forum, 106
Deng Xiaoping, 105, 109
Denmark, 24, 26, 30, 34, 36, 40, 48, 54, 56, 58, 66, 68, 102
Depression, The, **93**, 95
Descartes, René, 56, 58
Desert Storm, Operation, 106
Detroit, U.S.A., 67
Dezhnev, Cossack explorer, 59
Diadochi, the, 12
*Dialogues*, 56
diamonds, 84
Diana, Princess of Wales, 104, 108
Diaz, Bartholomeu, 41
Diaz, Porfirio, 85, 91
Diderot, Denis, 70
Dien Bien Phu, Battle of, 99
Dimitri, Prince of Moscow, 36
Dimitri, son of Ivan IV, 54
Diocletian, Roman emperor, 16
Directory, the, France, 74, 78
Disraeli, Benjamin, 84
*Divina Commedia, La*, 33
Djibouti, 98
Djugashvili, Josef, *see* Stalin
DNA structure, 98
Dnieper, river, 20
Dolly the sheep, 108
Domesday Book, 26
Don Carlos, Spanish pretender, 80
Don John of Austria, 49
*Don Quixote de la Mancha*, 54
Dong-son culture, 15
D'Orville, Albert, 61
Dover, Treaty of, 60
Downing Street declaration, 106
Drake, Sir Francis, 49, 50, 51
Dravidians, 9
*Dreadnaught*, 90
Dreyfus, Alfred, 86
Druze Muslims, 102
Dual Alliance, 84
Dubcek, Alexander, 100
Dublin, Éire, 28, 92
Dukas dynasty, 26
Duncan, King of Scotland, 42
Dunsinane, Scotland, 26
Duquesne, Marquis, 71
Dust Bowl, the, 95
Dutch, 48, 51, 54, 55, 57, 59, 60, 61, 63, 66, 71, 79, 80, 81, 84
Dutch East India Company, 54, 71
Dutch Guiana, 57
Dutch Republic, 58
Dutch Revolt, **48**, 55, 58
Duvalier, 'Papa Doc' and 'Baby Doc', 103
Dyer, General, 97
Dzungaria, Central Asia, 71

# E

Eannes, Gil, 38
Earth Summit Conference, 107
East Anglia, 22
East Berlin, 96, 98
East Germans, 100
East Germany, 96
East India companies
Dutch, 54, 71
English, 54, 55, 57, 61, 63, 67, 71, 73, 75, 79, 81, 83
French, 60, 63, 69
East Indies, 41, 45, 51, 55, 57, 59, 63, 79
East Jerusalem, 108
East Pakistan, 103, *see also* Bangladesh
East Prussia, Germany, 58
East Timor, 109
Easter Island, 27, 69
Easter Rising, Dublin, 92
Eastern Cape, 104
Eastern Church, 20, 26, *see also* Orthodox Church
Eastern Khanate, 33
Eastern Nigeria (Biafra), 100
Eastern Roman empire, 20 *see also* Byzantine empire
Eastman, George, 87
EC, *see* EEC
Eckert, John, 97
Ecuador, 7, 79, 81
Edict of Milan, 16
Edict of Nantes, 50
Edison, Thomas, 85
Edo (Tokyo), Japan, 49, 55, 75, 85
Edward of Wessex, 24
Edward the Confessor, 26
Edward I, King of England, 32
Edward II, King of England, 34
Edward III, King of England, 34
Edward IV, King of England, 40
Edward V, King of England, 40
Edward VI, King of England, 46
Edward VII, King of Britain, 90
Edward VIII, King of Britain, 94
EEC (European Economic Community), 98, 100, 102, 104
Egmont, Count, 48
Egypt, 21, 23, 25, 31, 33, 35, 45, 75, 78, 80, 82, 84, 86, 90, 92, 94, 96, 98, 102, 103, 104, 108
Egypt, Ancient, **7**, 8, **9**, 10, 11, 13, 14, 15, 16
Eiffel Tower, Paris, 86
Einstein, Albert, 90, 96
Éire, 94, 96, 102, 106, *see also* Ireland
El Alamein, Battle of, 96
El Cid, 26
El Mina, Ghana, 41, 57
El Niño, 109
El Salvador, 81, 95, 105
El Tajín, Central America, 11, 13, 21
Elba, Italy, 78
Eleanor of Aquitaine, 28
electric current, 80
electric dynamo, 80
electric telegraph, first, 80
Elissa, Princess of Tyre, 11
Elizabeth I, Queen of England, 48, 50, 54
Elizabeth II, Queen of Great Britain and Northern Ireland, 98
Elizabeth, Empress of Russia, 70
Empire State Building, New York, 95
Empty Quarter, the, 94
*Encyclopédie*, the first encyclopedia, 70
Engels, Friedrich, 82
England, 20, 22, 26, 32, 34, 36, 38, 40, 44, 46, 48, 49, 54, 56, 57, 58, 62
English, 24, 46, 50, 51, 59, 60, 66
English Civil War, **58**
English Poor Law, 48
English Royal Africa Company, 61
ENIAC, earl computer, 97
Enlightenment, the, 70
Entebbe, Uganda, 102
*Entente Cordiale*, 90
environment, 107
EOKA, 98
Equatorial Guinea, 98
Eric the Red, 25
Ericsson, Leif, 27
Eridu, Sumer, 6
Erie, Lake, 61
Eritrea, 86, 90, 96, 106
Estonia, 34, 56, 68, 106
Ethelred the Unready, King of England, 24
Ethiopia, 17, 21, 29, 31, 47, 67, 73, 100, 102, 104, 106
Etruscans, 10
EU (European Union), 106

Eugene, Prince of Savoy, 62, 66
Eumenes I, King of Pergamum, 12
Euphrates, river, 6
Euro, currency, 108
European Coal & Steel Treaty, 98
Everest, Mount, 99
Evesham, Battle of, 32
evolution, 82
Exclusion Crisis, 60
*Exxon Valdez*, 105
Ezana, King of Axum, 17

# F

Fahrenheit, Gabriel, 66
Faisal, King of Iraq, 92
Faisal, King of Saudi Arabia, 102
Falkland Islands, 73, 79, 81, 105
Falklands War, 105
famine,
African, 104, 106
Irish, 82
U.S.S.R., 94
Faraday, Michael, 80
farmers, early, **6**, 7
Farouk, King of Egypt, 98
Fascist movements, 92, 94
Fashoda Crisis, 86
Fath Ali, ruler of Persia, 75
Fatimid dynasty, 25, 29, 35
Fawkes, Guy, 54
Federated Malay States, 87
Fehrbellin, Battle of, 60
Feisal, King of Iraq, 98
Ferdinand, of Aragon, 40
Ferdinand II of Castile, 44
Ferdinand II, Holy Roman Emperor, 44, 46, 48
Fermi, Enrico, 97
Fertile Crescent, 6
Fez, Morocco, 25, 51
FFL (Free French Forces), 96
Field of the Cloth of Gold, 44
Fifth Republic, France, 98
Fiji, 59
Finland, 78, 92, 106
firearms, first, 36
First Empire, France, 78
First World War, **90**, *see also* World War One
Firuz, ruler of Delhi, 33
Five Year Plan, 92
Flanders, Belgium, 32
Fleming, Alexander, 92
Flemish, 34
flight, first solo across Atlantic, 93
first successful powered, 91
first woman solo across the world, 95
Flinders, Matthew, 75, 79
*Flyer I*, 91
flying shuttle loom, 68
Flodden, Battle of, 44
Florence, Italy, 36, 38, 40, 46, 68
Florida, U.S.A., 45, 49, 57, 75, 79, 83
Ford, Henry, 91
forest fires, 109
Formosa, 57, 63, 69, *see also* Taiwan
Fort Dauphin, Madagascar, 59
fossils, study of, 78
four-minute mile, first, 94
Fourteenth Amendment, 85
Fourth Republic, France, 96
France, 6, 20, 22, 24, 30, 32, 34, 38, 40, 44, 46, 48, 49, 50, 54, 56, **60**, 62, 66, 67, 68, 70, 71, 72, **74**, 82, 84, 86, 87, 90, 92, 94, 96, 98, 99, 102, 104, 106, 107
Franco, Francisco, General, 94, 102
Franco-Prussian War, 84
François I, King of France, 44, 46
Franklin, Benjamin, 71
Franks, 14, 16, 20, 22, 24
Franz Ferdinand, Archduke, 90
Frederick I Barbarossa, Holy Roman Emperor, 28
Frederick I, Elector of Brandenburg, 38
Frederick I, 'King in Prussia', 66
Frederick II, Hohenstaufen, Holy Roman Emperor, **30**, 31
Frederick II, ('the Great'), King of Prussia, **70**
Frederick III, Elector of Brandenburg, 66
Frederick VI of Hohenzollern, 38
Frederick William I, ('the Great Elector') of Brandenberg, 58
Frederick William I, King of Prussia, 66, 68
Free French Forces, *see* FFL
French, 32, 48, 54, 55, 58, 59, 61, 63, 66, 67, 69, 71, 73, 75, 78, 79, 84, 85, 86, 90
French Congo, 90
French Equatorial Africa, 90
French Guiana, 57, 95
French Revolution, **74**
French Somaliland, 90
French Wars of Religion, **48**
French West Africa, 90
Freud, Sigmund, 86
Friedland, Battle of, 78
Fronde, the, 58
Fujiwara clan, 23, 29
Fujiyama, Mount, 67

# G

Gabon, 98
Gadaffi, Colonel, 100
Gagarin, Yuri, 100
Galante, Maria, 59
Galatia, 12, 14
Galilei, Galileo, 50, 54, 56
Gallipoli, Turkey, 36, 38
Gama, Vasco da, 41
Gambia, 69, 78, 90, 98
Gandhara, India, 11
Gandhi, Indira, 101, 105
Gandhi, Mohandas (Mahatma), 93, 95, 97
Gandhi, Rajiv, 105, 107
Gang of Four, China, 103
Ganges, river, 9
Garibaldi, Giuseppe, 82, 84
Gascony, France, 30
Gaul (France), 14
Gauls, 12
Gautama Siddhartha, 11
Gaza, Egypt, 106
Geldof, Bob, 104
General Strike, in Britain, 92
Geneva, Switzerland, 46, 84, 99, 104, 106
Genghis Khan, 29, 31, 41
Genoa, Italy, 34, 36, 38, 70, 72
Geoffrey of Anjou 'Plantagenet', 28
geometry, 56
George I, King of United Kingdom 66
Georgia, Caucasus region, 55, 78
Georgia, U.S.A., 69
germ theory, 84
German African colonies, 90, 92
German South West Africa, 90, *see also* Namibia
Germanic peoples, 14, 16, 44, 46, 47
Germans, 67, 96
East, 100
Germany, 20, 22, 24, 30, 32, 54, 72, 78, 86, 90, 92, 93, 94, 96, 97, 104, 106
unification of, 84,
reunification of, 106
East, 98
West, 98
Gettysburg, U.S.A., Battle of, 85
Geza I, King of Hungary, 24
Ghana, 17, 23, 27, 55, 57, 80, 100, *see also* Gold Coast
Ghazan, ruler of Persia, 35
Ghent, Belgium, 50
Ghent, Pacification of, 50
Ghibellines, 30
Gibraltar, 66, 68, 72
Gilbert, Humphrey, 51
Giza, Egypt, 7
Gladstone, William, British prime minister, 86
Glarus, Switzerland, 32
*glasnost*, 104
Glencoe, Scotland, 62
Glendower, Owen, 38
gliders, 86
global warming, 109
Glorious Revolution, 62
Goa, India, 45, 47
Godaigo, Emperor of Japan, 35
Goethe, Johann Wolfgang von, 70
Gogra, India, 47
Golan Heights, Israel, 102
Gold Coast, 21, 41, 55, 57, 84, 90, *see also* Ghana
Gold Rush,
California, 83
New Zealand, 85
Golden Bull, 30
Golden Horde, khanate of the, 30, 32
Golden Temple, Amritsar, 61, 105
Gorbachev, Mikhail, 104, 106
Gordon, General, 86
Gothic style, architecture, 28, **30**
Goths, 14, 16
gramophone, first, 87
gravity, discovery of, 60
Great Britain, introduction of, 66, *see also* Britain, United Kingdom
Great Colombia, 79
Great Exhibition, 82
Great Fire of London, 60
Great Interregnum, 32
Great Lakes, 27, 61
Great Leap Forward, 99
Great Northern War, 66
Great Plague of London, 60
Great Pyramid of the Sun, 17
Great Schism, 26, **36**
Great Trek, Boer, 80
Great Wall of China, 15, 17
Great War, 90, *see also* First World War, World War One
Great Zimbabwe, 37, 39
Greece, 38, 48, 80, 86, 90, 92, 96, 98, 102, 104
Greece, Ancient, 6, **8**, **10**, 12, 14, 15
Greek alphabet, 22
Greek language, 20
Greek Orthodox, 20, 38, *see also* Orthodox Church
Greek War of Independence, **80**
Greeks, 80, 92, 100
Greenland, 25, 27, 32
Greenpeace, 105
Gregorian Calendar, 50
Gregory, Pope, 20
Gregory IX, Pope, 30
Gregory XIII, Pope, 50
Grenada, West Indies, 59, 73, 105
Grueber, John, 61
Guatemala, 7, 81, 95
Gudunov, Boris, 54
Guelphs, 30
guerilla warfare, 99, 101, 103, *see also* terrorists
Guevara, Che, 99, 101
Guiana,
British, 79
Dutch, 79
French, 79, 95
Guinea, 45, 84
Guinea Company, 61
Guinea-Bissau, 98
Guiscard, Robert, 26
Guiscard, Roger, 26, 28
Gujerat, India, 47, 49
Gulf War, 106
Gunpowder Plot, 54
gunpowder, invention of, 27
Gupta empire, 17, 21
Guru Nanak, 41
Gustav I, King of Sweden, 44
Gustavus Adolphus II, King of Sweden, 54, 56
Gustavus III, King of Sweden, 72, 74
*Gutenberg Bible*, 40
Gutenberg, Johann, 40
Guy Fawkes, 54
Guyana, 57, 95, 103
Guyenne, France, 30

# H

Habsburg family, 32, 38, 40, 44, 45, 46, 47, 48, 54, 62, 66, 74, 82
Habsburg, Albert I, Holy Roman Emperor, 32
Habsburg, Albert II, 38
Habsburg, Charles, *see* Charles V of Spain
Habsburg, Maximilian, 40
Habsburg, Rudolf of, 32
Hadrian, Roman emperor, 14
Hadrian's Wall, 16
Hague, Peace of the, 48, 58
Hahn, Otto, 94
Haile Selassie, Emperor of Ethiopia, 94, 102
Haiti, 49, 59, 75, 81, 91, 103, 107
Halley, Edmund, 62
Halley's Comet, 62
Hallstatt culture, 10
Hammurabi, King of Babylon, 8
Han dynasty, **15**, 17
Handel, Georg Friedrich, 66
Hankow, China, 95
Hannibal of Carthage, 14
Hanoi, Vietnam, 51, 97, 99
Hanover, Germany, 68
Hanover, house of, 66
Hanover, Treaty of, 68
Hanseatic League, 30, 36
Harald Bluetooth, 24
Harald Fairhair, 22
Harappa, India, 7
Hardie, Keir, 86
Hargreaves, James, 72
Harun al Rashid, Caliph, 23
Harvey, William, 54
Hashemite dynasty, 92
Hassan II, King of Morocco, 108
Hastings, Battle of, 26, 62
Hastings, Warren, 73
Hatshepsut, ruler of Egypt, 9, 108
Hattin, Battle of, 29
Hausaland, 25
Havel, Václav, 102, 104
Hawaii, U.S.A., 73, 87, 94, 97, 99
Hawkins, John, 49
Haydn, Franz Joseph, 72
heart transplant, first, 100
Hebrews, 8
Hebrides, Scotland, 32
Hebron, West Bank, 108
Heian Period, Japan, 23
Hejaz, Arabia, 92
helicopter, first, 95
Hellenistic Age, 12
Helsinki Convention, 102
Henri II, King of France, 46, 48
Henri III, King of France, 48, 50

Henri IV of Navarre, King of France, 48, 50, 54
Henri of Guise, 50
Henry I, King of England, 28
Henry II of Anjou, King of England, 28
Henry III, King of England, 32
Henry V, King of England, 38
Henry VI, King of England, 38, 40
Henry VII, King of England, 40, 41
Henry VIII, King of England, 44, 46
Henry VI, Holy Roman Emperor, 28
Henry VII of Luxembourg, Holy Roman Emperor, 34
Henry the Navigator, Prince of Portugal, 38
Henry I, of Saxony, 24
Henry Tudor *see* Henry VII of England
Henson, Matthew, 91
Heraclius, Byzantine emperor, 25
Herat, Persia, 37
heresy, **30**, 34
heretics, **30**, 38, 44, 46
Herod, King of Judea, 14
Herzegovina, 90
Hideyoshi, Toyotomi, 51
hieroglyphic writing, 7, 9, 75
Hillary, Edmund, 99
Hindu Kush, 25
Hindu religion, 9, 11
Hindus, 61, 67, 97
Hirohito, Emperor of Japan, 93, 105
Hiroshima, Japan, 97
Hispaniola, 49, *see also* Haiti
Hitler, Adolf, 94, 96
Hittites, 6, 8, 9
Ho Chi Minh, 97
Ho Chi Minh City, Vietnam, 99, *see also* Saigon
Hobart, Tasmania, 79
Hohenstaufen dynasty, 28, 30
Hohokam people, 15, 23
Hokkaido, Japan, 105
Holland, 72, 74, 78, 86, 98, *see also* Netherlands
Holocaust, the, 96
Holy Land, 27, 28, 29, 33
Holy League, 44, 62
Holy Roman Emperor, first, 24
Holy Roman Empire, 26, 28, 32, 38, 40, 44, 54, 56, 60, 62, 78
Home Rule, Irish, 84, 86
Home Rule Bill, 86
Home Rule League, 84
Homer, Greek poet, 10
Honduras, 81
Hong Kong, 81, 105, 109
Honshu, Japan, 105
Hooke, Robert, 58
Hoorne, Count, 48
Hopewell people, 13, 21, 27
horses, introduction of, 8
Hsin dynasty, 17
Hsiung-Nu, 15
Hsuan-tsang, 21
Huang Ho, river, 7, 21
Huari culture, 21, 27, 29
Huastec culture, 21, 29
Huayna Capac, 41
Hubble, Edwin, 93
Hubble Space Telescope, 107
Hudson Bay, 55, 61
Hudson, Henry, 55
Hudson's Bay Company, 61
Hugh Capet, 24
Huguenots, 48, 50, 56, 62
Hulagu Khan, 33
human rights, 100, 102
Humayun, Mogul ruler, 47, 49
Hundred Days, the, 78
Hundred Years' War, **34**
Hung Wu, Ming emperor, 37
Hungarian uprising, 98
Hungary, 22, 24, 26, 30, 34, 36, 38, 46, 48, 60, 62, 66, 70, 72, 82, 96, 98, 104, 106, 108
Huns, 15, 16, 17
Huron, Lake, 55, 61
Huron people, 59
hurricanes, 104, 109
Hurricane Mitch, 109
Hus, John, 38
Hussain, Ibn Ali, 67
Hussainid dynasty, 67
Hussein, King of Jordan, 98, 102, 108
Hussein, Saddam, 106
Hussite wars, 38
Hutu people, 106, 108
Hyderabad, India, 69
hydrogen bomb, 99
Hyksos people, 9

# I

IBM, 105
Ibn Ali Hussain, 67
Ibn Batutta, 35, 37
Ibn Saud, King of Hejaz and Nejd, 92, 94
Ibn Tughluk, Mohammed, Sultan of Delhi, 35
Iceland, 22, 27, 32, 84
Iceni tribe, 16
iconoclasm, 22
icons, 34
Idris Alooma, King of Kanem-Bornu, 51
Idris I, King of Libya, 100
Ife, 27, 29
Igbo Ukwu, 23
*Iliad, The,* 10
Il-Khan empire, 33, 35
Illinois, U.S.A., 67
Imperial Canal, China, 21
Inca people and culture, 31, 33, 35, **39**, 45, 47, 49, 75
Independence, American War of, **73**
India, **7**, 9, 11, 12, 13, 15, 21, 23, 25, 27, 29, 35, 37, 45, 46, **47**, 49, 51, 59, 61, 63, 69, 70, 71, **73**, 75, 79, 81, **83**, 91, 93, 95, 97, 101, 103, 105, 107, 109
India Act, 75
Indian Mutiny, **83**
Indian National Congress, 87, 93
Indochina, 87, 97, 99
Indo-Europeans, 9, 10
Indonesia, 25, 39, 51, 101, 109
Indus Valley culture, **7**, 9
Industrial Revolution, **72**, 78
industrialization, 84
influenza epidemic, 93
Innocent XI, Pope, 62
Inquisition, the, 28, 30, 46
Inuit people, 33
Investiture Controversy, 26
Iona, Scotland, 22
IRA (Irish Republican Army), 102, 104, 106
Iran, 8, 12, 45, 94, 99, 102, 104
Pahlavi II, 102
Iran-Contra scandal, 105
Iraq, 6, 21, 45, 55, 57, 92, 94, 100, 104, 106
Ireland, 22, 26, 28, 78, 82, *see also* Éire
Irish, 20, 58
Irish famine, 82
Irish Free State, 92, *see also* Éire
Irish Land Act, 84
Irkutsk, Siberia, 56
Iron Curtain, 98
iron-working, 10, 11, 17
Iroquois people, 23, 27, 59
Isabella of Castile, 40
Isandlwana, Battle of, 84
Isfahan, Persia, 51, 55
Ishme-Dagan, 8
Islam, **21**, 23, 25, 33, 35, 109
Isle of Man, 32
Ismail I of Persia, 45
Ismail, Mulai, 69
Israel, 8, 10, 94, 96, 100, 102, 103, 104, 108
Israelis, 102, 106
Issus, Battle of, 12
Istanbul, Turkey, 92, *see also* Byzantium, Constantinople
Italian Somaliland, 86, 90
Italy, 20, 22, 24, 26, 32, 34, 36, 38, 40, 44, 46, 48, 66, 74, 78, 82, **84**, 86, 90, 92, 94, 96, 98, 104
unification of, **84**
Itzcoatl, Aztec emperor, 39
Ivan I, Duke of Moscow, 34
Ivan III ('The Great'), Tsar of Russia, 40
Ivan IV ('the Terrible'), Tsar of Russia, 40, 46
Ivan VI, Tsar of Russia, 54, 70
Ivory Coast, 86, 98, 100
ivory trade, 106
Ivry, France, Battle of, 50

# J

Jackson, General 'Stonewall' 85
Jacobins, 74
Jacobites, 66, 70
Jacquerie, 36
Jahan, Shah, Mogul emperor, 57, 59
Jahangir, Mogul emperor, 55
Jamaica, 55, 59, 63
James Edward Stuart, ('the Pretender'), 66
James I, King of England, 48, 54, 55, 58, *see also* James VI, King of Scotland
James II, Duke of York, King of England and Scotland, 60, 62, 66
James IV, King of Scotland, 44
James VI, King of Scotland, *see also* James I, King of England, 48, 50, 54
Jameson Raid, 86
Jamestown, Virginia, 55
Jantszoon, Willem, 55
Japan, 7, 11, 13, 17, 21, 23, 27, 29, 33, 35, 37, 41, 46, 47, 49, 51, **55**, 59, 67, 72, 75, 83, 85, 87, 90, 91, 93, 94, 95, 97, 99, 107, 109
Japanese occupation of Manchuria, 95
Jarrow, England, 22
Java, East Indies, 25, 37, 51, 55, 61, 63, 71, 79, 81
Java Sea, 71
Java War, 81
*Jazz Singer, The,* 93
Jean II, King of France, 36
Jeanne d'Arc, 38
Jefferson, Thomas, U.S. President, 75
Jena, Battle of, 78
Jenkins' Ear, War of, 68
Jenner, Edward, 74
Jericho, Jordan, 6
Jerusalem, 10, 16, 21, 27, 28, 29, 31, 92, 96, 108
Jesuits, 46, 47, 55, 61, 72
Jesus Christ, 14, 16
jet rocket, first long-range, 96
Jews, 14, 16, 32, 34, 92, 94, 96, 106, 108, *see also* Hebrews
Jiang Jie Shi (Chiang Kai-shek), 93, 95
Jimmu, Emperor of Japan, 11
Johannesburg, South Africa, 86, 102
John I, King of England, 30
John of Luxembourg, 34
Johnson, Amy, 95
Johnson, President Lyndon B., 101
Johnson, Samuel, 70
Johore, Malaya, 67, 71
Jolliet, Louis, 61
Jomon Period, Japan, 7
Jordan, 6, 14, 92, 96, 98, 102
Jordan river, 106
José I, King of Portugal, 70
Joseph II, Emperor of Austria, 74
Juan Carlos, King of Spain, 102
Judah, 10
Judaism, 94
Judas Maccabeus, 14
Judea, Palestine, 14, 16
Jugurtha of Numidia, 15
Julian, monk, 21
July Revolution, 80
jumbo jet, first, 102
Justinian, Byzantine emperor, **20**, 21
Jutes, 14, 16

# K

K'ang Hsi, Emperor of China, 61, 67
Kabila, Laurent, 108
Kabul, Afghanistan, 45, 47, 59, 63, 109
Kaifeng, China, 25
Kairouan, North Africa, 21, 25
Kalmar, Union of, 36, 44
Kamakura Period, Japan, 29, 35
Kamchatka, Russia, 62
Kandahar, India, 51, 59, 63
Kanem-Bornu, 23, 37, 51
Kano, Nigeria, 69
Karamanli dynasty, 67
Karelia, Finland, 32, 54, 56, 68
Karlowitz, Treaty of, 62
Kashmir, India, 47, 51, 101
Katanga, Congo, 100
Kay, John, 68
Kazakhstan, Central Asia, 85
Kazembe, 71
Keating, Paul, 107
Kedah, Malaya, 81
Kei-ki, Japanese shogun, 85
Kemäl, Mustafa, 90, 92, *see also* Atatürk
Kennedy, John F., U.S. President, 101
Kennedy, Robert, U.S. Senator, 101
Kenneth MacAlpin, King of Scotland, 22
Kent State University, Ohio, 103
Kenya, 86, 90, 98, 100, 108
Kenyatta, Jomo, 100
Kepler, Johannes, 54, 56
Kerala, India, 25
KGB, 106
Khalij dynasty, 33
Khan Krum, 22
Khan, Genghis, 29, 31, 41
Khan, Hulagu, 33
Khan, Kublai, 33
Khan, Nadir, 69
Khan, Ogadei, 31
Khanate of the Golden Horde, 30, 32
Khartoum, Sudan, 86
Khayyam, Omar, 26
Khazars, 22, 24
Khitan kingdom, 25
Khiva, Central Asia, 85
Khmer dynasty, 23
Khmer Republic, 103
Khmer Rouge, 103
Khomeini, Ayatollah, 102, 104
Khorzim, Battle of, 60
Khrushchev, Nikita, 98, 100, 102
Khwarizm empire, 31
Kiev, Russia, 22, 24, 26, 60, 68
Kievan Russia, 24, 26

Kilby, Jack, 99
Killing Fields, the, 103
Kilwa, East Africa, 31
Kim Il Sung, 107
King George's War, 71
King James' Bible, 54
King, Martin Luther, 99, 101
Kingston, Jamaica, 63
Kleist, Ewald von, 70
Knights Hospitaller, 46
Knights Templar, 34
Knossos, Crete, 8
Knox, John, 46, 50
Kobe, Japan, 107
Kongo kingdom, 37, 41, 45, 61
Kongsompong, General Sunthorn, 107
Koprülü, Mohammed, 59
Korea, 13, 15, 17, 21, 25, 37, 51, 57, 85, 91, 97, 99, 107
North, 97, 99, 107
South, 97, 99
Korean Airlines 007, 105
Korean War, 99
Koryo, 25
Kosovo, Serbia, 108
Kosovo, Battle of, 36
Kowloon, China, 85
Krak des Chevaliers, Syria, 29
*Kristallnacht*, 94
Kuala Lumpur, Malaya, 79
Kublai Khan, 33
Kuchuck-Kainarji, Treaty of, 72
kulaks, 94
Kulikova, Russia, Battle of, 36
Kumbi, Ghana, 31
Kung Fu-tze, 11
Kuomintang, 93
Kurds, 108
Kush, 9, 11
Kushan empire, 17
Kuwait, 106
Kyoto, Japan, 37

# L

La Rochelle, France, 56
La Tène culture, 12
La Venta, Mexico, 9, 11, 13
Labrador, Canada, 27, 47
Labuan, Borneo, 83
Lagos, Nigeria, 86
Lahore, Pakistan, 71, 91
Laika, space dog, 98
Lake Peipus, Battle of, 30
Lalibela, Ethiopia, 29, 31
Lalibela, King of Ethiopia, 29, 31
Lamarck, Jean de, 78
Lancaster House Conference, 102
Landström, Battle of, 60
Landstuhl, Germany, Battle of, 44
Laos, 99, 103
Lao-tze, 11
Las Navas de Tolosa, Battle of, 30
Lascaux, France, 6
Latin empire, 32
Latin language, 8, 20, 24
Latins, 10
Latvia, 92, 106
Lavoisier, Antoine, 72
Law, John, 68
Lawrence, Colonel T.E., 92
League of Augsburg, 62
War of the, 62
League of Nations, 92, 93, 94
mandated territories, 94
Lebanon, 8, 10, 80, 92, 94, 96, 102, 104
Lechfeld, Battle of, 24
Leeson, Nick, 106
Leiden Jar, 70
Leif Ericsson, 27
Lenin (Vladimir Ilyich Ulyanov), 92
Lennon, John, 105
Leonardo da Vinci, 38, 40
Leonov, Alexei, 100
Leopold I of Austria, 34
Leopold I, Emperor of Austria, 66
Leopold II, Emperor of Austria, 74
Leopold, King of Belgium, 90
Lepanto, Battle of, 48
Lepenski Vir, Central Europe, 6
Lesotho, 98, *see also* Basutoland
Leszczynski, Stanislaus, 66, 68
Leuthen, Poland, Battle of, 71
Lewinsky, Monica, 109
Lhasa, Tibet, 61
Liao dynasty, 25
Liberia, West Africa, 80, 82, 90, 98
Libya, 17, 80, 90, 94, 96, 98, 100, 104
light bulb, first, 84, 85
Lilienthal, Otto, 86
Lima, Peru, 47
Lin Tse-hsu, 81
Lincoln, Abraham, U.S. President, 85
Lindbergh, Charles, 93
Lindisfarne, England, 22
Lindisfarne Gospels, 20
Linear A, writing, 8
Linear B, writing, 8
Linnaeus, Carolus, (Carl von Linné), 70
Lippershey, Hans, 54
Lisbon, Portugal, 70
Lisbon, Treaty of, 60
Lister, Joseph, 84
Li Ta-chao, 93
Lithuania, 36, 74, 92, 106
Little Big Horn, U.S.A., Battle of, 85
Liu Bang, Emperor of China, 15
Live Aid, 104
Livingstone, David, 82, 84
Livonia, 34, 48, 56, 68
Llewelyn, Prince of Wales, 32
Lockerbie, Scotland, 104
logarithms, 54
Lollards, 36
Lombards, people, 14, 20, 22
Lombardy, Italy, 84
Lon Nol, 103
London, England, 36, 60, 84, 90, 100, 102, 106
Long March, the, 95
Longshan period, 7
Lorraine, France, 68
Los Angeles, U.S.A., 75, 107
Louis of Anjou, 36, *see also* Louis of Hungary
Louis V, Carolingian king of France, 24
Louis IX, King of France, 31, 33
Louis XII, King of France, 40
Louis XIII, King of France, 54, 56
Louis XIV, King of France, 58, **60**, 66
Louis XVI, King of France, 74
Louis XVIII, King of France, 78
Louis the Great of Hungary, 34, *see also* Louis of Anjou
Louis III, King of Germany, 24
Louis II, King of Hungary, 46
Louis Philippe, King of France, 80
Louisbourg, Canada, 71
Louisiana Purchase, 79
Louisiana, U.S.A., 63, 75
L'Ouverture, Toussaint, 75
Lovelace, Ada, 80
Loyang, China, 9
Loyola, Ignatius, 46
Lübeck, Germany, 30, 56
Lucca, Italy, 84
Lucerne, Switzerland, 32
Lucknow, Relief of, 83
Luddites, 78
*Luftwaffe*, German air force, 94
Lund, Battle of, 60
Lunda kingdom, Central Africa, 70
Luther, Martin, 44
Lutheranism, 44, 46
Lützen, Germany, 56
Luxembourg, 34, 86, 98
Luxembourg dynasty, 34, 96
Luxor, Egypt, 103
Lvov, Ukraine, 72
Lydia, Turkey, 10

# M

Macao, 49
Macbeth, Earl of Moray, 26
MacDonald clan, 62
Macedonia, ancient, 12, 14
Macedonia, 106
Macedonian dynasty, Byzantine empire, 22
Machiavelli, Niccolò, 44
Mackenzie King, Canadian Prime Minister, 95
Madagascar, 59, 63, 86, 90, 98
Madeira, 39
Madras, India, 55, 59, 63, 67, 71, 107
Magadha, India, 13
Magdeburg, Germany, 58
Magellan, Ferdinand, 45
Magellan Straits, 45
*Magna Carta*, 30
Magnus the Good, King of Norway, 26
Magyars, 22, 24
Mahdi, the, Sudanese religious leader, 86
Mahmud, Sultan of, Ghazni, 25, 27
Maine, France, 30
Maine, U.S.A., 59
Majapahit kingdom, Java, 37
Majuba Hill, Battle of, 86
Makarios, Archbishop, President of Cyprus, 98
Makuria, 21
Malacca, Malaya, 45, 59, 79
Malacca Straits, 79
Malawi, 98, *see also* Nyasaland
Malaya, 45, 59, 67, 71, 75, 79, 81, 87, 91, 97, 101
Malcolm Canmore, 26
Malcolm IV, King of Scotland, 28
Malcolm X, civil rights leader, 101
Malden, Battle of, 24
Maldives, 39
Mali, 31, 35, 37, 41, 45, 47, 98
Mallia, Crete, 8
Malta, 46
Mamelukes, Egyptian, 33, 37, 78
Manchu dynasty, 55, **59**, 63, 83, 91
Manchukuo, Republic of, 95
Manchuria, 57, 59, 91, 95
Manco Inca, 47
Mandalay, Burma, 83
Mandela, Nelson, 106, 108
Manhattan, U.S.A, 55
Manila, Philippines, 49
Mansa Musa, King of Mali, 35
Manuel Comnenus, Byzantine emperor, 28
Manzikert, Battle of, 26
Mao Zedong, 93, 95, 97, 99, 101, 103
Maori people, 23, 27, 83
Marathas, 61, 63, 67, 69, 71, 73
Marathon, Greece, Battle of, 12
Marchfeld, Battle of, 32
Marco Polo, 33
Marconi, Guglielmo, 86, 91
Marcos, Ferdinand, 101, 105
Margaret, Queen of Denmark & Norway, 36
Margaret, Queen of Scotland, 32
Maria Galante, 59
Maria Theresa of Austria, 68, **70**
Mariam, Mengistu, 104
Marie of Burgundy, 40
Marienburg, Prussia, 34
Marignano, Battle of, 44
Marius, Roman general, 14, 15
Marlborough, Duke of, John Churchill, 66
Marquette, Jacques, 61
Mars, 109
Marshall Plan, 97
Marx, Karl, 82, 84
Marxist Party, Russia, 86
Marxists, 86, 99
Mary I, Queen of England, 48
Mary II, Queen of England, 62
Mary, Queen of Scots, 46, 48, 50
Maryland, U.S.A., 57
Masada, Israel, 16
Masai people, 73
Massachusetts Bay Colony, 57, 59, 63
Massachusetts, U.S.A., 51, 57, 59, 63
Massawa, Ethiopia, 47
Mataram dynasty, 55
Mataram, Java, 25, 55, 71
Mathilda, Queen of England, 28
Mau Mau, 98
Mauchly, John, 97
Mauretania, 17, 98
Mauritius, 51, 59, 67, 69, 79
Maurya dynasty, 13, 15
Maximilian of Bavaria, 54
Maximilian Habsburg, 40
Maximilian II, Holy Roman Emperor, 48
Maximilian, Emperor of Mexico, 85
May '68, **100**
Mayan culture, 9, 11, 13, **17**, 31, 33, 35, 41
Mayapán, Mexico, 31, 41
*Mayflower, The*, 57
Mazarin, Cardinal, 58
Mazowiecki, Tadeusz, 104, 106
Mazrui dynasty, 71
Mbeki, Thabo, 108
McCarthy, Senator, 99
Mecca, Arabia, 21, 35, 82
mechanical adding machine, 58
Medes, 8, 10
Media, 10, 12
Medici family, 38, 46, 68
Medici, Catherine de', 48
Medici, Cosimo de', 38
Medici, Lorenzo de', 38, 40
Medina, Arabia, 21
Meerut, India, 83
megaliths, 6
Mehemet Ali, viceroy of Egypt, 78
Mehmet II, Sultan of Turkey, 41
Meiji Restoration, Japan 85
Meir, Golda, 100
Mekong, river, *61*
Melbourne, Australia, 81
Mendel, Gregor, 84
Menelik, ruler of Ethiopia, 86
Menes, King of Egypt, 7
Mengistu Mariam, 104
Mercator, Gerardus, 50
Mercia, England, 22
Meroë, 17, 45

Merovingian dynasty, 16, 22
Mesopotamia, **6**, 8, 10, 12, 14, 16
Methodist movement, 68
Metropolitan Police Force, 80
Mexico, 7, 9, 11, 13, 15, 17 21, 23, 31, 37, 39, **45**, 47, 81, 83, 85, 91, 95, 97
*mfecane*, 78
Michael, Tsar of Russia, 54
Michael Paleologus, Byzantine emperor, 32
Michelangelo Buonarroti, 38
Michigan, Lake, 61
Midway, Battle of, 97
Mieszko I of Poland, 24
Milan, Italy, 32, 38, 40, 44, 82
Milan, Edict of, 16
millennium, 109
Minamoto, Yoritomo, 29
Minamoto, Yoshitsume, 29
Ming dynasty, China, 37, 39, 59
Minoans, **8**
Minos, King of Crete, 8
Mississippi Company, 68
Mississippi mound-builders, 21, 23, 31, 33
Mississippi, river, 29, 57, 61, 63
Mississippi Valley Culture, **23**
Missouri, river, 29
Mitanni, 8
Mithridates I, King of Parthia, 14
Mithridates I, King of Pontus, 12, 14
Mitterand, François, 104
Mixtec culture, 25
Mobuto Sese Seko, 100, 108
Moche, Peru, 15, 29
Model Parliament, 32
Modena, Italy, 84
Mogadishu, Somalia, 106
Mogul empire, 45, **47**, 51, 55, 57, 59, 61, 63, 67, 69, 71, 79, 83
Mohacs, Hungary, 46, 62
Mohammed, prophet, **21**
Mohammed Koprülü, 59
Mohenjo-Daro, India, 7
Moldavia, 34, 74
Molucca Islands, 45
Mombasa, East Africa, 51, 69, 71
monasticism, 17, 20
Mongolia, 17, 23, 25, 29, 63, 67
Mongols, 30, **31**, 32, 33, 35, 36, 37, 40, 47, 48, 49
Monmouth, Duke of, 62
Monroe Doctrine, 81
Monroe, U.S. President, 81
Mons people, 47, 71
Monte Albán, Mexico, 11, 13
Monte Cassino, Italy, 20
Montenegro, 84, 90
Montevideo, Uruguay, 69
Montezuma, Aztec ruler, 39
Montfort, Simon de, 30, 32
Montgomery, General, 96
Montreal, Canada, 47, 59, 71, 73
Montségur, France, 30
Moon, first man on, 101
Moors, 22, 26, 54
Moravia, 22, 32, 38
Morgarten, Switzerland, 32
Morgarten, Battle of, 34
Morocco, 17, 23, 41, 51, 69, 82, 90, 92, 98
Morse Code, 83
Morse, Samuel, 83
Moscow, Russia, 28, 34, 36, 40, 48, 50, 68
motion pictures, 86
motor car,
first, 86
mass production of, 91
Mount Everest, 99
Mountbatten, Lord, 102
Mozambique, 45, 84, 90, 98, 100, 102
Mozart, Wolfgang Amadeus, 70, 72
Mubarak, Hosni, 104
Mugabe, Robert, 104
Muhammed, Aga, ruler of Persia, 75
Muhammed Ali, ruler of Persia, 90
Muhammud of Ghur, 29
Muhlberg, Germany, 46
Mukden, Manchuria, 57, 59
Mulai Ismail, 69
multiracial elections, first in South Africa, 106
Munich, Germany, 94, 102
Munich Conference, 94
Munich Olympics, 102
Münster, Germany, 46
Murad III, Sultan of Turkey, 49
Murat I, Sultan of Turkey, 38
Mururoa atoll, 107
Muscat, 59
Muscovites, 36
Muscovy Company, 32
Muslims, 21, 23, 26, 27, 30, 33, 34, 40, 47, 97, 102, *see also* Islam
Mussadeq, 99
Mussolini, Benito, 92, 94
Mustafa Kemäl, 90, *see also* Atatürk
Mwenemutapa kingdom, 57
Myanmar, *see also* Burma
Mycenae, Greece, **8**
Myriokephalon, Turkey, 28
Mysore, India, 75, 81

# N

Nabataeans, 10, 12, 14, 16
Nabopolassar, King of Babylon, 10
Nadir Khan, 69
Nagasaki, Japan, 49, 57, 59
Nagy, Imre, 98
Namibia, 98, 106, *see also* South West Africa
Nanak, Guru, founder of the Sikhs, 41
Nanking, China, 29, 91, 95
Nanking, Treaty of, 81
Nantes, Edict of, 48, 50
Napier, John, 54
Naples, Italy, 38, 40, 44, 68, 84
Napoleon Bonaparte, 74, 75, **78**, 80
Napoleon III, 82
Nara, Japan, 23
Narai, King of Siam, 61, 63
Narai, Phra, ruler of Siam, 51
Narva, Battle of, 66, 68
Nasser, Gamal Abdul, 98
Natal, South Africa, 80, 82, 84
National Assembly, France, 74
National Convention, France, 74
Nationalist Party, China, 97
South Africa, 96
Native North Americans, 61, 73, 81, 85, 87
Native Titles Bill, 107
NATO (North Atlantic Treaty Organization), 97, 108
Navarino, Battle of, 80
Navarre, Spain, 30, 44
Nawab of Bengal, India, 71
Nazca people, 15
Nazca, Peru, 15
Nazi Party, 94, 95, 96
Nebuchadnezzar II, King of Babylon, 10
Nehru, Jawaharlal, 101
Nejd, Arabia, 92
Nelson, Admiral, 78
Netanyahu, Benjamin, 108
Netherlands, 44, 48, 50, 54, 60, 68, 74, 96, 98, *see also* Dutch Republic, Holland
Neva, Battle of the River, 30
Nevsky, Alexander, 30, 32
New Albion, 51
New Amsterdam, 57
New Deal, 95
New England, 57, 61
New France (Canada), 55, 67, 71
New Granada, 79
New Guinea, 67
New Hampshire, U.S.A., 59
New Haven, Connecticut, 67
New Hebrides, 73
New Jersey, U.S.A., 61
New Mexico, U.S.A., 55, 97
New Model Army, 58
New Netherlands, 61
New Orleans, U.S.A., 67
New South Wales, Australia, 75
New Spain (South America), 79
New World, 44, 45
New York, U.S.A., 57, 61, 69, 71, 87, 93, 95, 101, 102, 105, 107
New Zealand, 23, 27, 59, 73, 83, 85, 87, 91, 99, 105
Newcomen, Thomas, 66
Newfoundland, Canada, 27, 41, 45, 51, 55, 67, 71, 91
Newton, Isaac, 60, 62
Ngong Hills, East Africa, 73
Niagara Falls, 61
Nicaea, Anatolia, Council of, 16, 22
Nicaragua, 81, 95, 103, 105, 107
Nicholas II, Tsar of Russia, 86, 92
Nicolet, Jean, 57
Nicot, Jean, 48
Niépce, J-N, 80
Niger, 51, 98
Niger, river, 75, 78
Nigeria, 13, 35, 63, 86, 90, 98, 100, 106
Nigerian Civil War, 100
Nightingale, Florence,
Nijmegen, Peace of, 60
Nile, Battle of the, 75
Nile, river, 7, 82
Nineveh, Assyria, 6, 8, 10
Nixon, Richard, U.S. President, 103
Nkrumah, Kwame, Prime Minister of Ghana, 98, 100
No plays, 35
Nobatia, 21
Nobunaga, Oda, 41, 49
Nok people, 13
Nördlingen, Battle of, 56
Noriega, General, 105
Normandy, France, 22, 24, 30
Normandy, William of, 26, *see also* William I ('the Conqueror') King of England
Normandy landings, 94
Normans, 24, 26, 28
North Carolina, U.S.A., 63, 69
North German Confederation, 84
North Korea, 97, 99, 107
North Pole, 91
North Vietnam, 15, 101
Northern Ireland, 92, 100, 102, 106, 108
Northern Rhodesia, 98, *see also* Zambia
Northern Sung dynasty, 25
Northumbria, England, 22
Norway, 22, 24, 26, 32, 56, 90
Nova Scotia, Canada, 55, 67, 71
Novgorod, Russia, 22, 40
Nubia, 9, 13, 17, 21, 45
nuclear accidents, 103, 104, 109
nuclear missiles, 105
nuclear reactor, first built, 97
Nuclear Test Ban Treaty, 100
nuclear testing, 105
nuclear weapons, 97, 100, 105, *see also* atomic bombs
Numidia, 15
Nuremberg, Germany, 46
Nuremburg Laws, 94
Nuremburg Trials, 96
Nyasaland, 90, 98, *see also* Malawi
Nystadt, Peace of, 68
Nzinga Nkuwu of the Kongo, 41

# O

O'Neill, Hugh, Earl of Tyrone, 50
OAU (Organization for African Unity), 100
Oaxaca, Mexico, 11, 13, 21
Obote, Milton, 100
Octavian, 14, 15, *see also* Augustus, Emperor
October Revolution, 92
*Odyssey, The*, 10
OEEC (Organization for European Economic Cooperation), 96
Oersted, Hans, 80
Offa, King of Mercia, 22
Ogadei Khan, 31
Ohio, river, 11
oil industry, 83, 98, 99, 102
oil spills, 102, 105, 106
Okhotsk, Siberia, 58
Okinawa, Japan, 97
Oklahoma City, U.S.A., 107
Olaf II, King of Norway, 26
Olaf Skötkonung, King of Sweden, 24
Olaf Tryggvason, King of Norway, 24
Oleg the Wise, ruler of Russia, 22
Oliva, Treaty of, 60
Olmec culture, 9, 11
Olympic Games, 10, 86, 95, 102
Oman, Arabia, 67, 71
Omayyad caliphate, 21, 22
Omdurman, Battle of, 86
*On the Origin of the Species*, 82
Onin War, 41
Ontario, Lake, 61
OPEC (Organization of Petroleum Exporting Countries), 100, 102
opium, 79, 81
Opium Wars, 69, **81**, 83, 85
oracle bone, writing, 9
Oran, North Africa, 45
Orange Free State, South Africa, 82, 86, 90
Orkney, Scotland, 6, 40
Orléans family, 38
Orléans, France, 38
Orthodox Church, 20, 26, 34, 38
Osman I, Sultan of Turkey, 33
Ostrogoths, 14, 16, 20
Otago, New Zealand, 83
Otrepieff, Grigoriy, Russian pretender, 54
Ottawa river, 55
Otto I, Holy Roman Emperor, 24
Otto, Prince of Bavaria, King of Greece, 80
Ottokar II, King of Bohemia, 32
Ottoman empire, 33, 36, 51, 72, 80, 92
Ottoman Turks, 33, 38, 40, 41, 44, **45**, 46, 47, 49, 55, 57, 59, 60, 62, 80
Oudh, India, 83

Outremer, Christian kingdom, 33
Owens, Jesse, 95
Oxenstierna, Axel, 56
Oxford, England, 30, 68
oxygen, discovery of, 72
Oyo kingdom, 55, 67
ozone layer, hole in, 105

# P

Pachacuti, Inca, 39
Pacific, 45, 58, 63, 73, 75, 94, 97, 105
Pacification of Ghent, 50
Pagan, Burma, 27
Paine, Thomas, 74
Pakistan, 13, 97, 99, 101, 103, 105, 107, 109
Palaeolithic people, 6
Palatinate, Germany, 62
Palestine, 8, 10, 14, 27, 33, 45, 92, 94, 96
Palestine Liberation Organization, *see* PLO
Palestinians, 102, 104, 106, 108
Palmyra, Syria, 16
Panama, 45, 91, 95, 105
Panama Canal, 87, 91
Panipat, Battles of, 47, 73
Panmunjon, Treaty of, 99
Papadopoulos, George, 102
Papal States, 84
paper, invention of, 17
Papua, 91
Paracas culture, 13
Paracas Necropolis, 15
Paraguay, 47, 55, 79, 95
Paris, France, 28, 30, 36, 50, 58, 78, 82, 84, 86, 96, 108
Paris Commune, 84
Paris Exposition, 86
Paris, Peace of, 72, 73
Paris, Treaties of, 75, 82
Park, Mungo, 75, 78
Parliament, birth of English, 30
Parma, Italy, 84
Parthenon, Athens, 12
Parthia, 12, 14
Parthians, 15, 17
Pascal, Blaise, 58
Passarowitz, Peace of, 66
Pasteur, Louis, 84
Pathans, 41
Patzinaks, 28
Paul of Tarsus, 16
Pavia, Battle of, 46
Pearl Harbor, Hawaii, 94, 97
Peasants' Revolt, 36
Pedro I, King of Brazil, 81
Pedro II, King of Brazil, 87
Peel, Sir Robert, 80
Pegu, Burma, 47, 71
Peleset, 8
Peloponnese, Greece, 62
Peloponnesian Wars, 12
Penang, Malaya, 71, 75, 79
penicillin, discovery of, 92
Peninsular War, 78
Penn, William, 63
Pennsylvania, U.S.A., 63, 83
Penny Black, the, 82
Pepin III, 22
Pequot War, 57
*perestroika*, 104
Pergamum, Turkey, 12, 14
Pericles, 12
Perlis, Malaya, 91
Perón, Eva, 99
Perón, Isabel, 103
Perón, Juan, 97, 99
Pérouse, François de la, 75
Persepolis, Persia, 12
Persia, 10, **12**, 13, 14, 16, 20, 21, 25, 27, 33, 37, 45, 51, 54, 55, 57, 69, 75, 80, 90, 94
Persian Gulf, 39, 106
Persians, 8, 10, 12, 21, 35, 55, 67
personal computer (PC), 103, 105
Peru, 7, 9, 11, 13, 15, 29, 31, 35, 39, 41, **45**, 47, 49, 75, 85, 95, 109
Peter I ('the Great'), Tsar of Russia, **62**, 66, 68
Peter III, Tsar of Russia, 72
Petra, Jordan, 12, 14
Phaistos, Crete, 8
pharaohs, 9
Philadelphia, U.S.A., 63
Philadelphia Congress, 73
Philby, Harry, 94
Philip II, King of Macedonia, 12
Philip II, King of Spain, 44, 48, 50
Philip IV, King of Spain, 56
Philip V, King of Spain, 66, 68
Philippe II, King of France, 29, 30, 36
Philippe the Good of Burgundy, 36
Philippines, the, 45, 49, 79, 81, 87, 99, 101, 105
Philistines, 8
Phoenicia, 10, 12
Phoenicians, 8
photograph, first, 80
photographic process, first practical, 80
Phrygia, 10
piano, first, 66
Piedmont-Sardinia, 82, 84
Pilgrims, 57
Pilsudski, Jósef, 92
Pinkie, Battle of, 46
Pinochet, General, 103, 108
Pitt, William, the Younger, 74
Pizarro, Francisco, 45
planets, movement of, 46
Plassey, Battle of, 71, 73
Plataea, Greece, Battle of, 12
Plate, river, 47
PLO (Palestinian Liberation Organization), 102, 104, 107
Plymouth, England, 57
Podolia, 60, 62
Poitiers, France, 22, 34
Poitiers, Battle of, 22
Pol Pot, 103
Poland, 24, 26, 30, 34, 36, 46, 48, 50, 56, 58, 60, 62, 66, 72, 74, 82, 92, 94, 96, 98, 104, 106, 108
Poles, 38, 60, 68
polio, first inoculations against, 99
Polish Succession, War of the, 68
pollution, 107, 109
Polovtsy, 26
Poltava, Battle of, 66, 68
Polynesian islands, 23
Pombal, Marquis de, 70
Pomerania, 72
Pompey, 14
Pondicherry, India, 61, 63, 73
Pontius Pilate, 16
Pontus, 12, 14
Poor Laws, English, 48
Port Philip Bay, Australia, 81
Port Royal, Jamaica, 55
Portsmouth, Treaty of, 91
Portugal, 27, 28, 36, 38, 46, 47, 54, 55, 58, 59, 60, 66, 70, 72, 80, 82, 90, 94, 102, 104
Portuguese, 38, 39, 41, 45, 47, 49, 50, 51, 57, 59, 61, 63, 67, 69, 100
Portuguese Guinea, 90
Posen, Poland, 74
postage stamp, first, 82
Potala Palace, Lhasa, 61
Potsdam, Germany, 58
Pragmatic Sanction, 68
Prague, Czech Republic, 34, 56, 58, 70, 82, 100
Prague Spring, 100
Premsyl dynasty, 34
Presbyterianism, 50
Pretoria, South Africa, 82
Priestley, Joseph, 72
*Principia*, 52
printing press, first, 40
printed book, earliest, 23
Pripet region, 20
Proclamation Line, 73
Prohibition, 93, 95
Protestantism, 44, 46, 48, 54, 56, 58
Protestants, 58, 62, 74
Provinces of Rio de la Plata, 79
Prussia, 34, 46, 53, 60, 66, 68, 70, 72, 74, 84
Prussians, 30
psychoanalysis, 86
Ptolemaic dynasty, 13
Ptolemy, 12, 13
Pu Yi, Emperor of China, 95
Pueblo Bonito, 31
pueblo builders, 23, 25, **31**, 33
Pugachev, 72
Punic Wars, 12, 14
Punjab, India, 15, 37, 47, 71, 83
Puritans, 57, 58
Pyongyang, North Korea, 21, 99
pyramids, 7, 11, 13
Pyrenees, Peace of the, 58

# Q

Qaja dynasty, Persia, 75
Qin (Ch'in) dynasty, China, **15**
Quadesh, Battle of, 9
Quadruple alliance, 66
Quakers, 63, 69
Quebec, Canada, 55, 57, 61, 71, 107
Queensland, Australia, 83
Quetzalcoatl, 25
Quito, Ecuador, 33, 41

# R

Rabin, Yitzhak, 106, 107
radioactivity, discovery of, 86
radium, discovery of, 86
Radzin, Treaty of, 60
Raffles, Sir Stamford, 79
railway,
first passenger, 80
first trans-continental, 85
*Rainbow Warrior*, 105
Rajara I, King of Chola dynasty, 25
Rajputana, India, 23
Raleigh, Walter, 51
Rama I, King of Siam, 75
Rama II, King of Siam, 79
Ramesses II, King of Egypt, 9
Ramesses III, King of Egypt, 9
Ramlah, Peace of, 29
Rangoon, Burma, 71
Ras Tafari, 94
Rashtrakuta, India, 23
Ravenna, Italy, 16, 20, 22
Reagan, Ronald, U.S. President, 104, 105
*reconquista*, 26
record player, invention of, 85
Red Cross Society, 84
Red Guards, China, 101
Red Terror, U.S.S.R., 92
Reform Acts, 80, 84, 86
First, 80
Second, 84
Reformation, **44**, 46
Reichstag, the burning of the, 94
Reign of Terror, France, 74
Relativity, Special Theory of, 90
Renaissance, 36, **38**
reservations, Native North American, 87
Restoration, the, 66
Revere, Paul, 73
Revocation of the Edict of Nantes, 62
Reykjavik summit, 104
Reza Pahlavi I, Shah of Persia, 92
Reza Pahlavi II, Shah of Iran
Rhineland, German, 94
Rhode Island, U.S.A., 59
Rhodes, 8
Rhodes, Cecil, 84, 86
Rhodesia, 86, 90, 102, 104
*see also* Northern Rhodesia (Zambia), 98
Southern Rhodesia, (Zimbabwe), 90, 100
Rhodesian Front Party, 100
Rhodi Mawr, Prince of Wales, 22
Rhone-Saone, Burgundian kingdom, 16
Richard I, King of England, 28, 29
Richard III, King of England, 40
Richelieu, Cardinal, 56, 57
Richmond, Virginia, 69
Riga, Latvia, 34
*Rights of Man, The*, 74
Rijswick, Treaty of, 62
Rio de Janeiro, Argentina, 47, 73
Rio de la Plata provinces, 79
Rio De Oro, 86, 90
Rio Muni, 90
Robert Bruce, King of Scotland, 34
Robespierre, Maximilien, 74
Robinson, Mary, 106
*Rocket, The*, 80
Rococo style, 68
Rocroi, Battle of, 58
Roger II, King of Sicily, 28
*see also* Roger Guiscard
Roggeveen, Jacob, 69
Rollo, Duke of Normandy, 24
Romagna, Italy, 84
Roman Empire, **14**
eastern, 20
western, 16
Roman Republic, 10
Romans, Ancient, **10**, 12, 14, 16
Romania, 84, 90, 98, 104, 106
Romanov dynasty, 54
Rome, Ancient, **10**, 12, **14**
Rome, Italy, 28, 46, 74, 92, 96
Rome, Treaty of, 98
Romero, Archbishop, 105
Rommel, General Erwin, 96
Röntgen, Wilhelm, 86
Roosevelt, President Franklin D., 95, 96
Roses, Wars of the, **40**
Rosetta Stone, Egypt, 75
Roskilde, Peace of, 58
Rossbach, Battle of, 70
Rostock, Germany, 60
Rousseau, Jean-Jacques, 66
Royal Niger Company, 86
*Rubaiyat, The*, 27
Rub' al-Khali Desert, 94
Rudan, Battle of, 36
Rudolf of Habsburg, 32
Rupert's Land, Canada, 61
Rurik dynasty, 50
Rurik the Rus, 22
Rus tribe, 22
Rushdie, Salman, 104
Russia, 20, 22, 24, 26, 30, 32, 34, 37, 46, 48, 49, 50, 51, 54, 56, 58, 60, 62, 66, 68, 69, 78, 80, 82, 84, 85, 86, 87, 90, 91, 92, 106, 108
Russians, 71, 83, 91
Russian civil war, 92
Russian Orthodox Church, 34, 38
Russian Republic, 106
Russian Revolution, **92**
Russo-Turkish War, 72, 84
Rutherford, Ernest, 90, 92
Rutli, Pact of, 32

Rwanda, 98, 104, 106, 108

# S

Sabaea, 12
Sacramento, Uruguay, 63
Sadat, President, 102, 104
Safavid dynasty, Persia, 45, 49, 55, 69
Sahara Desert, 7, 11, 17, 23, 31, 51, 80
Saigon, Vietnam, 97, 99
Sailendra kingdom, 23
Saints, The, 59
Saïs, Egypt, 11
Saladin, Sultan of Egypt, 29, 31
Salazar, Antonio, 94
Salic Law, 34
Salle, Robert de la, 61, 63
SALT treaty, 103
*Salyut 1*, 102
Salzburg, Austria, 72
Samanid dynasty, 25
Samarkand, 25, 37
Samoa, 69
samurai, **27**, 49, 57
San Agustín, South America, 29
San Lorenzo, Mexico, 9, 11
San Francisco, U.S.A., 73, 91, 97
San Martín, José de, 79
Sandinistas, 103, 107
Sante Fé, U.S.A., 55
Sao Paulo, Brazil, 49
Sapa Inca, 39
Sarajevo, Bosnia, 90
Sardinia, 82, 84
Sargon II, King of Assyria, 10
Saro-Wiwa, Ken, 106
Sassanid dynasty, Persia, 16, 21
*Satanic Verses, The*, 104
satellite, relaying TV and phone calls, 101
Saud, Ibn, King of Hejaz and Nejd (Saudi Arabia), 92, 94
Saudi Arabia, 92, 96, 102
Saul, King of the Hebrews, 8
Savery, Thomas,
Savoy, 62, 66, 68
Saxon dynasty, 24
Saxons, 14, 16, 20
Saxony, 24, 62
Scandinavia, 22, 44
Schiller, J.C.F. von., 70
Schism, Great, 26, **36**
Schmalkalden, League of, 46
Schouten, Willem, 55
Schwyz, 32
Scotland, 20, 22, 26, 28, 32, 34, 36, 40, 44, 46, 48, 50, 62, 66, 108
Scots, 22, 24, 32
Scramble for Africa, **84**
scutage, 28
Scythians, 10, 14
SEATO (Southeast Asia Treaty Organization), 99
Sea Beggars, 48
Sea Peoples, 8
Sebastian, King of Portugal, 51
Second Empire, France, 82, 84
Second Republic, France, 82
Second World War, **94**, *see also* World War Two
Segu, West Africa, 75
Sekigahara, Battle of, 55
Selangor, Malaya, 67, 71
Selassie, Haile, Emperor of Ethiopia, 94, 102
Seleucia, 14
Seleucid empire, 12, 14
Selim II of Turkey, 45, 49
Seljuk Turks, 26, 28, 31, 33
Sempach, Switzerland, 32
Sena, East Africa, 45
Senegal, 55, 57, 59, 98
Senlis, Peace of, 40
Sennacherib, King of Assyria, 10
Seoul, South Korea, 99, 109
Septimius Severus, Roman emperor, 17
Serbia, 28, 44, 62, 84, 90, 108
Serbs, 108
serfdom, 58
serfs, 74, 84
Seven Years' War, 70, 72
sewing machine, first, 83
Seychelle Islands, 69
Sforza, Francesco, 40
Shabra and Shatila refugee camps, 104
Shah Abbas the Great, of Persia, 57
Shah Alam, Nawab of Bengal, 71
Shah Jahan, Mogul emperor, 57, *59*
Shah Reza Pahlavi I, of Persia, 92
Shah Reza Pahlavi II of Iran, 102
Shah, Sher, 47, 49
Shailendra dynasty, Java, 29
Shaka 'the Great', Zulu military leader, 78
Shakespeare, William, 48
Shamshi-Adad, King of Assyria, 8
Shan states, Burma, 71
Shang dynasty, 9
Shanghai, China, 95
Shapur I, King of Persia, 16
Sharifian dynasty, 51
Sharpeville massacre, 100
Shetland, Scotland, 40
Shi Huangdi, Emperor of China, 15, 103
Shia Muslims, 102
Shi'ites, 21, 23, 27
Shikubu, Lady Murasaki, 27
Shinto religion, 17
Ship Money, English tax, 56
Shiva, Hindu god, 25
shogun, 29, 35, 49, 55
Siam, *see also* Thailand, 39, 51, 55, 61, 63, 73, 75, 81, 87, 91, 97
Siberia, 50, 51, 54, 56, 58
Sicilian Vespers, 32
Sicily, 20, 26, 28, 30, 32, 82, 84
Siddhartha, Gautama, 11
Sidon, Lebanon, 8, 102
Sierra Leone, 41, 49, 75, 78, 90, 98
Sikh religion, 41
Sikhs, 61, 105
Sikorsky, Igor, 95
Silesia, 70
silk-making, start of, 7, 44
silver, 47
Simnel, Lambert, 40
Simpson, Mrs., 94
Simpson, O.J., 107
Sinai, 96, 100, 102
Sind, India, 11, 47, 51, 83
Singapore, 35, **79**, 101, 106
Singer, Isaac, 85
Singhalese people, 105
Single European Market, 106
Sioux people, 85, 87
Sis, Armenia, 37
Sivaji Bhonsla, 61, 63
Six Days' War, 100
Skara Brae, Orkneys, 6
Slave Dynasty of Delhi, 31
slave revolt, 75
slave trade, 49, **67**
slaves, 45, 49, 69, 78, 80
slavery, 47, 72, 74, 78, 80, 85
Slavs, 20, 22
Slovakia, 106
Slovenia, 106
Sluys, Battle of, 34
Smith, Adam, 72
Smith, Ian, 100
Smolensk, Russia, 58
Sobieski, Jan, 60
solar eclipse, 92
Solidarity, 104, 106
Solomon, King of the Hebrews, 10
Solomon Islands, 69, 75
Solon, 10
Somalia, 98, 104, 106, 108
Somerville, 78
Somoza family, Nicaragua, 103
Songhai kingdom, 37, 41, 44, 47, 51
Sony, 105
Sophia, regent of Russia, 62
South Africa, 39, 41, 78, 80, 82, 84, 86, 90, 98, 100, 104, 106
South Carolina, U.S.A., 63, 69, 75
South Korea, 99, 109
South Pole, 91
South Sea Bubble, 68
South Sea Company, 68
South Vietnam, 99, 101
Southern Netherlands, *see* Spanish Netherlands
Southern Rhodesia, 90, *see also* Rhodesia, Zimbabwe
Southern Sung dynasty, 29
Soweto, South Africa, 102
Space Shuttle, 103, 105
space station, world's first, 102
space travel, 100, 103, 105
Spain, 6, 16, 20, 22, 24, 26, 27, 30, 40, 44, 48, 49, 50, 51, 54, 55, 56, 58, 60, 62, 66, 68, 72, 73, 74, 75, 78, 80, 82, 84, 85, 86, 92, 94, 102, 104
Spanish/Spaniards, 69, 73 75, 79, 87
Spanish-American War, 87
Spanish Armada, 50
Spanish Civil War, 94
Spanish Netherlands, *66 see also* Southern Netherlands
Spanish Succession, War of the, **66**
Sparta, Greece, 12
*Special Theory of Relativity*, 90
spectacles, first lenses, 30
Speke, John, 82
Speyer, Germany, 46
Sphinx, the, Egypt, 7
Spinning Jenny, 72
*Sputnik 1*, 98
Sri Lanka, 25, 101, 103, 105, 105, *see also* Ceylon
Srivijaya kingdom, 23, 29
St. Augustine, 20
St. Bartholomew, 59
St. Bartholomew's Eve Massacre, 48
St. Basil's Cathedral, 40
St. Benedict, 20
St. Columba, 20
St. Croix, 59
St. Cyril, 22
St. Denis, Paris, 28
St. Helena, 59, 78, 80, 82
St. Lawrence River, 27, 47, 57, 73
St. Lucia, 59, 79, 81
St. Martin, 59
St. Methodius, 22
St. Paul's Cathedral, London, 66
St. Petersburg, Russia, 62, 66, 68, 72, 90, 92
St. Sophia, Constantinople, 20, 45
St. Vincent, 73
Stalin, Josef, 92, 94, 96, 98
Stanley, Sir Henry, 84
*Starry Messenger, The*, 54
Statue of Liberty, New York, built, 87
stealth bomber B-2, 105
steam engine, first practical working, 66
Watt's, 72
Stephenson's, 80
steam train, first to run on a track, 78,
Stephen I, King of Hungary, 24
Stephen of Boulogne, 28
Stephenson, George, 80
Stephenson, Robert, 80
Stettin, Peace of, 48
Stewart, house of, 36
Stirling Bridge, Battle of, 32
Stockholm, Treaty of, 56, 68
Stock Market Crash, 93, 105
Stolbovo, Treaty of, 54
Stone Age, 6
stone circles, 6
Stonehenge, 6
Stralsund, Peace of, 36
Strassman, 94
Straw, Jack, 36
Strongbow, 28
Stuart dynasty, 54, 58, 66
Stuart, Charles Edward, 70
Stuart, Mary, *see also* Mary, Queen of Scots, 46
Stuart, Charles, 58
Sturt, Charles, 83
Styria, 40
Sudan, 9, 45, 80, 86, 98, 104, 106, 108
Sudetenland, Germany, 94
Suevi, 14
Suez Canal, 82, 84, 90, 94, 98
Suez Crisis, 98
suffrage, women's, *see* votes for women
sugar industry, 69
Suger, Abbot, 28
Suharto, President, 109
Sui dynasty, 21
Sukothai kingdom, 31
Suleiman II, the Magnificent, Sultan of Turkey, 45
Sulla, Roman general, 14
Sumatra, East Indies, 55, 71, 79
Sumer, Mesopotamia, 6, 8
Sun Diata Keita of Mali, 31
Sun Yat-sen, 91, 93
Sung dynasty, 33
Sung empire, 39
Sunni Ali of Songhai, 41
Sunni Muslims, 102
Superior, Lake, 61
supersonic plane, 102
Surat, India, 55, 63
Surinam, 95 *see also* Dutch Guiana
Suryavarman I, King of Cambodia, 27
Suryavarman II, King of Cambodia, 29
Susa, Persia, 12
Swabian League, 40
Swan River Settlement, Australia, 81
Swan, Joseph, 84
Swaziland, 90, 98, 100
Sweden, 24, 26, 30, 32, 34, 48, 54, 56, 58, 60, 62, 66, 68, 70, 72, 78, 106
Swedes, 60
Sweet Track, England, 6
Swiss Confederation, 32
Switzerland, 34, 40, 44, 46, 74, 82, 102
Sydney, Australia, 75, 95, 103
Sydney Opera House, 103
Synod of Whitby, 20
Syria, 10, 16, 21, 23, 27, 29, 33, 45, 49, 67, 80, 82, 92, 94, 96, 98, 102, 104

# T

T'ai tsung the Great, Emperor of China, 21
T'ang dynasty, 21, 25
Tabriz, Persia, 55
Ta-chao, Li, 93
Taharka, King of Kush, 11
Taiping Rebellion, 83

Taira clan, 29
Taiwan, *see also* Formosa, 57
Taj Mahal, India, 57
Taksin, King of Siam, 73, 75
Talas river, Battle of, 23
Taliban, 109
Tamerlane, **37**, 39, 41, 47
Tamils, 105, 109
Tamil Tigers, 109
Tanganyika, 86, 90
Tangier, North Africa, 41, 61
Taninganway Min, King of Burma, 67
Tanjore, India, 79
Tannenburg, Prussia, Battle of, 38
Tanzania, 98, 100, 102
Taoism, 11
Tao-kuang, Emperor of China, 81
Tarim Basin, Central Asia, 71
Tartars, 48, 55
Tarxien, Malta, 6
Tashkent, Central Asia, 85
Tasman, Abel, 59
Tasmania, 59, 79, 81
telegraph, first electric, 80
telephone, first, 85
*Telstar*, 101
Temujin, *see also* Genghis Khan, 29, 31
Tenochtitlán, Mexico, 33, 35, 39
Tensing, Sherpa, 99
Teotihuacán, Mexico, 11, 13, 15, 17, 21, 23, 25
Tereshkova, Valentina, 100
terrorists, 102, 104, 107, 109
test-tube baby, first, 102
Tet offensive, 101
Tete, Mozambique, 45
Teutonic Knights, 28, 30, 34, 36, 38
Texas, U.S.A., 81, 83
Texas Instruments, 99
Texcoco, Mexico, 35, 39
Thailand, 31, 97, 99, 107, 109, *see also* Siam
Thais, 37, 49
Thatcher, Margaret, 102, 106
Thebes, Egypt, 9
Theodor, Tsar of Russia, 50
Theodora, Byzantine empress, 20
Theodoric, King of the Ostrogoths, 16
Theodosius, Roman emperor, 16
Thera, 8
thermometer,
Centigrade, 70
Fahrenheit, 66
Thessalonika, Greece, 38
Third Republic, France, 84
Thirteen Colonies, 71, 75
Thirty Years' War, **54**, 56, 58
Thomas à Becket, 28
Thonburi, Thailand, 71, 73
Thorn, Poland, 74
Three Mile Island, 103
Thule Eskimo people, 27
Tiahuanaco, South America, 15, 17, 21, 27, 29
Tiananmen Square massacre, 105
Tiber, river, 10
Tibet, 21, 23, 61, 69, 71, 75, 91, 99
Tientsin, China, Treaty of, 83
Tigris, river, 6
Tikal, Mexico, 11
Timbuktu, West Africa, 23, 37, 41, 51, 80
Timor, 109
Tippoo of Mysore, 75
*Titanic*, 91
Titu Cusi Inca, 49
Titicaca, Lake, Bolivia, 17, 41
Tito, President of Yugoslavia, 98, 104
Titus, Arch of, 16
Tlacopán, Mexico, 39
tobacco, 48, 55, 109
Tobago, 79, 81, 101
Togo, 86, 90, 98, 100
Tokugawa dynasty, **55**, 83, 85
Tokugawa, Hidetada, 55
Tokugawa, Iemitsu, 57
Tokugawa, Ieyasu, 55
Tokyo, Japan, 49, 55, 93
Toledo, Spain, 26
Tolpuddle Martyrs, 81
Toltec culture, 25, 29
Tomsk, Siberia, 54
Tondibi, Battle of, 51
Tone, Wolfe, 74
Tonga, 73, 91
Tongking, Indochina, 47
Tonkin, Indochina, 81, 85
Topa Amaru, Inca ruler, 49
Topa Inca, Inca ruler, 41
Tordesillas, Treaty of, 41
Torricelli, Evangelista, 58
Totonac culture, 21
Toulouse, France, Burgundian kingdom, 16
Toungoo, Burma, 47, 49
Trafalgar, Battle of, 78
train,
first steam, to run on a track, 78
Stephenson's *Rocket*, 80
*see also* railway
Trajan, Roman emperor, 14, 16
transatlantic cable, first, 85
transistor, first invented, 97
Transjordan, 92, 96
Transvaal, South Africa, 82, 84, 86, 90
Transylvania, 34, 62
Trengganu, Malaya, 91
Trent, Council of, 46
Trevithick, Richard, 78
Trier, Germany, 44
Trinidad, 41, 75
Tripoli, Libya, 49, 67, 80, 101,
Tripoli, Syria, 102
Trojan Wars, 8, 10
Troy, Turkey, 8
Trudeau, Pierre, 101
Truman, Harry, U.S. President, 97
Trutor, 78
tsars, first, of Russia, **40**
Tsushima, Japan, 91
Tudor dynasty, 40, 54
Tudor, Henry, 40, *see also* Henry VII, King of England
Tula, Mexico, 25, 29
Tulunid dynasty, 23
Tunis, Tunisia, 15, 21, 47, 49, 59, 67
Tunisia, 49 84, 86, 96, 98
Tupac Amaru II, Inca ruler, 75
Tupac Amaru, 109
Turcoman dynasty, 35
Turenne, France, 30
Turkestan, 33, 67, 71
Turkey, 6, 8, 10, 12, 16, 26, 33, 38, 46, 51, 56, 66, 72, 74, 82, 90, 92, 94, 108
Turkish Republic, 92
Turkmenistan, 87
Turks, 36, 38, 58, 94, 102,
Ottomans, 33, 38, 40, 41, 44, **45**, 46, 47, 49, 57, 60, 62, 67, 75
Seljuks, 21, 26, 27, 31, 54, 55
Turre, Mohammed, ruler of Songhai, 45
Tuscany, Italy, 68, 84
Tutsi people, 106
Tutu, Desmond, 104
Tyler, Wat, 36
Tyre, Lebanon, 8, 102
Tz'u-hsi, Empress of China, 85, 87

# U

U-boats, 93
UDI (Unilateral Declaration of Independence), 100
Uganda, 85, 90, 102
Uighur empire, 23
Ujiji, East Africa, 84
Ukraine, 58, 60, 62
Ukrainians, 74
Ulundi, South Africa, 84
Ulyanov, Vladimir Ilyich, 92, *see also* Lenin
underground railway, first, 84
Union, Act of, 78
Union of England and Scotland, 66
Union of South Africa, *see* South Africa
Unionists, Northern Ireland, 100
Unionist States of American Civil War, 85
United Arab Republic, 98
United Kingdom, 96, 100, 102, 108, *see also* Great Britain
UN (United Nations), 96, 99, 102, 106, 107, 108
United Provinces of Central America, 81
United Provinces, 50, 58, 62, *see also* Dutch Republic
U.S.A. (United States of America), 72, 75, 78, 79, 82, 83, 85, 87, 90, 91, 93, 96, 97, 99, 100, 101, 103, 105, 107, 108, 109
U.S.S.R. (Union of Soviet Socialist Republics), 92, 94, 96, 97, 98, 99, 100, 101, 102, 103, 104, 106
universities, first, 30
Unterwalden, Switzerland, 32
Upper Burma, 71
Upper Niger, 61, 67
Upper Volta, 98
Ur, Sumer, 6
Uranus, 105
Urartu, 10
Urban II, Pope, 26
Urban VI, Pope, 36
Uri, Switzerland, 32
Urnfield culture, 8
Uruguay, 63, 69, 79, 81, 95, 105
Uruk, Mesopotamia, 6
Utah, U.S.A., 83
Utrecht, Peace of, 66
Utrecht, Union of, 50

# V

V-2 rocket, 96
vaccinations, first, 74
vacuum pump, 58
Valens, Roman emperor, 16
Valerian, Roman emperor, 16
Valois dynasty, 34, 48
Van Dieman's Land, 59, *see also* Tasmania
Vandals, 14, 16, 17, 20
Vargas, Getulio, 95
Vasa dynasty, Sweden, 50
*Vasa, The*, 56
VE Day, 94, 96
VJ Day, 94
*Vedas* 9
Vedic Period, India, 9
Venezuela, 45, 47, 71, 79, 95
Venice, Italy, 28, 33, 36, 40, 48, 58, 60, 62, 84
Vereeniging, Peace of, 90, 92
Versailles, France, 60
Versailles, Treaty of, 92
Verwoerd, Prime Minister of South Africa, 100
Vesalius, Andreas, 46
Vespucci, Amerigo, 41, 45
Vesuvius, volcano, 16
Victor Emmanuel II, first King of Italy, 84
Victoria Falls, southern Africa, 82
Victoria, Australia, 82
Victoria, Lake, 82
Victoria, Queen of Great Britain, 80, 85, 90
Vienna, Austria, 46, 62, 66, 82
Vienna, Congress of, 78
Vienna, Treaty of, 68
Viet Cong, 99
Viet Minh, 101
Vietnam, 15, 39, 47, 51, 61, 85, 97, 99, 100, 101, 103
North, 103
South, 99, 101, 103
Vietnam War, **99**, 100, 101, 103
Vietnamese, 41, 99
Vijayanagar kingdom, India, 35
Vikings, **22**, 24, 25, 26, 27, 35, 101
Vilcabamba, Peru, 47, 49
Viracocha Inca, Inca ruler, 39
Virginia, U.S.A., 51, 55, 69
Virtual Reality, 107
Visconti, Mateo, 32
Vishnu, Hindu god, 17
Visigoths, 14, 16, 20
Vivaldi, Antonio, 66
Vladimir I, of Kievan Russia, 24
Vladislav Lokiekek, 34
Volta, Alessandro, 78
Voltaire, 62
von Braun, Wernher, 96
von Goethe, Johann Wolfgang, 70
von Kleist, Ewald, 70
von Linné, Carl, *see also* Linnaeus, 70
*Vostok I*, 100
votes for women, 91, 92, 93, 94, 96, 102
*Voyager 2*, 105
Vratislav of Bohemia, 26

# W

Waco, U.S.A., 107
Waitangi, Treaty of, 83
Wales, 22, 32, 34, 38
Walesa, Lech, 104, 106
Wall Street Crash, 93
Wallace, William, 32
Wallachia, 34
Walpole, Robert, 68
Warbeck, Perkin, English pretender, 40
Wars of the Roses, **40**
War of the League of Augsburg, 62
War of the Spanish Succession, **66**
Warsaw Pact, 98
Warsaw, Poland, 74, 82
Washington, George, U.S. President, 73, 75
Washington, U.S.A., 105, 107
water frame, 72
Watergate, 103
Waterloo, Battle of, 78
Watson, James, 98
Watt, James, 72
*Wealth of Nations*, 72
Welsh, 22, 46
Wenceslas III, King of Hungary and Bohemia, 34
Wenceslas of Bohemia, 24
Wesley, Charles, 68
Wesley, John, 68
Wessex, England, 8, 22
West Bank, of River Jordan, 108
West Berlin, Germany, 90
West Galicia, 74
West Germany, 96, 98, 102
West India Company, 57
West Indies, 41, 57, 70
Western Australia, 81
Western Roman empire, 16
Western Sahara, 98
Westminster, Statute of, 94

Westmoreland, England, 28
Westphalia, Germany, 58, 78
Wheatstone, C., 80
wheel, invention of, 6
Whitby, England, Synod of, 20
White Mountain, Battle of, 56
White Russians, 74, 92
Wilberforce, William, 74, 78, 80
Wilhelm I, Kaiser of Germany, 84
Wilhelm II, Kaiser of Germany, 86
Wilkes, Captain, 83
William I, King of England ('the Conqueror'), 26
William III (of Orange), King of England and stadtholder (ruler) of the Netherlands, 60, 62
William of Orange, stadtholder of Dutch Republic, 50
Wills, William, 85
Winter Palace, St. Petersburg, 62
wireless,
first, 86
first transmission, 91
Witte, Sergei, 86
Wittenburg, Germany, 44
Wolfe, General, 71
Wolfe Tone, 74
Woodstock, U.S.A., 101
World Trade Center, 107
World War One, **92**, *see also* First World War, Great War
World War Two, **94**, *see also* Second World War
World Wide Web, 104
Worms, Germany,
Concordat of, 26, 28
Diet of, 44
Wounded Knee, Battle of, 87
Wright, Orville, 91
Wright, Wilbur, 91
writing, introduction of, 6, 7, 9, 17
materials, 35
written exams, first, 21
Wu, Empress of China, 21
Wu-ti, Emperor of China, 15
Wycliffe, John, 36
Wye Mills Agreement, 108

X

Xavier, Francis, 47
Xerxes I, King of Persia, 12
X-group culture, 17
Xia dynasty, 7
x-rays, 86

Y

Yale University, 67
Yalta, Ukraine, 96
Yamato government, 17, 21
Yang Chien, General, 21
Yangshao culture, 7
Yangtu, China, 25, *see also* Beijing
Yangtze, river, 7, 21
Yaroslav the Wise, ruler of Russia, 26
Yayoi culture, 13
Yeltsin, Boris, 106, 109
Yemen, Arabia, 98, 100
Yenan, China, 95
Yom Kippur War, 102
York, England, 40
York, House of, 40
York, Richard Duke of, 40
Yorktown, U.S.A., 75
Yoruba kingdom, 67, 78
Yoshimune, Shogun of Japan, 67
Young Turks, the, 90
Yuan dynasty, 33, 37
Yucatán, Mexico, 25, 33, 35
Yugoslavia, 92, 98, 104, 108
Yung-Lo, Emperor of China, 39
Yunnan province, China, 91
Yuri Dolgoruky, Prince of Kiev, 28

Z

Zaire, 108
Zama, Battle of, Tunisia, 15
Zambezi, river, 45, 82
Zambia, 98, *see also* Northern Rhodesia
Zanzibar, 67, 100
Zapolya, John, King of Hungary, 46
Zapotec culture, 13, 17, 21
Zela, Battle of, 14
Zelankemen, Battle of, 62
Zenobia, Queen of Palmyra, 16
Zenta, Battle of, 62
Zhou dynasty, China, 9
Zia al-Haq, General, 103, 105
ziggurat, 6
Zimbabwe, 86, 98, 102, 104
Zimbabwe, Great, 37, 39
Zogu, Ahmed, 92
Zulu people, 78, 80, 84
Zuravno, Peace of, 60
Zurich, Switzerland, 32, 44
Zwingli, Ulrich, 44

# Acknowledgements

b, bottom; m, middle; l, left; r, right; t, top.

**Alamy**
/qaphotos.com
p106 bl In a Channel Tunnel rail tunnel

**Corbis**

/Roger Ressmeyer
2-3 Pyramid

/Wolfgang Kaehler
4-5 Minoan dolphins

/Angelo Hornak
18-19 Tree of Jesse stained glass window

/Bettmann
42-43 Spanish map

/Angelo Hornak
52-53 Gosain Narain takes poison

/Hulton-Deutsch Collection
64-65 Storming of the Bastille

/Burstein Collection
76-77 Toulouse Lautrec poster

/Peter Turnley
105 bl Student Protesters Tiananmen Square

/AFP
106 br Nelson Mandela

/Yann Arthus-Bertrand
107 cl Aerial view of flooded Bangladeshi village

/Howard Davies
107 bl Aung Sang Suu Kyi

/Sean Aidan; Eye Ubiquitous
108 cl Tony Blair

/Dave Bartruff
108 cr Queen Hatshepsut's mausoleum

/Mike Zens
108-109 b New York fireworks

/Philip Gould
109 tr Palm trees

**Hong Kong Tourist Association**
109 cl Hong Kong street scene

**Illustrated London News**
82 cl Karl Marx

84 br Cecil Rhodes

85 tr Abraham Lincoln

86 rc General Gordon

87 lc Indian troops in Burma

92 tl Tsar Nicholas II & family

92 cb Benito Mussolini

92 tr Lawrence of Arabia

93 tl Mao Zedong

93 cl Tokyo after earthquake

94 cl Spanish civil war republican soldiers

95 tl Gandhi

96 cl Churchill, Roosevelt and Stalin

96 cr Rommel's troops after capture

**Mary Evans Picture Library**
/Sueddeutsche Zeitung Photo 90 lc Albert Einstein

**PETER NEWARK'S MILITARY PICTURES**
91 cl Battle of Tsushima

**Struan Reid**
16 cr Palmyra Roman ruins

29 bl Krak des Chevaliers

**Stockbyte/Cadmium**
88-89 Spaceman

**Turkish Information Office**
92 br Mustafa Kemäl 'Ataturk'

Cover design: Amy Manning. Cover Illustration: Ian McNee.
Additional design: Tom Lalonde. Additional editor: Rachel Firth.

First published in 2016 by Usborne Publishing Limited, 83-85 Saffron Hill, London EC1N 8RT, United Kingdom. usborne.com
Copyright © 2016, 2002, 2000, 1998 Usborne Publishing Limited. The name Usborne and the Balloon logo are registered trade marks of Usborne Publishing Limited. All rights reserved. No part of this publication may be reproduced, stored in a retrieval system or transmitted in any form or by any means without prior permission of the publisher. First published in America 2016. This edition published 2024. UE.